Contemporary Theatres in Europe

'This is a remarkably good book – not only are the essays and the editors' comments incisive and stimulating, but the idea of the book as an intervention into contemporary scholarly discourse is also provocative at the metatheatrical-metapedagogical level.'
From Janelle Reinelt's Foreword

Europe at the turn of the twenty-first century is a place where the practice of theatre still matters. Theatre remains a place and a practice in which pressing questions of political and personal identity, desire, imagination and dissent can be explored.

Contemporary Theatres in Europe: A Critical Companion offers a series of essays about some of the most interesting theatre currently being made in Europe. It also presents a range of different approaches to the challenge of writing about the experience of theatre and performance. The book includes essays on some of the most celebrated European theatre companies of the last twenty years (Théâtre du Soleil, Societas Raffaello Sanzio), as well as considerations of work that is still only to be found in the more secluded parts of the European theatrical landscape. It also includes essays on music theatre, dance and dance theatre and theatre for children: theatrical practices which are often marginalised in critical writing but which are clearly still central to the work of theatre makers in Europe.

This book offers the student, the scholar and the theatre-goer an informed and vivid critical introduction to contemporary theatre in Europe and an open invitation to the reader to extend their theatrical imaginations.

Joe Kelleher teaches drama, theatre and performance studies at Roehampton University.

Nicholas Ridout is Lecturer in Performance at Queen Mary University of London.

Contemporary Theatres in Europe

A critical companion

Edited by Joe Kelleher
and Nicholas Ridout

Routledge
Taylor & Francis Group

LONDON AND NEW YORK

First published 2006 by Routledge
2 Park Square, Milton Park, Abingdon, Oxon OX14 4RN

Simultaneously published in the USA and Canada
by Routledge
270 Madison Ave, New York, NY 10016

Routledge is an imprint of the Taylor & Francis Group, an informa business

© 2006 Joe Kelleher and Nicholas Ridout; individual chapters, the
contributors

Typeset in Baskerville by Florence Production Ltd, Stoodleigh, Devon
Printed and bound in Great Britain by MPG Books Ltd, Bodmin

British Library Cataloguing in Publication Data
A catalogue record for this book is available from the British Library

Library of Congress Cataloging in Publication Data
Contemporary theatres in Europe : a critical companion / edited by
Joe Kelleher and Nick Ridout.
          p. cm.
       Includes bibliographical references and index.
    1. Theater–Europe–History–20th century.   2. Theater–Europe–
History–21st century.   I. Kelleher, Joe.   II. Ridout, Nick.
PN2570.C665 2006
792.094'0904–dc22   2005035565

ISBN 10: 0–415–32939–6 (hbk)
ISBN 10: 0–415–32940–X (pbk)
ISBN 10: 0–203–32129–2 (ebk)

ISBN 13: 978–0–415–32939–2 (hbk)
ISBN 13: 978–0–415–32940–8 (pbk)
ISBN 13: 978–0–203–39129–7 (ebk)

Contents

List of illustrations   vii

Notes on contributors   ix

Acknowledgements   xiii

Foreword from 'across the pond'   xiv
JANELLE REINELT

Introduction   1
JOE KELLEHER AND NICHOLAS RIDOUT

1 Human stuff: presence, proximity and pretend   21
JOE KELLEHER

2 Investigating the entrails: post-operatic music theatre in
Europe   34
NICHOLAS TILL

3 Encountering memory: Acco Theatre Center's *Arbeit
macht frei MiToitland Europa*   47
HEIKE ROMS

4 On the border as theatrical space: appearance,
dis-location and the production of the refugee   61
SOPHIE NIELD

5 Foreign bodies: performing physical and psychological
harm at the Mladi Levi festival, August 2003   73
SARAH GORMAN

6 Dying bodies, living corpses: transition, nationalism and
resistance in Croatian theatre   87
MARIN BLAŽEVIĆ

7 Desire amongst the dodgems: Alain Platel and the
   scene of seduction   106
   ADRIAN KEAR

8 'Constitutive ambiguities': writing professional or
   expert performance practices, and the Théâtre du Soleil,
   Paris   120
   SUSAN MELROSE

9 Marshfield Mummers: The Old Time Paper Boys   136
   MIKE PEARSON

10 The gift of play: *Übung* and the secret signal of
   gesture   149
   ANDREW QUICK

11 Authority, empowerment and fairy tales: theatre for
   young people   163
   BRIDGET ESCOLME

12 Make-believe: Socìetas Raffaello Sanzio do theatre   175
   NICHOLAS RIDOUT

13 After the fall: dance-theatre and dance-performance   188
   ADRIAN HEATHFIELD

14 What state am I in? Or, How to be a spectator   199
   SIMON BAYLY

   Index   212

Illustrations

1.1 Baktruppen, *Homo Egg Egg*. Photograph: Carlo F. Prelz.   30
2.1 Heiner Goebbels and the Ensemble Modern, *Black on White*.
    Photograph: Wonge Bergmann.   40
5.1 Uninvited Guests, *Offline*. Photograph: Thomas Hall.   76
5.2 Kuno Bakker in Dood Paard, *40,000 Sublime and Beautiful
    Thoughts*. Photograph: Sanne Peper.   80
6.1 Montažstroj-Performingunit, *Fragile*, designed by Borut
    Šeparović.   95
6.2 Montažstroj-Performingunit, *Fragile*, designed by Borut
    Šcparović.   96
6.3 Zagreb Youth Theatre, *The Grand Master of All Scoundrels*,
    directed by Branko Brezovec. Photograph: Sandra Vitaljić.   98
6.4 Nikolina Bujas-Pristaš and Jelena Vukmirica in BAD.co,
    2, choreography by Nikolina Bujas-Pristaš. Photograph:
    Marko Čaklović.   100
6.5 Damir Bartol Indoš and Zlatko Burić in Kugla, *War Kitchen*,
    directed by Damir Bartol Indoš.   101
7.1 Victoria, *Bernadetje*. Photograph: Kurt Van der Elst.   108
7.2 Victoria, *Bernadetje*. Photograph: Kurt Van der Elst.   110
7.3 Victoria, *Bernadetje*. Photograph: Kurt Van der Elst.   113
8.1 Ariane Mnouchkine in rehearsal at the Théâtre du Soleil.
    Stills from *Au soleil même la nuit, Scènes d'accouchements*,
    É. Darmon and C. Vilpoux, Théâtre du Soleil/Agat Films/
    La Sept Arte, 1997.   123
8.2 Ariane Mnouchkine in rehearsal at the Théâtre du Soleil.
    Stills from *Au soleil même la nuit, Scènes d'accouchements*,
    É. Darmon and C. Vilpoux, Théâtre du Soleil/Agat Films/
    La Sept Arte, 1997.   131
9.1 The Marshfield Mummers. The fight. Photograph:
    Mike Pearson.   137
12.1 Societas Raffaello Sanzio, *Tragedia Endogonidia (C.#11)*.
    Photograph: Luca del Pia.   184

13.1 Jan Minarik, Malou Airaudo and Dominique Mercy in
      Pina Bausch's *Café Müller*. Courtesy Pina Bausch and
      Ulli Weiss. Photograph: Ulli Weiss.   192
13.2 Jan Minarik, Malou Airaudo and Dominique Mercy in
      Pina Bausch's *Café Müller*. Courtesy Pina Bausch and
      Ulli Weiss. Photograph: Ulli Weiss.   193
13.3 La Ribot, *Another Bloody Mary*. Photograph:
      Hugo Glendinning.   196

Notes on contributors

Simon Bayly is a Research Fellow in the School of Arts at Roehampton University, London, and Director of the theatre group PUR. After ten years working in theatre and performance, Simon completed a Ph.D. entitled 'The Pathognomy of Performance: Theatre, Philosophy and an Ethics of Interruption' in 2002. His current work is on new forms of creative research and assembly and on the function of stupidity, idiocy and not-knowing in the ever-expanding monoculture of excellence.

Marin Blažević is Assistant Lecturer in the Department of Dramaturgy and Theory at the Academy of Drama Arts, University of Zagreb (Croatia). He is also Assistant Researcher for the project '*Branko Gavella: History, Theory and Culture of Theatre*' at the same academy. He is a member of the editorial board of performing arts magazine *Frakcija* and editor of the *Akcija (Action)* book series, which publishes books on performing arts and performance theory (www.cdu.hr). He has published widely on contemporary performance practice, in particular on the 'new theatre' in Croatia. Most recently he co-edited, together with Matthew Goulish, a special issue of *Frakcija – Reflections on the Process/Performance: A Reading Companion to Goat Island's When Will the September Roses Bloom? Last Night was Only a Comedy*, and, together with Nikola Batušić, a book, *Branko Gavella: Teorija Glume – Od Materijala do Ličnosti (Branko Gavella: Theory of Acting – From Material to Personality)*.

Bridget Escolme is a Senior Lecturer in Drama at Queen Mary, University of London, and has held lecturing posts at the University of Leeds and Wimbledon School of Art. Her interest in theatre for young people emerged from an early career in secondary-school drama teaching and Theatre in Education. She has worked in comprehensive schools in Surrey and Nottinghamshire, a further education college in Hull, and for Theatre Centre young people's theatre company in London. She has a long-standing connection with the theatre company Blah Blah Blah, featured in her essay here, and has edited a collection of plays for young people commissioned by the company, and published an essay on their participatory work in Leeds. Her other main research interest is in early modern drama in performance. Both research areas are bound by an interest in the meanings produced by the relationship between performer and audience. Bridget's book *Talking to the Audience: Shakespeare, Performance, Self* was published by Routledge in 2005.

Sarah Gorman is a Senior Lecturer in Drama Theatre and Performance Studies at Roehampton University, London. Her current research focuses upon contemporary British, North American and European experimental theatre, comprising articles on New York City Players, Forced Entertainment, desperate optimists, Stan's Cafe and Janet Cardiff. Her work has been published in a number of journals (*Performance Research, Contemporary Theatre Review, The Drama Review, Theatre Journal, New Theatre Quarterly*) and she is currently preparing contributions to *Making Contemporary Theatre: International Rehearsal Processes* (Harvie & Lavender – due 2007) and Blackwell's *Concise Companion to Contemporary British and Irish Drama* (Luckhurst & Holdsworth – due 2007).

Adrian Heathfield writes on and curates contemporary performance. He is the editor of *Live: Art and Performance* (Tate Publishing, 2004), *Small Acts: Performance, The Millennium and the Marking of Time* (Black Dog Publications, 2000), *On Memory*, an issue of *Performance Research* (Routledge, 2000) with Andrew Quick, and the box publication *Shattered Anatomies: Traces of the Body in Performance* (Arnolfini Live, 1997) with Andrew Quick and Fiona Templeton. He co-curated *Live Culture*, a four-day performance series and two-day international state-of-the-artform symposium at Tate Modern, London, in March 2003 with Lois Keidan and Daniel Brine. He is a Principal Research Fellow at Nottingham Trent University.

Adrian Kear is Principal Lecturer and Subject Leader for Drama, Theatre and Performance Studies at Roehampton University, London. He is the author of numerous articles investigating the relationship between critical theory, cultural politics, performance and ethics. He is the co-editor of *Psychoanalysis and Performance* (Routledge, 2001) and *Mourning Diana: Nation, Culture and the Performance of Grief* (Routledge, 1999). He is a contributor to the academic journals *Contemporary Theatre Review, Parallax* and *Journal for the Psychoanalysis of Culture and Society*, as well as writing regularly for *Performance Research*. He is currently completing a book entitled *Theatre and Event: Performance and the Ethic of Interruption* (Palgrave, forthcoming), supported by funding from the AHRC.

Joe Kelleher teaches in the School of Arts at Roehampton University, London. He has been writing recently on contemporary theatre, performance and performance rhetorics, and his work has appeared in journals such as *Contemporary Theatre Review, Frakcija, Performing Arts Journal* and *Performance Research*, and books such as Deborah Lynn Steinberg and

Richard Johnson's *Blairism and the War of Persuasion* (Lawrence & Wishart, 2004) and Adrian Heathfield's *Live: Art and Performance* (Tate Publishing, 2004). He is the author of a series of essays on Socìetas Raffaello Sanzio's *Tragedia Endogonidia*, published in *Idioma, Clima, Crono* (Cesena, 2002–4), and is currently collaborating, as co-author or contributing author, on books with the Socìetas and with Italian performance collective Kinkaleri. Joe is a member of London-based theatre group PUR.

Susan Melrose is Professor of Performing Arts and Research Convenor for Dance, Music and Theatre Arts at Middlesex University, London. She completed her postgraduate research in the early 1980s with Patrice Pavis and Annie Ubersfeld at the Institut d'Études Théâtrales of the Université de Paris III. She is widely published in performance analysis and her most recent work critiques dominant discourses in Performance Studies in the university. She is a major contributor to the national debate, in the British university, on the 'knowledge status' of professional arts practices, viewed from within the mainstream research context of the university. Her *Semiotics of the Dramatic Text* was published by Macmillan in 1994, and her co-edited *Rosemary Butcher: Choreography, Collisions and Collaborations* was published by Middlesex University Press in 2005.

Sophie Nield is Head of the Centre for Excellence in Training for Theatre at Central School of Speech and Drama, University of London. She has previously taught at the Universities of Roehampton and Glamorgan, and Goldsmiths College, University of London. Sophie writes on questions of space, theatricality and representation in political life and the law, and in nineteenth-century magic shows. She is currently completing a book, *The Social Theatre of Power: Space, Theatricality, Resistance*, and is Director of the AHRC Mander and Mitchenson Theatre Collection Access for Research Project.

Mike Pearson trained as an archaeologist. For the past thirty years he has pioneered innovative approaches in the practice, theory, pedagogy and documentation of performance in Wales and further afield. He was an Artistic Director of Cardiff Laboratory Theatre (1973–80) and Brith Gof (1981–97). Since 1997 he has worked with Mike Brookes in the Pearson/Brookes group, most recently creating multi-site, mediated works in urban contexts. He is co-author with Michael Shanks of *Theatre/Archaeology* (Routledge, 2001); his forthcoming monograph is entitled *'In Comes I': Performance, Locality, and Landscape* (University of Exeter Press, 2006). He is currently Professor of Performance Studies in the Department of Theatre, Film and Television Studies, University of Wales, Aberystwyth.

Andrew Quick is a Senior Lecturer at Lancaster University, where he is also the co-director of the Centre for the Advanced Study of Contemporary Performance Practice. He is co-editor of *On Memory* (2000), an issue of *Performance Research Time and Value* (1998), and *Shattered Anatomies* (1997). He is currently completing two monographs, *The Event of Performance* and *The Wooster Group Book*, both to be published in 2007. His writing on contemporary performance and related art practices has appeared in numerous journals and books. Since 1998 he has also been working with imitating the dog, a performance company based in Leeds. He is co-writer and director (with Pete Brooks) of their latest multimedia work *Hotel Methuselah*, which tours in Europe in 2007.

Nicholas Ridout is Lecturer in Performance at Queen Mary, University of London. He is the author of *Stage Fright, Animals and Other Theatrical Problems* (Cambridge University Press, 2006). He has written extensively on contemporary theatre and performance, publishing articles in *Theatre Research International, Performing Arts Journal, Performance Research, Contemporary Theatre Review, Frakcija* and *TheatreForum*. He was co-editor of the special issue of *Performance Research*, entitled 'On Theatre' (with Richard Gough). He has written a series of eight essays on the work of Socìetas Raffaello Sanzio, in a series of publications entitled *Idioma Clima Crono*, published in conjunction with *Tragedia Endogonidia*. He is currently working with the company and with Joe Kelleher on *The Theatre of Socìetas Raffaello Sanzio: Theatre of Revelation*, to be published by Routledge in 2007.

Heike Roms is Lecturer in Performance Studies at the University of Wales, Aberystwyth. She publishes on contemporary performance practice, in particular on work originating in Wales. Future plans include a history of Welsh performance art and a book on the relationship between performativity and waste. Originally from Germany, she worked in the early 1990s as Head of Press and Publicity for the Internationales Sommertheater Festival Hamburg, where she first saw Acco Theatre Center's *Arbeit macht frei (MiToitland Europa)* in 1993. In 1995, she was Production Manager and Dramaturg for the staging of the work at the *Ruhrfestspiele Recklinghausen*.

Nicholas Till is Director of the Centre for Research in Opera and Music Theatre at the University of Sussex and co-artistic director of the experimental music theatre company Post-Operative Productions (www.post-operative.org). Formerly Course Leader of the MA in Art and Performance Theory at Wimbledon School of Art, London, his publications include *Mozart and the Enlightenment* (Faber, 1992) and 'I Don't Mind if Something's Operatic Just as Long as it's Not Opera: A Critical Practice for New Opera and Music Theatre' (*Contemporary Theatre Review*, February 2004). He is an occasional contributor on contemporary music to *The Wire* magazine, and current research includes a three-year theory-practice project on the 'voice in modernity'.

Acknowledgements

The editors would like to thank the many artists, performers, writers, producers and promoters across Europe whose work, conversation and – in many cases – hospitality has contributed greatly to the development of this book. We would also like to acknowledge the day-to-day contribution of colleagues and students at Queen Mary, University of London and Roehampton University – the sort of contribution to the development of thought that is indispensable to any project of this sort.

Joe Kelleher would also like to gratefully acknowledge Roehampton University and the Arts and Humanities Research Board for study leave support towards the completion of this project.

Foreword from 'across the pond'

Janelle Reinelt

When Joe Kelleher and Nick Ridout approached me with their ideas for *Contemporary Theatres in Europe: A Critical Companion*, my first reaction was to welcome a book that would provide a link to European theatre experiences – very desirable to an American scholar like myself who must negotiate the Atlantic in order to approach the European theatre scene. In the United States, few contemporary European plays are translated and produced, and few companies travel beyond occasional engagements in New York or Los Angeles. To say that it is difficult, without a major investment of time and resources, to keep up with European theatre is only stating the obvious. However, when I'd read the collection of essays, I realised something much more important about this volume. The preoccupations, themes and categories that drive these contributions open up comparative possibilities for modes of theatre scholarship, and triangulate relationships between, on the one hand, UK and US scholarly discourse and European theatrical practice, and on the other, roles of theatre making, theatre theory/criticism and theatre spectatorship. In their introduction Kelleher and Ridout address questions arising from their title: When is the *contemporary*, what are *theatres* and where is *Europe*? These questions become provocative in a transatlantic dialogue as well, since there will be some shared and some divergent ideas about these issues. In what follows, I would like to suggest the characteristics of this book of/on European scholarship from the perspective of my 'Yankee' eye.

First, I am struck by the taken-for-granted seriousness of theatre as a cultural practice when treated by my British colleagues. Missing are the familiar American anxieties about the worth of theatre as an institution. In this book, attending the theatre is an activity that can be presumed to be practised by many – adult citizens, children, civic leaders, townspeople, university students, intellectuals and artists. The theatre is a part (even if only a limited part) of public discourse. An argument does not seem to need to be made so stridently for the worth of the whole theatrical enterprise. On the other hand, several essays do query the future of theatre, imagine its limitations and its utopian possibilities, especially in Simon Bayly's conclusion to this volume, when he asks: What if theatre is stupid?

Along with anxiety about the worth of theatre in the contemporary world, often American scholars have been preoccupied with the status of live theatre in an age of mediatisation. One thinks immediately of Peggy Phelan's and Philip Auslander's contrary formulations of this issue and the way it has continued to occupy an important position in journals and conferences during this past decade. While some essays in *Contemporary Theatres in Europe* discuss aspects of mediation or the context of globalisation, I do not detect any radical scepticism about the worth of the live event. Several essays are explicit about the effects of real bodies on the stage and in the audience (Blažević, Kear and Roms, for example). I would argue that these two concerns are linked in American experience – if the live theatre is not a vibrant form of public discourse, and if the media is the dominant form of representation in a vast country of 300 million diverse inhabitants, then questions about the efficacy of theatre may come more naturally to the fore than they do for Europeans, even if these colleagues are also inevitably circumscribed by globalisation/mediatisation.

Although Americans share with Europeans a Western performance tradition that still tends to trace its origins to Aristotle, this book highlights a European preoccupation with the sense of tradition and its reworking. In particular, the move to define a distinction between 'a European history rather than a universal one', as the editors put it, has consequences for an examination of old problems such as mimesis (in Kelleher, Kear and Quick) and emerging new ones such as Sophie Nield's location of the border as a theatrical space where the person who appears at the border 'must simultaneously be present and be represented'. The history of Europe and its contemporary crucible provokes issues of memory and membership, past events and future possibilities. The colonial past, two world wars and the Holocaust, the breakup of the Soviet Union – all of these European matters are in fact inflected, appropriated and processed differently and with great specificity among the various performances examined here, and the British scholars who conduct the examinations are themselves interrogating their own Europeaness. This seems from the outside something like an insider conversation, but Sarah Gorman's essay on her British spectatorship of the Mladi Levi festival in Ljubljana, Slovenia struck me as profoundly useful for raising questions about American spectatorship in similar settings. The puzzle will have different pieces if the players change, but the problematics of the dislocation of the spectator (and, in the case of festivals, also of the performances) can be analysed to the benefit of spectators/scholars of many identity positions.

This collection affords an opportunity to see how British theatre scholars have been developing their own version of Performance Studies. Involved in the early institutionalisation of the field through, for example, the journal *Performance Research*, the UK seems to be developing an understanding of performance studies that is related to American versions, but also unique to the British situation. A strong community-based theatre tradition, born of deep commitments to place and heritage, shows up in Mike Pearson's essay on the Boxing Day mummers' play in Gloucestershire where performance studies can signify folkloric practices, ludic play and ways of adaptation and transformation in light of concrete material circumstances.

In recent years, the concept of 'performance as research' has been the source of much debate and practical evolution as British academics have sought to work out appropriate scholarly protocols through which to understand performance research, performance as research, and how these practices might be effectively evaluated/valued. Susan Melrose's essay points out how scholars in our field have tended to write from the position of spectators, and urges a deeper engagement with practitioners' expertise. This essay connects in interesting ways with a phenomenon I am seeing with increasing frequency in the States. Many theatre departments are now hiring one or more new faculty who have been explicitly trained in performance studies. Their integration into the previous department does not make much difference at the level of theory or history, when theatre and performance scholars share basic bibliography; rather, it makes a difference at the level of curriculum and programme definition when scholars who are themselves practitioners, and who value the pedagogy and research conducted through practice, encounter departments where often the scholars only read and write while the practitioners try to become trained for the 'professional theatre'. New ways of understanding doctoral training, scholarly achievement, appropriate research projects – all of these things are in flux in the American as well as the British situation, but the inflections are different because of the different histories and academic practices of the two countries.

Many of the topics in this collection will bring welcome new information or perspectives to North American readers. While most of us who study theatre will be very familiar by now with the work of Ariane Mnouchkine or Pina Bausch (although a much smaller number may have seen performances), few will have seen, or perhaps even heard of, Belgium's Victoria company, Italy's Socìetas Raffaello Sanzio or Latvia's New Riga Theatre. The excellent performance analyses of Kear, Quick, Ridout and Kelleher provide rich introductions to their work. A fresh perspective, too, appears in the treatment of children in the volume, both representations of and by them, and in the questions about theatre used as a form of pedagogy (Escolme). In the United States, children's theatre is an underdeveloped genre, nor does it get extensive scholarly attention. There are some excellent scholars of youth theatres such as Manon Van de Water, and some specialised emphases or programmes at a few universities such as Madison (Wisconsin), Austin (Texas) or Tempe (Arizona). But on the whole this is a neglected field, as I became acutely aware when travelling in Scandinavia, where theatre for children is an exceptionally rich aspect of contemporary performance, taken quite seriously by performance scholars. I hope the European perspective on children's theatre as well as the ethical and aesthetic questions asked about the use of children in this collection will be provocative for future transatlantic conversations on these matters.

The last major difference I wish to remark on between British/European theatre and scholarship and the North American variety concerns the deployment of and involvement with philosophy. Americans and Canadians have not been averse to critical theory – but the dominant strains have been cultural studies theory via Edward Said and Gayatri Spivak, literary versions of theory via Derrida or psychoanalysis through Lacan and Kristeva. Americans have pursued feminist theory, critical race theory and post-colonial theory. They have rarely, however, engaged with continental philosophy – Hegel, Kant, Nietzsche, Schopenhauer, Heidegger and, more recently, Agamben, Badiou, maybe Rancière. Some notable American scholars, including Herb Blau from an 'older generation', and Elin Diamond, Jon Erickson, James Harding and Stan Garner have engaged with primary texts from European philosophers. By and large, however, that tradition has not dominated the American scene. Cultural critics (Baudrillard, Benjamin, Stuart Hall) – yes; philosophers, well, maybe not (although in recent years Judith Butler, who is a serious philosopher, has dominated much theatre and performance scholarship). In regard to several of the essays collected here (for example, Kear, Bayly, Kelleher), it is difficult not to describe them as 'philosophical', although some might argue that the term 'theoretical' does just as well. But the self-conscious interest in and involvement with the philosophical tradition is pronounced. The editors of the volume say, '[P]erhaps a feature of the European theatre discussed in this book [is] that it operates in proximity to philosophical thought'. It is worth thinking through what that actually means in the essays here, and whether North Americans would inflect that proximity differently; I believe that they would/do. On the other hand, although many of the essays collected here would probably be considered by their authors as 'political' or having a 'political concern' at their core, the kind of identity politics and overt political activism familiar to American and Canadian theatre scholars is not really found in this volume. Politics may mean something else to Europeans at this historical juncture.

From time to time, two uncomfortable conflations surface in this Foreword. One has to do with the interesting issue of the 'New Europe'. What is Britain's relationship to it? Are these mainly British scholars also Europeans? If so, is it in a particularly designated sense? The other uncomfortable reference is to North America, which sometimes means the US and Canada, but sometimes necessitates a distinction between Canada and the States, and resists an easy umbrella term. In my Foreword, neither of these has been satisfactorily resolved. The book, as well as my remarks, offers instances of trying to work with and in between these unsatisfactory categories, which nevertheless mark the geographies of our discourse.

This is a remarkably good book – not only are the essays and the Editors' comments incisive and stimulating, but the idea of the book as an intervention into contemporary scholarly discourse is also provocative at the metatheatrical-metapedagogical level. I learned a great deal from 'across the pond', some of which translates differently in the context of my own national traditions of scholarly practice. I admire this work and have learned from it and, I hope, dear readers, that you will too.

Introduction

Joe Kelleher and Nicholas Ridout

This is a book about experiences of theatre. It takes as its starting point the encounters that take place in the theatre between the spectator and the performance. These encounters are located, and part of the project of this book is to account for the ways in which the experience of a particular theatre event is marked by its location, be that geographical, cultural or social in nature. Almost inevitably, the experiences of which we are writing here are experiences that you, the reader, will not have shared. You were not there, that night, in that theatre, when it happened. More than that, many of the artists and companies of whom we are writing here are not widely known in the English-speaking world. Even in the UK, separated from so-called 'continental' Europe by a narrow stretch of water, much of this work will only have been seen by those with the time and the resources to travel. This situation is, of course, far more acute for those living in parts of the English-speaking world that are much further away from Europe than that. So you might want to think about the essays in this volume as reports from travellers, from people who have had the chance – the time and the resources – to make the journeys.

This is one of the reasons why this book does not claim to be a survey. There is no attempt here to be comprehensive, either in the kinds of work that are discussed or in the locations to which the writers have travelled. The individual contributors have been guided in their work by their interest in writing about those encounters with theatre that have provoked, troubled, intrigued or enchanted them. Many of these encounters have been recent, and this means that much of the work discussed has not received sustained critical attention (or, in some instances, any critical attention at all) in English-language scholarship. We hope, therefore, that for many of our readers this book will serve as an introduction to a range of theatres, and to theatre practices that are among those that we think may turn out to be significant for the immediate future development of theatre in Europe. It is not, though, an attempt to predict the canon of the future or to define – either by inclusion or exclusion – what should be considered important in the theatre of the present moment. What it attempts, instead, is to offer a range of different ways of thinking and writing about the kinds of encounter that take place, these days, in the theatre. Each essay in this book might be read, then, as an attempt – this is what an essay is, after all – and each attempt has been written in the expectation that those readers who also want to be writers will make their own attempts, develop their own strategies of writing and response to theatrical performance.

This is also, in a minor way, a book about Europe, or at least a book in which a certain reckoning with the fact of Europe – European history and cultural institutions (including, of course, theatre in its European forms) – is made. During the writing of this book there has been much talk and considerable resources devoted to the project of 'European' expansion, with the accession, in May 2004, of nine new member countries (mainly from the former Eastern bloc) to the European Union, and the initiation, in October 2005, of negotiations between the EU and Turkey on Turkey's future accession. The Europe of this book is not identical with the Europe of this other, grander project. Some of the thinking and conversation that has contributed to the composition of this book has taken place in Brussels (which is, of course, the administrative heart of that other project), in St Petersburg (surely one of the great European theatrical locations, but not part of that other project at all), in Riga (recently welcomed into the other project), in Belgrade (which still maintains a distinctly difficult relationship with the other project) and in Israel and Palestine (which sit firmly outside the geographical and political space of the European Union, but whose present and whose past, as Heike Roms shows in her chapter here, have so much to do with the ways in which we might think of ourselves as European or not). The idea of Europe as an imaginary space is something that surfaces in many of these essays, and the theatre as a place where that imaginary space gets imagined is a recurrent theme across the volume as a whole. But Europe is also, as Sophie Nield will show (in an essay that thinks about theatre as something that extends beyond the space of the theatre itself, into social and political realities) far from imaginary. It has borders which are often fiercely defended against those that Europe wants to keep out. At the time of writing the European (Spanish) enclaves of Ceuta and Melilla in Moroccan North Africa are the locations for violent acts of exclusion in which people trying to enter Europe are being expelled to die in the desert. The imaginary and the real are not opposites where Europe is concerned. It is a particular imagination of what Europe should be that leads to the expulsion and death of those whose presence might challenge such imaginaries, or open up alternative possibilities.

The encounters about which the writers who have contributed to the present volume have written seem to have thrown up difficulties that might initially be addressed by asking the obvious questions about the title of the book itself: When is the *contemporary*, what are *theatres* and where is *Europe*? Clearly no book, of this or any other kind, is likely to offer definitive answers to such questions. Our aim here is rather to suggest interesting ways in which these questions might be explored. We have already suggested a few of the ways in which we imagine where Europe might be, as far as this project is concerned. The 'contemporary' and the 'theatres' of our title perhaps require a little further comment.

Two ways of thinking about the contemporary might emerge from such explorations, for example. On the one hand, the contemporary might be thought of as the time of the encounter; the time around a particular theatrical experience in which you might be enfolded. This could be a very short contemporary – the time in which you are face to face with the theatrical production itself, the time of the present during which you are in your seat in the theatre and the event is taking place on stage. It could be thought of as a longer time, however – the time of thought and research around a particular event or, indeed, a particular theatrical practice. The different temporalities of the performer and the spectator might be worth thinking about here. As Susan Melrose observes in her chapter, the theatrical production is usually a once-only affair for the spectator, whereas it might be the experience of months, if not years, of work (in preparation, rehearsal and performance) for those who make the theatre. In the cases of companies like Ariane Mnouchkine's Théâtre du Soleil, for example (the focus of Melrose's chapter), or of Socìetas Raffaello Sanzio, or indeed any of the companies whose work constitutes an ongoing exploration, the notion of the contemporary might be defined in terms of the lifetime of the company itself, its members and its projects. On the other hand, an alternative sense of the contemporary might be derived in relation to historical time. It is striking, for example, how frequently, in the essays contributed to this volume, the theatre discussed is engaging with, or at least working within the context created by, the events of the mid-twentieth century: the Second World War and the Shoah. This historical catastrophe and its ramifications in today's culture and social relations seems, at least in this book, to determine a particular contemporary (perhaps a particularly European contemporary).

Our use of the term 'theatres' is perhaps an attempt to preserve a sense of a cultural and institutional tradition of theatre making in Europe, and to suggest that even those experimental practices that we might be tempted simply to file under 'performance' still enjoy (or suffer) some historical relationship with practices that have commonly been accepted as theatre. At the same time, our use of the plural form perhaps betrays an anxiety around definition. Perhaps we are not comfortable with the idea that there is any such thing as 'theatre'. Perhaps we simply don't want to worry too much about whether something is theatre or performance. Perhaps we want to have our cake and eat it, too. At least that is one way of trying to hold on to the experiences of the encounters, and to stay faithful to them, in all their ambivalence and promiscuity.

Joe Kelleher starts our consideration of contemporary theatre with a suggestion that some of the most distinctive theatre practices of the early twenty-first century are worrying away at some of the same questions that preoccupied theatre makers at the start of the twentieth. In particular, Kelleher suggests, the conception of 'theatre as a mechanism of human interaction, or more elaborately a means of representing reality from – and to – a human point of view', is shared by Stanislavsky and Gorky one hundred years ago as well as by today's TV 'reality shows' and the theatre practices of Alvis Hermanis in Riga and the Norwegian experimental performance group Baktruppen. For Kelleher, one might speculate, the 'contemporary' of our title is one in which Stanislavsky himself remains our contemporary.

The idea of a return to 'theatrical basics' that Kelleher notes in the work of these artists might be taken further, to suggest that what looks, superficially, to be a product of a very particular historical moment (the last decade, perhaps) – with its live video relays – is also the latest instalment in a centuries-long struggle over the ways in which we, as humans, represent ourselves to one another. Kelleher's chapter, then, invites us to think historically about the present, and to think of the practice of theatre itself as a constant returning to some very old problems – how to put human beings on stage and have them imitate human beings and their actions. An historical thinking along these lines will also have to recognise that it is a European history that is being thought rather than a universal one: Aristotle may be seen not as the transcendent origin of all theatre so much as the adopted father of a European theatre that can't keep its hands off the problems and the possibilities the Greek philosopher first articulated in his famous *Poetics*.

It is perhaps a feature of the European theatre discussed in this book that it operates in proximity to philosophical thought. That is perhaps why a significant number of contributors to this volume articulate relations between theatrical and philosophical practice. They do so not because 'theory' – to which philosophical texts are all too often reduced in the contemporary study of culture (as Simon Bayly protests in his chapter) – can be used to explain or interpret specific theatre events or works (we prefer here to resist such approaches), but because the practices of theatre and philosophy have for so long worked hand in hand (or wrestled arm against arm) over similar questions (representation, human nature, truth, illusion).

Kelleher suggests the presence of this very long European history (as, in various ways, do Melrose and Ridout in later chapters) while also drawing specific attention to a particular, shorter-term historical relationship: a history in which representations of the human at the dawn of revolutionary socialism in Russia come into startling contact with representations of the human not long after the twilight of Soviet Communism.

That they should do so in Riga is itself significant as an occasion for thinking about history and theatre history, since the Latvian capital was one of those European cities that suffered most intensely from the political conflicts of the twentieth century, enduring occupation by both the Nazis and the Soviet Union.

History is also at the heart of Nicholas Till's account of contemporary 'post-operatic' music theatre. In the work of Christoph Marthaler, Heiner Goebbels and Salvatore Sciarrino, Till identifies a range of strategies for dealing with the compromised history of opera as a theatrical form. Opera, he argues, is not only an art form that has survived its own death; it staggers onward under the terrible burden of complicity with European totalitarianism. It is no accident that it is in Italy and Germany, the nations most acutely aware of their own role in mid-century fascism and Nazism, that these developments have been taking place. In post-operatic music theatre, then, we are dealing with an attempt to move beyond the living deadness of opera itself by confronting explicitly, in musical and theatrical languages, the realities of twentieth-century genocide and fascist aggression. Again, there is an invitation to think about contemporary theatre in Europe in historical terms, not just as the outcome of a specifically European historical process, but also as part of that history, as an attempt to engage with it, account for its continued power over us, both intellectual and emotional.

Heike Roms' chapter on Israeli Acco Theatre Center *Arbeit macht frei MiToitland Europa* looks at just one instance of recent theatrical production to engage with related problems of history, memory and feeling. The theatre event is an encounter between people with their own memories and histories; in the case of this production, an encounter between Jewish and Arab citizens of Israel and spectators in Germany. The affective dynamics of the theatre encounter seem to offer a way of getting at what matters, subjectively, in history. Acco Theatre Centre's work is in part a critique of the official acts of memorialisation that stand in for history in so much contemporary public discourse. Roms suggests that theatre's capacity to bring the process of making history into the present of the face-to-face encounter gives it a particular emotional power and political efficacy. In part, that power derives from ways in which, in the production that she addresses in her chapter, 'Historical time and theatrical time become superimposed'. In this respect Roms draws our attention to an ambivalence of the term 'work' – the *Arbeit* of the show's title – which might refer at the same time to the production itself, the labour of theatrical devising that went into making the production, but also to the 'death-bringing labour regime of the camps', as well as the critical work of remembering that is stretched out, as it were, between an accumulation of historical 'knowledge' and the immediate now-time of the theatrical encounter. An effect of this superimposition of historical and theatrical time is to challenge the 'innocence' of the theatrical spectators, who are provoked instead to respond to the performance as bearers of knowledge and memory, and provoked too to consider their complicity in what – and how – they remember. For Roms, the effect is compounded as she recognises the impossibility of separating her initial impressions of the performance from subsequent attempts to engage with the work, either as a participant or returning spectator, or as a writer on this and other occasions. Any present spectating, then – any way in which one might attempt again to look upon the scene and see things anew – is, in one way or another, infected by remembering. This remembering may, of course, be the sort of enriched recognition that would see the work of Acco Theatre Center as belonging to a tradition of experimental European theatre making that would include the likes of Grotowski and Kantor, as Roms allows at the end of her chapter. However, even to allow such a recognition is to acknowledge at the same time the eventual dissolution of historical memory (might Acco really be the 'last representative' of this tradition?) and – not least in the theatre – the breaking up of remembering, whether in the face of an immediate and personal theatrical challenge or else in the face of that wasted landscape that lies outside, beyond (but only just beyond) the 'contemporary' theatrical scene: 'the "deathland" that was twentieth-century Europe'.

Sophie Nield would also draw our attention to the landscape of European history, and ways in which we might think of that landscape as being constituted in theatrical terms. Nield, in the first of three chapters (along with chapters by Melrose and Bayly) that pose challenges to the activity of theatre scholarship, invites us to think theatrically about one of the pressing political issues in contemporary Europe – the movement of people. Nield offers an extension of the concept of theatricality that works to illuminate the structure of events such as the appearance of a refugee at a border. In so doing, she asks us to consider the value – and the dangers – of a theatrically informed thinking for our attempts to understand the world we live in and our encounters with the people who appear (and disappear) in the making up of this world. For Nield, it is appearance that matters. She suggests that we think of the theatrical in terms of 'the production of a space in which "appearance" of a particular kind becomes possible'. This is a complex operation, which involves the fictional space of a drama or fantasy just as much as it involves the supposedly actual space of a stage, and where both are subject to the localisations of judgement and point of view – call these the spaces of the audience – across which all such appearances are encountered. An aspect of this complexity is the sort of 'double exposure' that seems endemic to any theatrical appearing. We might think of this double exposure in terms of the ways in which one appearance is contingent upon another; for example, the ways in which the appearance of the 'refugee' as such is dependent upon the conception of a 'border', and vice versa the ways in which the border impinges as a political fact at the moment in which someone appears who would cross to the other side. Nield, however, takes the matter further by considering any of these appearances as, in themselves, double exposures. According to the theatrical logic at work here, the person who appears at the border 'must simultaneously be present and be represented'. They must be there, as it were, in person; and they must be there as the person they are supposed to be. This is to say, too, that they must be there for someone else, for whoever it may be – or whatever 'legal/juridical mechanisms' there may be – that will see and acknowledge these performances. This someone else is the audience, the spectators who will consider, and pass judgement upon, the relations between who (or what) presents themselves and who (or what) these presentations may be taken to represent. Nield's engagement, then, of a 'theatrical' argument to consider such matters, returns us to important political considerations. Among the questions she poses there is the question of how 'we' – we humans, we Europeans – represent ourselves to each other, and how these representations might function in relation to those occasions where we choose, perhaps, to represent nothing, but simply appear to each other (if this were ever possible) *as* 'each other', as fellows *and* others, as familiars and strangers. Then again, to turn the matter upon its blind side as it were, there is the question of how and under what conditions 'we' – or 'they' – might choose instead strategies not of appearance but of invisibility. There are questions, too, of how we might act – how we might think when such strategies appear chosen for us, before our journeys are even begun.

Kelleher, Till, Roms and Nield all write with an awareness of the defining force of a particular European historical experience. 'Contemporary Europe' is therefore a social, political and cultural reality and imaginary shaped by the ways in which this particular sequence of events has been experienced by the different people who now imagine themselves really to be part of contemporary Europe. It should be no surprise that theatre makers will be found worrying away at the impact of these experiences, not because theatre 'reflects reality' but because this historical experience has shaped what it means to be a maker of theatre in contemporary Europe. We are not suggesting that all the theatre makers whose work is discussed in this volume set out to make work that is somehow 'about' this historical experience, but rather that they, and we, and you, all experience theatre, and its meanings, in a way that is shaped, at least to some extent, by that history.

Sarah Gorman detects consequences of particular historical experiences in a variety of experimental performances seen at the Mladi Levi festival in Ljubljana, Slovenia, while also reflecting upon the cultural, political and linguistic particularity of her own experience as a spectator of performance and as someone trying to account for it in writing. She also introduces a (perhaps otherwise rather submerged) theme which the attentive reader might like to trace through the various chapters of the book – the theme of the festival.

The theatre festival in twentieth-century Europe seems to have been one of those initiatives designed in the aftermath of catastrophe (the Second World War) in the hope that if we performed enough of these ameliorative actions the future might be better. The theatre festival, bringing us together around a common fascination and a set of values that we might somehow agree to be European, would help heal the wounds and bind back together the diverse communities whose lives had been torn asunder by war and by genocide. In this perspective the theatre festival looks like part of a wider project, of which the European Union itself – a political organisation that today includes twenty-five nations – is perhaps the most substantial instance. The theatre festival has come under fire, or at least it has been questioned in recent years, on the grounds that it encourages a mode of cultural consumerism in which the same familiar productions – often by celebrated auteurs, visually sumptuous and universally appealing – circulate from festival to festival. The festival, once perhaps an occasion for discovery and community, becomes simply a further site for the consumption of the spectacular familiar.

Gorman's chapter questions this consumption of the seemingly familiar, by focusing on her own situation as a British spectator-scholar at the Mladi Levi festival. She asks how the sort of perspectives and competences she brings to her understanding of a range of experimental performance work that she encounters in the Slovenian capital might be formed and disrupted by conditions of cultural dislocation. For Gorman, any attempt on her part to account for the socio-geographical complexities of Europe – or European performance – will raise the issue of how she may understand her own identity as a 'European'. Gorman's approach to this issue is to begin with descriptions – from the point of view of a theatre spectator – of the performances she has witnessed in Ljubljana. Immediately, though, the work of description raises a question of interpretation. What sort of knowledge and expectation go into the selecting and framing of a 'reading'? How far, and under what conditions, does a work of performance 'translate'? And how far, given the various dislocations involved here – the dislocation of the spectator, but also the dislocations of the works themselves in the context of an international festival – can a reader trust his or her intuition, even at the level of his or her 'intuition as to what the show might be "about"'? Such questions, however, do not absolve the spectator-scholar from the responsibility of making a reading and trying to account for what happens in the theatrical encounter. Gorman therefore organises her understandings of the works, in the first instance, in relation to the situation of socio-geographical dis-location according to which she encounters them. That is, she sketches a 'crudely distinguish[ed]' map of Northern European and Southern European experimental theatre cultures and sensibilities. Then, across that map, she explores the variations of a theme – the theme of 'harm' – as this appears to emerge for her in the internalised, confessional rhetorics of certain Dutch or British performance work, or else in the more violent and more explicitly political work of the Spanish company Conservas.

As Gorman acknowledges, there are limitations to this thematic mapping – not least the danger of constructing a reductive analytical binary – although at the same time certain possibilities are opened up: a possibility at least of reading performance practice (and the practice of performance analysis) in relation to different sorts of historical experience, and *not least* in relation to a specifically Slovenian experience which might frame the context within which these works are being presented together. The effect of Gorman's analysis is to draw our attention to the contexts wherein our interpretations are performed, and to challenge us to recognise the contradictions that inform our attempts to make sense. If we go to the theatre with the hope that we might understand things better by understanding differently – for example, by encountering ourselves in the reflection of an other, of 'someone who sees differently' – we should also understand that 'the images we get back, and those we make of "others" are not, and can never be, mirrored directly back'. And if, in this era of expanding European 'unification', there appears a tendency towards the obscuring of cultural difference for the sake of a certain cultural hegemony – a festivalising, let's say, of a generic Western European sensibility – we may do well, as we consume the products of this festivalisation, to 'attest to the difficulty' of the mechanisms of communication by which the festival appears to be sustained.

It's probably fair to say that a great deal of the theatre seen by the authors of this collection in recent years – by the editors perhaps above all – has been presented at festivals (Avignon, Edinburgh, Homo Novus, Zürcher Theaterspektakel, Bitef, Santarcangelo, Kunstenfestival des Arts, to name but a few). The theatre festival thus enables a certain kind of theatre scholarship, too, a certain kind of expert spectatorship. Is this a problem? To what extent is theatre now something which is only encountered once it has been detached from its 'real', 'authentic' context – the site of its production – and reassembled in some alien and inauthentic context of consumption in which its 'real' meanings vanish? Or is the idea of the 'real' and the 'authentic' actually just some sort of fetish of theatrical desire, all the more perverse when you recall that theatre has always, surely, traded in the non-real and the inauthentic?

Both Marin Blažević and Adrian Kear address the question of theatre's desire for the 'real' by considering the ways in which theatrical practices engage human bodies in mimesis, i.e. engage real bodies in the business of pretend, the business (and pleasure) of the 'as if', the 'what if?' and – of course – the 'if only'. Again, a 'double exposure' is involved since, in both of these chapters, there is an analysis of the sorts of demands made upon those performing bodies that are given, on the one hand, to serve the agendas (the fiction, the fantasy if you will) of the theatrical representation by standing in *for* something other than themselves and, on the other hand, sustain the authenticity of that fantasy by standing in *as themselves*: real bodies, really there, as real as you or I.

Marin Blažević writes about a series of transitions in Croatian theatrical culture during the 1990s – on the professional theatrical stage, but also on the theatricalised 'stage' of the Croatian state since the communist period, through the years of nationalism and after. The theatre under discussion, then, may well be the performance of a dramatic fiction for an audience of specialist spectators, but it might also be a 'popular' state spectacle (a military parade, for example) or indeed an actual battlefield. The theatre, in this argument, appears wherever human bodies are put under a particular representational pressure, whereby they are obliged both to serve as inviolate signs of this or that theatrical operation, and at the same time suffer the vulnerability of any actual fleshly body, a vulnerability that involves a capability of being replaced, hurt, or even killed. Blažević's historical-political argument is detailed and complex, not least in his insistence on the very different conditions and possibilities that pertain in specific representational situations, where the body's 'real' is on each occasion in a particular, transitional relation to the sorts of theatrical 'realisms' that would both exploit and obscure that actuality. However, what plays throughout the argument is a suggestion that these historical specificities might be approached, whatever the performance, by asking each time a version of the same question, which would be a question about the agency of the performing bodies. To look after the bodies, as it were, is a way of taking care, in the sense of an assumed responsibility for others (a 'caring for'), but also in the sense in which one might heed a warning for oneself ('take care') – in the face of a theatre that has its own eye upon the bodies, its own sense of what it wants the bodies to be or do.

This caring eye upon the performing bodies is at the heart of Adrian Kear's analysis of a performance by the Victoria company from Belgium, in which the majority of the bodies on stage were those of young children and teenagers. In a sense, Kear's chapter is an exemplary instance of a key procedure that runs throughout this book, in that it addresses the question of a contemporary European theatre through the optic of a particular theatrical encounter that disturbs the thought of the spectator, and in such a way that this disturbance seems to impact on the wider theatrical landscape within which the encounter took place. For Kear, though, the Victoria performance was itself 'exemplary', in that this was one of those rarer occasions – for this particular spectator – when the theatre 'worked'.

What works, however, in this encounter is inextricable from what disturbs, not least because the theatrical logic of the performance would appear to implicate the adult spectator, at some level, in a paedophilic gaze upon the young performers, a gaze which would seem to coincide with the actual situation of the paying spectators in the theatre auditorium on that particular evening. As with the previous chapter by Blažević, Kear does not seek to excuse himself from the theatre's disturbing logic but embarks rather on a logical analysis – as far, that is, as the theatrical encounter, reapproached *after the event*, over a distance of time, will allow anything like a logical procedure to be sustained. In this instance a psychoanalytic analysis is brought to bear that might provide the tools for an examination of the theatre's 'affective dynamics', which is to say the ways in which a performance might produce a 'gut reaction'. This is a reaction that relates, not just to the bodies that perform on stage, but also to the body of the spectator that registers that performance. It is also, though, a reaction that is involved in a theatrical operation, a 'mimetic' operation according to which structures of meaning may be other than they seem, and mean something other than they seem to say.

As Kear suggests – and again the suggestion could apply to both the chapters under discussion here – if we can understand better the mimetic operations involved, particularly on those occasions when the theatre appears to 'work', then we might understand better the ways in which theatre appears both 'to mark and to mask the materiality and historicity of its signifying practice'. This understanding might lead us into questions that both Blažević and Kear, along with several others in the book, might want to ask of the theatre's workings – questions such as 'Work for whom?' and 'Work to produce what?' In the context of a study of theatre practices in contemporary Europe, such questions would appear in the first instance to produce a focus upon issues of violence, community, spectacle and the production of meaning as a function of ideology. That last, though, whether one is at home encountering the work of a visiting 'international' company or reflecting upon the transitions in one's 'own' national theatrical culture, is always a production of meaning *for* someone. Spectators that find themselves before 'a battlefield of identities and bodies' (Blažević) are particular spectators, who must come to terms with their personal implication (a political, moral and even physical implication) in the spectacle and its violent performatives. However, as Kear allows in his conclusion, a better understanding of theatrical seduction and of the mimetic operations that implicate *me* in its event might serve as 'bearing witness to the culture of abuse that is represented, almost literally, as our shared, complicit, but nonetheless collective responsibility'.

Susan Melrose is also concerned with what we might mean when we say that a theatrical production appears to 'work'. And, like the authors who precede her in this collection, she will locate that working – in large part – in operations of affect, as well as crediting the theatre's affective transformations (of whatever resistant materials it takes hold of) to the labours of 'moving bodies'. However, Melrose also insists in her chapter that we also think of the professional expertises that inform these movements, in particular the performance practice expertises that go into the production of a theatrical 'work'. She proposes, too, that we consider how these differ from the sorts of writerly expertises that inform the labours of the 'expert spectator', who tends to approach the work from some very particular – and somewhat limiting – perspectives. As such, Melrose challenges us to think very carefully about what we are doing when we write about theatre and performance. She suggests that what we are doing, not least in the universities, is not really performance studies, but spectator studies.

Melrose's argument, however, is not that we tend to ignore performer perspectives but rather that, even when we attend to them, we tend to incorporate such perspectives within the sorts of points of view that support the concerns of a theatrical spectator, whose regular mode of expression is a form of writing, predicated usually upon a backward glance, a remembering of what is gone, that is ill-equipped to articulate the different sorts of knowledge and practice – often collaborative, mixed-mode, affectively driven, future-oriented practices – that go into the making of professional theatre. Melrose suggests, for example, through a consideration of approaches to the work of Ariane Mnouchkine and the Théâtre du Soleil, that the collaborative aspect of much performance making is misrecognised in performance studies' need to give a name to 'signature' practices; or that an academic tendency to privilege radical, 'cutting-edge' practice might tend to misrecognise the ways that such radicality is dependent upon a professionalism, a 'disciplinary mastery' even. Furthermore, she argues that any attempt to understand this sort of expertise will have to deal with the fact that even this mastery bears – or can appear to bear – a certain fragility, for example when the work of performance making, projected as it is towards a future event, appears to run ahead of the present knowledge of the performance makers themselves. Melrose finds this and other possibilities evidenced in a video of Mnouchkine and her collaborators in rehearsal, an 'insider' document which – Melrose argues – better 'theorises' this practice than any expert writing could. Not least, the video would appear to evidence the fact that, for the practitioner too, there is an affective encounter, in her case with the unknown known of the 'work itself' (a phrase that Melrose warns us to guard ourselves against). In short, the practitioner does not know exactly what will emerge from her labours. However, she – along with her collaborators – has a sense of how one can work towards whatever *might* emerge. This working towards, this being able to carry through, is a hard-won expertise. It is also (and this theme will be touched on again soon enough in subsequent chapters of this book) something of a gift: both in the sense, perhaps, in which we might think of a 'gifted' practitioner (in that case an acquired gift, a gift of disciplinary mastery) and also in the sense of the gift that is brought, after all, before the spectators, who will best acknowledge the encounter, not so much in their academic writings as in the generosity of their applause.

Melrose's concern with practitioner perspectives finds a forceful echo in Mike Pearson's chapter, which will assert, at its conclusion, 'an increasing personal urge to reorientate the enquiry of performance studies from spectatorship – both aesthetic and academic – and towards a more acute concern with – a closer listening to – what practitioners themselves perceive that they are doing'. Pearson's urge is also, in large part, the urge *of* a practitioner, who receives – from the gift of the theatrical encounter – a provocation to better understand performance practice, in terms of where it has come from and to whom it belongs, but also as opening on to a set of possibilities of what might still be *done*. As such, Pearson's chapter looks towards a concern – or we might say a tendency – that runs throughout the book, which relates to the academic tendency Melrose identifies to privilege the 'radical' in contemporary arts, and which is evidenced in several analyses in this volume that explore the European theatrical scene by way of practices that appear, themselves, to privilege an alternative, reflexive, experimental approach to their work.

Part of the provocation, however, that Pearson offers us in his chapter is that these possibilities for an 'alternative' contemporary theatre are not located in an experimental performance practice as such, nor any sort of professional theatre, and nor are they gathered home by casting into the immediate future for the next new thing, or even looking abroad for the strange familiar. Rather, the encounter takes place (more or less) *at* home, in relation to the performer expertises that sustain a traditional mummers' play that is given every Boxing Day on the streets of Marshfield in Gloucestershire, England. The encounter here is not so much singular as seasonal. Pearson suggests it has the nature of a returning 'visitation'. And, in the returns of the mummers, what returns also is a set of reflections upon the politics and economics, the material histories, the ergonomics, the ways of remembering and doing, the survivals and transformations of any localised, contemporary performance practice. This is to say, too, that the work is 'contemporary' to the extent that it bears with it, on the one hand, a sense of ambiguous continuity marked by historical rupture. Pearson is careful to point out, for example, ways in which the 'authentic' oral tradition is, in part, sustained thanks to an archival-folkloric 'reconstitution'; and how the function of the performance has changed over the centuries, from a means–ends activity (a performance offered in hard times by out-of-work labourers in exchange for the gift of alms) to a form of 'ludic play' that itself constitutes a 'gift' towards the local community. The other aspect of this theatre's contemporaneity has to do, though, with what these particular practices might share with other performance practices in other climates. That *other* contemporary European theatre is also *here*, wherever 'here' is, although it takes, perhaps, an ear – rather than an eye – to attend to it: as Pearson says, 'a closer listening to'. Again, what this listening will attempt to attend to is what the performers think they are 'doing', because 'to actually do it, that's something else'.

The phrase 'something else', which Pearson borrows from one of the Marshfield Mummers, does, however, serve to register a return to a theme that has been at work throughout the book so far, and which we have already remarked upon. That theme involves an attention paid by most, if not all, of these authors to the pleasures and challenges of *mimesis*, as if any investigation of a European theatrical landscape cannot help but uncover all sorts of ambivalently imitative acts – a range of mimetic doublings that seem to unsettle, even as they constitute, the very substance of the contemporary 'here and now'.

Andrew Quick considers this 'something else' of mimetic performance in terms of a 'revolutionary' – we might even say utopian – possibility. Quick draws his analytical framework from a very 'old European' source, the Marxist-inflected cultural theory of Walter Benjamin, which was written during (and in the face of) the rise to power in Germany of Adolf Hitler in the 1920s and 1930s. What this move allows, however, is the consideration of utopian possibility as an actuality that might appear still, within the materiality of an act of performance, or more specifically within a theatrical 'gesture', even more specifically within the gestures of a children's theatre. The gesture of the child performer, according to Benjamin (and in an analysis that will recall arguments set out by Adrian Kear earlier in the volume), is a 'secret signal' that draws its life from some other place, a world beyond adult comprehension, a place seemingly withdrawn from 'meaning', so that it seems to involve the sort of mimetic labour that might force a break in what tends to stand for knowledge, a rip in time, so that 'something' else, a future meaning, might appear to present itself. This is, as Quick says, a 'future that has yet to be conceived as knowledge'. Again, as was the case with Kear's chapter – and in a gesture of return on Quick's part, of looking again and otherwise, that the editors hope will serve to point up the sort of exploratory further thinking that this book seeks to support – Quick finds his theatrical encounter in another project with child performers by the Belgian company Victoria. What he recognises in this 2003 work is a putting-into-practice of the possibilities of Benjamin's 1929 'Program for a Proletarian Children's Theater', a practice which manifests itself, however, not so much in Marxist (or even proletarian) terms, but rather as a peculiar stop–start mimesis, a doing – or rather 'being done' – that imitates, as it were in real time, a particular given world, while refusing to participate or even identify with that world outside of this act of imitating (and to an extent transforming) its gestures, as these are given to appear within the same theatrical frame. In Quick's reading, it is, then, the interrupted time of the children's mimetic play that is differentiated from the time of the represented adult world out of which those actions are derived, even as these two worlds seem to co-exist simultaneously, the one on stage, the other on a film screen at the back of the stage. And it is out of this differentiation – this doubling of time, this mimetic opening up of the world of play – that the unnameable 'something else' might emerge, as a gesture towards the past on behalf of the future, a possibility for the fulfilment – and also, of course, betrayal – of a promise that was laid down long ago and still awaits its articulation.

Perhaps, though, that 'long ago' might give us further pause, particularly in the context of a book that claims to be addressing *contemporary* European arts. We have already pointed out that several authors in this book would persuade us to think about our encounters with current performance practice in Europe in historical and/or technical-mimetic terms. That is, our encounters here with theatrical meaning are likely to be inflected by particular European histories that impinge upon the work, whether at the levels of its production or its reception or both; and, furthermore, these meanings are indeed the effects of a particular set of material practices engaged in the production of material *fictions* that manifest as so many 'double exposures' or 'constitutive ambiguities', so many 'scenes of seduction', so many somethings or somewheres else. In other words, other times and other places, other points of view, are likely to be involved in any 'contemporary' theatrical event. That is all well and good. What might give us pause, however, is the currency of the theatrical fiction as such. In short, we might want to ask – given our familiarity, say, with technological media that would seem capable of effecting whatever displacements, imaginings and transformations we might call for and doing so, as it were, immediately, without any of the theatre's phoniness, without any of its laborious huff and puff – we might want to ask whether the theatre is really a contemporary art form at all.

Both Bridget Escolme and Nicholas Ridout, in their chapters, address this question, and do so by relating contemporary encounters with the production of theatrical fiction to the larger scene of a modern European imaginary. In both of these chapters a predominantly bourgeois, rational-scientific 'modern Europe' is given as the context within which theatre appears – or, rather, professional theatre makers labour – both metaphorically and literally – to work a certain 'magic'. This is theatre made out of some decidedly pre-modern materials (for example, classical rhetoric, folk tales and – in both chapters – acts of mimetic conjuring), but which would appear – explicitly so in the case of the educational theatre for children that Escolme writes about – to seek out, even to contribute to the formation of, a certain *post*-modern spectator, a future citizen perhaps of an *other* Europe, a re-imagined Europe that hovers as it were just beyond the edge of whatever stories we might feel we can believe, whatever acts and events we feel we can take seriously, or whatever values (dread word) we imagine we uphold and consider ourselves to act upon when we do the things we do. As such, these are theatres concerned, after all, with the agency of the spectator, which is to say, indeed, the (political, intellectual, moral) freedom of the spectator – although that is a freedom also to 'fall for' the theatrical fiction, and to keep falling even though we can't really credit it, can't quite credit that this is anything like 'real life'.

Bridget Escolme approaches these issues through an examination of the theatricalisation of folk tales in recent European theatre for children. She opens, on the one hand, an historical perspective by considering the development of these tales from their pre-modern, oral, folk context towards their appropriation by modern bourgeois literary cultures, and the ambivalence of their deployment in therapeutic and moral-pedagogic contexts – particularly in relation to the 'training' of children's imaginations. On the other hand, Escolme opens what we referred to above as a technical-mimetic perspective by focusing closely on the theatrical methods of particular performances through which some of these tales are retold. She examines ways in which, for example, a shift from a reading-to towards a performing-for might effect shifts in the power relationship between the teller (adult) and told (child), enabling the child spectator to see through – or around – the storyteller's rhetorical authority, enabling the child, too, to take a certain control of the meanings they might make of the fiction, and to give empathy so to speak where it is due rather than where it is demanded. Running throughout Escolme's chapter, however, we might also find a suggestion that we should not take this theatrical enabling of spectator agency totally on trust. Escolme asks, at the head of her chapter, a question about 'what happens to these tales when we make theatre out of them, and the kinds of children we imagine and produce when we do so'. If we can hear in this question something like a tone of unease or even warning – or at least a certain vigilance with regard to the arts practices we support and the reasons we think we support them – we might find that vigilance at work in those moments of the analysis where the 'agency' of the child spectator is given in part by an apparent 'loss of control' on the part of the adult performer (a loss of control that might seem to be suspended somewhere between play and violence) or where the deployment of theatrical realism in an otherwise 'empowering' production seems to conjure up – alongside the future citizen's imaginative capabilities – the ghosts of some rather older misogynist stereotypes. The suggestion throughout the chapter – indeed the premise of much of the work that Escolme's chapter examines – is that these productions of fiction might have certain 'real' effects, for which one might want to take care.

Real effects – or perhaps, rather, effects of the real as they are produced in the theatre – are what concern Nicholas Ridout in his chapter,the only one in this book dedicated to the consideration of a range of work by a particular company (a company whose work is also touched on in Till and Escolme's chapters), the Italian group Societas Raffaello Sanzio. As was Escolme, Ridout is interested in the relation between a theatrical fiction and how that fiction is produced by performers and spectators alike, particularly when – in this day and age – the spectator seems to be invited to 'make-believe' that something real is going on, even as – at the same time – it is manifestly clear that whatever is going on is being 'made up'. Also, though – and again one might find echoes with the sorts of issues identified as emerging from Bridget Escolme's chapter (among others) – Ridout is concerned to pursue this interest in relation to an historical framework, so that the sorts of instants of theatrical 'magic' he examines are only to be understood in the lights of the (supposedly) 'rational' late modern European sensibility for whom these instants happen, a sensibility predicated to an extent on scepticism and solitude, for whom nothing it would seem is unimaginable, but to whom even the closest and most familiar thing – even something as old-style as theatrical pretending – can appear unnervingly strange.

We might suggest, then, that the wider concern of Ridout's chapter – although it borrows all of its performance examples from the writings and theatrical practice over twenty years of a particular company – has to do with the historicity, or the cultural currency, of any theatrical pretending. The sort of questions that Ridout asks with regard to the work of Societas Raffaello Sanzio – questions such as, How can we make out the difference between a thing and a copy of a thing? or, How do we make truth in a place (the stage) which is not the real world? or, Why is it that real things on stage often look like fictional representations of themselves? – are questions that might crack open the historical-cultural status of theatrical mimesis in any particular place and occasion.

In the event – and here we might recall chapters by Till, Roms, Nield, Blaževć and others – these questions about the status (or even the 'nature') of mimesis become sooner or later political questions, to the extent that they may persuade us to ask of ourselves, for example, What sort of mimetic spells are our imaginations in thrall to these days? How do we tear our gaze away from shadows and cast the scales from our eyes? Although, as it were in the same breath, we might also want to ask how we should believe in magic after all, and ask what sorts of seeming fiction – what sorts of unlikely transformation – might be worth making-believe in, so as to make real, so as to try to make true. Ridout, however – who does, it would appear, believe in magic – leaves those sorts of questions for the moment to the fairies. His analysis of the status of theatrical mimesis in the moments he examines in his chapter is more mordant. He suggests that if mimesis can – or does – restore magic to the rational, post-realist stage, it can only do so through illusion, and therefore at the expense of a certain loss, the loss of the 'real' that might have been evoked by that illusion. In the end – although it is only the end of his chapter, it is not the end of theatre, not quite, not yet – he offers a figure for that end of illusion. That figure is death, a figure that would seem to have haunted this book since its earliest chapters, particularly those chapters that consider 'contemporary' European theatre in relation to the long twentieth century of European history that this theatre often draws in its wake. Perhaps when Ridout writes that 'it is death that we really came here to experience', he touches on an intimation that several of these authors share, a feeling that this seemingly liveliest of the arts is indeed haunted – and perhaps *especially* in Europe – by a sense of its happening – even *as* it happens – as it were 'after the event'. To that extent, rather than pointing to the ephemerality of performance as the essence of the theatre's constitution, we might propose instead that the contemporary European theatre seems, somehow, to be perpetually surviving itself, if only just.

It is to this sense of theatre and performance as spaces of ambivalent 'survival' that Adrian Heathfield addresses himself in his chapter towards the close of the book, and in a way that rehearses – as it were in 'real time' – another key concern that might be taken as a link between all of the chapters here. That is a concern for the relation between the theatrical experience and the writing of that experience, which, as was suggested at the start of this introduction, we might assume involves a certain kind of knowledge being produced *in the wake* of the encounter, *in the aftermath* of the experience. Heathfield's chapter, however, might go some way to confounding such an assumption. For one thing his engagements with particular scenes from the 1980s dance-theatre work of Pina Bausch or a more recent gallery-situated dance-performance piece by La Ribot are woven, in Heathfield's text, through a present-tense voicing that – while it explores too many slippages and uncertainties to fall into the 'ontologising' trap of spectator studies that Susan Melrose writes about – is explicit in its staging of the spectator's real and present implication in the production of theatrical meaning. This is an implication which takes the form, Heathfield argues, of a spectatorial entangling in these performances' complex stagings of temporality. At the same time, however, Heathfield would also draw our attention to the varying ways in which the performances themselves do not quite occupy a simple present tense (in the ways in which, for instance, we might imagine live performance to be a matter of something coming into presence 'in the moment', something happening here and now in front of our eyes), but seem rather to take place in an 'after-space' of performance, 'a space of remembrance and re-enactment within the present'. To think historically about performance – for example, to read La Ribot's early twenty-first-century work as a reconsideration, however distanced or attenuated, of the sorts of concerns over femininity, relation, spectacle and the dancer's fall that Bausch was engaged with decades before – is already to recognise each appearing as something of a reappearing, the earlier interior impulse to move recaptured, perhaps, in the later artist's work, as an imperative from outside that would have that movement recuperated and fixed *as* image. However, we might also, Heathfield suggests, consider each of these performance examples as constructing their own sorts of after-space, spaces of care perhaps where certain sorts of 'wounds' – psychosexual wounds, or wounds inflicted by or upon the social body – may be exposed *and* treated. This treatment might be a matter of a set of repetitions that effect an 'un-learning' of the relations between a particular meaning and a particular image, or else a durational extending of a more or less still image so that what appears to appear for the spectator – *this* image in *this* instant – might somehow be unfixed from the consciousness with which he or she encounters it. It is, then, in such instances, such after-spaces of performance – even as the performance would appear to lend itself directly to the 'aftermath' of writing – that the theatre or the performance might really unsettle us with its suggestion that it is not *it* that is pressed for time, but rather *us* and our writings, mere contemporaries of the event.

Writing after the event has a double meaning. The first and obvious sense is temporal (we write after we have witnessed the event). The second and less immediately obvious is that of pursuit. The event is what we are after. The event is for the writer a kind of quarry or prey, to be captured or, to offer a slightly less lethal formulation, chased down so that it may be identified, named, described. If theatre and performance criticism works from a pursuit vehicle, this is because it so passionately wants to know what the theatre event is after is all about. We love the act of writing about it, and that love may be destructive as well as productive. In Simon Bayly's chapter, which concludes this collection, the event appears as something that is central both to a thinking about theatre and to the practice of philosophy. For Bayly, philosophy is always struggling against writing. Philosophy is a dialogical practice, the practice of talking towards the truth, perhaps, which is always going to be falsified in some way by the act of writing it down. Theatre, too, when it happens as event, as something that interrupts the state of things as they are, is always falsified and betrayed, not simply by the writing that comes after or that pursues it, but by itself. The theatre event that Bayly is after, it seems, is something that appears almost outside the attention of the spectator, or something to which the spectator (whether scholarly or not) would normally try not to pay any attention. The moment the spectator (whether Bayly or not) starts to see that thing appearing within an existing understanding of what theatre is supposed to be, that thing ceases to be that thing. It stops being an event and becomes part of the state of things. Bayly is compelled, therefore, to follow the lead of 'the contemporary philosopher of the event and part-time dramatist' Alain Badiou, in resisting altogether any naming of any specific theatrical practice. Badiou does this by presenting a series of names from recent theatrical history, as if to underline their interchangeability, and the way in which this naming simply contributes to the stabilisation of the state of things as they are. Bayly does this by refusing to write about any particular theatre at all. In this refusal – which is perhaps better under-stood as a certain reticence – there is, of course, an invitation, an invitation that could stand as well at the beginning of this book as at its end, an invitation to encounter the theatrical event yourself, 'dear spectator'. We started out claiming that this is a book about experiences of theatre. On the face of it, Bayly's essay would seem to refute that claim – there are no experiences of theatre in it – but upon reflection you might conclude that there might be, if you want to take up the invitation to make them your own experiences.

Chapter 1

Human stuff

Presence, proximity and pretend

Joe Kelleher

In a prospectus for the 2003–4 season at Latvia's Jaunais Rigas Teatris (JRT – the New Riga Theatre) artistic director Alvis Hermanis advertised two productions, *By Gorky* and *Long Life*, to be rehearsed together in a programme of experimental work that would engage the entirety of the company's creative labours for the foreseeable future.[1] The 2003–4 programme was proposed as a response to a perceived 'technological crisis' in the acting profession, namely the usurpation of the actor's 'monopoly' (as exercised largely in cinema and theatre) on the production of imitations of reality, by the expansion of television 'reality shows'. According to Hermanis this expansion 'has totally changed the level of credibility which a spectator is ready to accept or – using Stanislavsky terminology – believe'.[2] The response of the theatre will be to take the reality shows on at their own game, deploying the professional actors' mimicking skills so as to produce as it were reality portraits, but with a particular twist. Hermanis uses the word 'artificiality'. While one piece (*By Gorky*) will function after the fashion of photography, with the actors appearing supposedly as themselves, 'using their own names and relationships', *Long Life* will involve young actors imitating geriatric citizens of Riga at a hyper-realistic level of pictorial detail that 'makes no secret of its artificiality', in the mode of a 'circus artist who demonstrates a trick and at the same time shows how it is performed'.

What struck me on seeing these works presented during a showcase of Latvian performance hosted by the New Theatre Institute of Latvia[3] was that this return to 'theatrical basics' – i.e. the expertise of pretend – appeared to go along with a certain anthropological focus, a directing of our attention towards human stuff and its worldly situation. Perhaps this should go without saying. Reality, it will be pointed out, as it is conceived in the theatre, tends to be on a human scale. Theatre tends to privilege the representation of human life. It tends to be enjoyed – when it is enjoyed – by human beings, so much so that a general account of theatre as a mechanism of human interaction, or more elaborately a means of representing reality from – and to – a human point of view, hardly seems worth elaborating. Indeed it may well be objected that one major problem of theatre lies in these same anthropocentric tendencies, which have deployed that generality to mask the sorts of privileges that cause things to go harder in the world for some humans than for others. My contention, however, in this chapter – which will consider the JRT shows alongside work of a different sort by the Norwegian company Baktruppen – is that there is something in the *return* of contemporary performance to 'basic' theatrical materials and mechanisms that involves neither the recuperation of a transcendental humanism *nor* a deconstruction of human being for a supposedly 'post-human' age; but rather contributes towards an understanding of how humans and non-humans struggle (alongside as well as against each other) over the privileges of representation, struggle we might say over the ways in which their representations will count *as* real.

I shall come to the Norwegians later, but we begin in Latvia with a testimonial. Across the front of the set for *By Gorky*, in bold red lettering against a black strip that runs from one side of the stage to the other, there is a slogan 'CILVĒKS – TAS SKAN LEPNI', which remains in place throughout the two-hour show. The phrase translates as 'HUMAN – THAT SOUNDS PROUD', or perhaps 'MANKIND – THAT HAS A PROUD RING TO IT'. Above the slogan are screens showing recorded footage from rehearsals, alongside live action (largely facial close-ups, individual features cut out from the group) relayed by a hand-held video camera. The action itself takes place below the slogan in a glass room with a built-in ceiling, divided by further glass walls deeper into the stage. The space is part living quarters, part workspace, part exercise room – there is movable bedding, light plastic furniture, a massage table and exercise equipment, a cooker and water cooler, entertainment gear such as a video karaoke machine and so on. It is occupied by twenty or so mainly youngish people, dressed in regular contemporary casual clothes, who spend the best part of two hours in this human goldfish bowl doing the sort of things one might think of to do in such a place. There are occasional set pieces: a massage session set to Wagner; an acrobatics display at the evening's end; or the very opening of the piece in which nothing and nobody moves except – eventually, and then only gradually – various objects and pieces of furniture, the inert elements of the environment teased into animation by the actors, who pull imperceptibly on lengths of twine that gather after some minutes into a giant cat's cradle that entangles and defines the human group, linking them and separating them from the things that constitute their world. Otherwise, the action amounts to an exhibition of games, tasks, embraces, flare-ups, mating rituals, time-killing, makings-up and makings-do, a circulation of energies and materials that appears to stabilise here and there around this or that point of focus (a karaoke performance of 'Killing Me Softly', a face made out of spaghetti and ketchup, a slap, a kiss, the smashing of a plastic chair), and then breaks up again.

This activity gathers up a way of life and a history of sorts, but a history that appears cooked up in a laboratory under predetermined conditions, an 'everyday' that images the everyday of the world without quite belonging to it. There is a peculiar ambivalence to all this. *By Gorky* is promoted as being devoted to the ideas of cultural theoretician Hakim Bey, and there is indeed something here of Hakim's notion of the 'temporary autonomous zone', the sort of 'free enclave' in which modes of insurrection might be realised, in part according to a praxis of social withdrawal ('the best and most radical tactic will be to refuse to engage in spectacular violence, to *withdraw* from the area of simulation, to disappear'), and in part through the exploration of a 'festal sodality' or sort of secret society 'devoted to the overcoming of separation'.[4] However, the sort of 'immediacy' we might associate with the passionate play of Hakim's writing is touched here with a sense of something unredeemed, a feeling of melancholy. The actors take breaks during the show, exiting the glass environment as if stepping out to breathe 'real' air, on to a small time-out area on the forestage (there are a few chairs, some magazines, a place to smoke and chat) where they slump down and hang out with each other in small groups while the activity continues behind them. The words they speak here, though, even as the actors appear to come out of the fiction 'as themselves', are not their own. Their conversation, read off photocopied rehearsal scripts, is lifted from a play first produced just over a hundred years ago, in 1902, at Stanislavsky and Nemirovich-Danchenko's Public Art Theatre in Moscow: Maxim Gorky's *The Lower Depths*.

Gorky's drama was set in an urban dosshouse, populated by a semi-transient group of people who have been scraping along the bottom of life's pit and are unlikely now to claw themselves out. At the level of the narrative the play is unremittingly grim, depicting a complex of poverty, addiction, exhaustion, despair, terminal illness, violence, meanness, betrayal and self-delusion. It is, however, from the text of this drama that the slogan is taken that adorns the JRT *mise-en-scène*. The phrase belongs to the fourth-act set-piece monologue delivered by the alcoholic cardsharp Satin (Stanislavsky's role in the 1902 production), a speech that rehearses an inclusive and celebratory humanism on behalf of the socially excluded and dispossessed:

> (*Outlines the figure of a man in the air*) You understand? It's tremendous! In this are all the beginnings and all the ends. Everything in man, everything for man. Only man exists, the rest is the work of his hands and his brain. Man! It's magnificent! It has a proud ring![5]

The sentiment is unambivalent. Nor is the basic humanism of this and other passages undermined by their being woven together in a tapestry of sharp but weary epigrams on humankind that deliver a dry running commentary on the species. At the same time this creature 'mankind' remains compromised – even as prime examples are made present on the stage of the drama, serving up their juice as it were to reflective wisdom – by a certain failure to appear. Either that or a superfluity that amounts to the same thing, a seeming invisibility given by a condition (for *certain* humans, at least) of being too much in the world. 'You're not needed anywhere. For that matter all humans on this earth are not needed'. 'When you die you'll have rest, folks say. It's true, my dear. For where can a human being find rest in this world?' 'I have no name here. Do you realise how it hurts to lose one's name? Even dogs have names. Without a name there's no man'. Satin's fanfare, too, is haunted by the fictive rhetoric that has run throughout the play (talk, for instance, of an imaginary 'true-and-just land' where there are even hospitals for alcoholics – 'They've decided, you see, that a drunkard is a human being like everybody else'[6]), and which, without either reifying or decimating the human ideal, puts it into question by subjecting it to the conditions of a theatrical producing. So that in the shadow of the most pressing reality (or at least its most exact imitation) the human essence is given as an outline traced in the air by a cynical fantasist, an ephemeral gesture, a sound effect.

There would seem to be more than one way to trace the *historical* play between Gorky's drama and the JRT production. A technical, or art-historical line of enquiry could make a comparison between the different rhetorics of realism, between on the one hand the naturalist verisimilitude of the early Stanislavsky stage technique (research for the 1902 production involved a company field trip to Moscow's Khritov Market, the city's large underground dormitory labyrinth[7]) – inflected as that was by Gorky's proto-socialist realism, and on the other hand the 'post-modern' simulacra of the television reality show, itself inflected in turn by the JRT's virtuoso *self*-imitation. Another line, more sensitive perhaps to the particular histories of the players involved, might consider the relation between the way Gorky's romantic brand of socialism prefigures some of the purest hopes of a society living on the lip of revolution (a true-and-just land indeed), and the way the JRT's application of that discourse to 'lives and relationships' in early twenty-first-century Riga draws attention to the historical betrayal of such hopes (most violently in Latvia during the 1940s[8]) and what appears still to be their perpetual deferral, thirteen years since Latvia declared independence from the Soviet Union – and only a few months before the country's 2004 accession to the European Union. If, though, there is a particular axis upon which to turn such enquiries, it may reside in Satin's clarion call to humankind, which Hermanis appropriates and imprints upon the contemporary scene as the most enigmatic of judgements. *This* sounds proud? And what is this exactly? How, for instance, might what I see chime with what I am supposed to hear? And is this humanity on each occasion the *same* thing?

It depends what one means by humanity. Or perhaps what one *doesn't* mean by humanity, since the concept of the human animal would seem to have turned largely upon the exclusion of other animals from definitions of human being, indeed the separation of humans from 'the animals' as such, whatever the specific defining criteria (conceptual thought or reason, language, culture, self-consciousness, tool-using, productivity, laughter, a sense of the future, 'and all the rest'[9]). Late twentieth-century philosophers have taken this history to task, arguing for example as Mary Midgley did in her 1979 book on the matter *Beast and Man*, that 'it is really not possible to find a mark that distinguishes man from "the animals" without saying *which* animals. We resemble different ones in different ways'.[10] The pertinence of the point being underlined by the fact that the sort of reasoning that establishes categorical differentiation between human and animal and even the institution thereby of 'human rights' – has also been used (not least in the twentieth century, since Gorky's Satin recited his hymn to the species) to effectively exclude some people from the human category.

Was the centrality of the human category as such the problem? An 'avant-garde' response to such issues would appear to have involved a decentring of the human figure in accounts of the world, or – as Paul Virilio has put it recently – a pitiless 'smashing to smithereens of humanism'.[11] In theatrical terms, this involved unmasking the hero of the humanist drama so as to expose the theatrical machinery itself as the means of production within which the human fiction is cooked up, and the stage meanwhile as the sort of place where actual humans (as well as non-humans, i.e. animals and things) find themselves lost or ill-fitting or overexposed.

A philosophical return might take us to the formulations of Martin Heidegger's 1929–30 lecture series *The Fundamental Concepts of Metaphysics*, which considers differences between nonliving beings (e.g. a stone), animals and humans in terms of how they each relate to their world or environment, and according to which 'the stone is worldless; the animal is poor in world; man is world-forming'.[12] Contemporary philosopher Slavoj Žižek points out that Heidegger's notion of the animal being 'poor' in relation to the world (i.e. according to Heidegger merely 'captivated' by whatever in its environment affects its instinctual activity, an analysis which we should note is largely confined to a consideration of lizards and insects) is already anthropomorphic because such a concept is only thinkable if we presuppose world-conceiving humans as the 'measure of all things'.[13] Žižek also suggests, however, that if we consider – with Heidegger – the animal's deprivation as 'a kind of pain and suffering',[14] then this offers us a means to think against the grain of the sort of 'naïve evolutionist approach' that sees historical development simply in terms of progress, whereby higher stages (humans?) would be a positive fulfilment of the lower stages' potential for growth, decay and transformation. Rather we might think of the 'new' as having been already present in the 'old' in the guise of grief, frustration and longing: as a vague intimation of another dimension that remained just out of reach, on the other side (as it were) of a transparent barrier. That is, the present must conceive its contemporaneity in relation to the compromise of utopian hopes *in the past*; conceive itself indeed as the 'outcome' of those 'crushed potentials'. So it is that 'we, the "actual" present historical agents, have to conceive of ourselves as the materialization of the ghosts of past generations, as the stage in which these generations retroactively resolve their deadlocks'.[15] And so it is we might understand what happens on stage in Riga in 2004 not so much as an adaptation or updating of the 1902 Moscow piece, but as an exploration of the ways in which that earlier event was already 'open' to this later occasion, the channel between the two inaugurated by the broadcast of a 'human' hope (already back then ironically framed) that still awaits a place and time in which that shape drawn in the air and that proud sound might fit the creatures who go about their business in its name. A place and time when human beings become fully human.

However, we fail to arrive at that redeemed humanity as long as humans are consigned to subhumanity by the conditions of the market.[16] As Giorgio Agamben remarks, it is unclear 'whether the well-being of a life that can no longer be recognized as either human or animal can be felt as fulfilling'.[17] This is an indecision underwritten as it were by the slogan across the stage of the JRT during *By Gorky*, which reads now less like a philosophical, religious or poetic pledge than a logo, a brand name, slapped across a shop window or an exhibition stand. Life, so to speak, for sale or rent. As for the life that fails to measure up on this market, the life abandoned by well-being's dispensation, perhaps the contemporary theatre is the best companion for it. They can both make as much noise as they like, without mattering too much.[18] As it is, *Long Life*, the other piece in the JRT 2003–4 season, is quiet enough (there is no text and no one speaks above an indistinct mumble), although it is possible to hear in the background the grinding of the gears of what Agamben has called the 'anthropological machine', the conceptual machinery that threshes out human value from the other stuff. 'Since the 1990s', Hermanis writes in the prospectus, 'contemporary capitalism in Eastern Europe has discriminated against our older citizens, to a level that can be equalled to some anthropological experiment or peculiar reality show whose rules are still uncertain – whether the winner is the one who dies first or who stays last'.[19] In the show performed at the JRT studio there are no obvious winners nor losers, just an exploitation of that peculiar phenomenon that the theatre specialises in, the sense of a human reality close enough to touch and at the same time out of reach, presented *and* re-presented, at once familiar and irredeemably alien.

The action takes place slap up against the knees of the first of three rows of spectators arrayed before a wide and shallow stage, which – after

painted boards representing a tenement front are taken down at the start
of the performance – exposes (at the level at least of the *theatrical* invitation) an Aladdin's cave of acutely detailed mundanity. There is a strip of
five rooms, three cell-like bedsits, a kitchen and a bathroom. The inhabitants are five retirees (played by actors in their late twenties and early
thirties) who, in their cut-away living spaces, perform their daily business:
from the snores and whistles and twitchings of sleep and the elaborate
labours involved in engaging again with the waking world, through the
occupations that make up their meagre enough stake in this world. These
include ordinary (though never less than intricate and, necessarily, given
the straightened circumstances, inventive and collaborative) routines of
ablution, cooking and feeding and general self-conservation; as well as
more singular occupations (one couple appear to have a minor cottage
industry producing small painted plaster decorations moulded in condoms;
the man two doors away has a battered Casio keyboard and a microphone through which he broadcasts wheezing pop ditties); and also social
rituals – there is an evening birthday party in one of the tiny rooms,
involving all five neighbours in a resourceful game of hide-and-seek.

However, to go along with Hermanis' observation on the social and
economic marginalisation of older people in post-Soviet societies (and the
serving up of this marginalisation as an entertainment for the society of
the spectacle), much as we might respect the resourcefulness of these characters with regard to the business of living, and respect too the virtuosity
of the production in rendering this slice of life as a credible verisimilitude,
there is still something about the experience of spectating this exhibition
that chimes with Barbara Kirschenblatt-Gimblett's insistence – in an essay
on museum culture and 'ethnographic' performance – that 'to make people
going about their business objects of visual interest and available to total
scrutiny is dehumanizing'. This was 'a quality of exhibition that was not
lost on some nineteenth-century viewers in London who complained about
live displays on humanitarian grounds'.[20] This last is a point picked up by
Jane Goodall in her recent book on scientism and popular performance
in the 'Age of Darwin', where she also develops the argument that nineteenth-century ethnology – the 'science of savages' – was compromised as
it were at source by the modes of theatricality demanded of (and often it
appears professionally delivered up by) the 'exhibits' who were supposed
to provide live supporting evidence of this or that 'savage' fantasy; and,
by extension, of the values of those more 'advanced' forms of life whose
own humanity was to be defined in these same lights.[21] Theatrical lights,
that is. All of which – as the ethnological 'reality show' is recaptured in
an early twenty-first-century experiment that makes no bones about
its own 'artificiality', and in a way that *even so* might not fail to move us
(that is, provoke in us a response that profoundly unsettles us, that attaches
us, however briefly, to a life outside of our own) – may give us pause

to consider the forms of life 'our' stages are home to. Can anything really 'live' there at all?

A contemporary work with a different sort of lineage than the JRT productions, Norwegian performance group Baktruppen's 2002 show *Homo Egg Egg* (dedicated to an investigation of 'the identity, difference and evolution of mankind including the Neanderthals'), meets such questions head-on.[22] In contrast to the JRT's detailed and densely populated *mises-en-scène*, Baktruppen's performance presents a stage-space devoid of actual life, a space indeed of images drawn in the air and presumptuous words, as if in mockery of that strictly virtual space in which the 'savage' of ethnology (or the 'missing link' of early evolutionary science) was supposed to appear; a stage-space akin, that is, to Agamben's conception of the 'perfectly empty' zone carved out by the anthropological machine, in which the 'truly human being' is always failing to make a truly *definitive* appearance.[23] Furthermore, the project proceeds with barely a hint of the sort of imitative competence in which Hermanis' actors excel. This is not to say that Baktruppen don't 'do' pretend.[24] What they don't do (any more than the Latvian actors) is the sort of persuasively 'sincere' (i.e. rhetorical) face-pulling, posturing and gesticulation that amounts to a commodification of the human image – *real* reality-show stuff, which makes a demand upon the spectators that they 'believe it' (i.e. buy it), and for the actor's sake. Baktruppen appear unconcerned with what their spectators believe, saving all their seriousness for the Neanderthals. They also – at least in this particular work – appear unconcerned with that most basic theatrical pay-off, human presence, to the extent that they barely appear on stage at all. Where presence and appearance fail, however, something much more touching and troubling may step in: proximity. Baktruppen get very near to us in this performance, so that our attention is pulled between whatever images of the 'us unit' are drawn on the air before us and the sort of stuff that we *feel* to be closer by, and upon which the justice of those images depends. That stuff involves actors, but there is something more than human to be included in that term: urine, hazel leaves, stones, mud and water, among other things. Along with the world's oldest tune (or so we are told). And, of course, the Neanderthals.

Homo Egg Egg is constructed around a presentation of findings from Baktruppen's trip to the Neanderthal valley near Düsseldorf in Germany. Here in 1856 workers digging out a cave for limestone mining discovered fossilised bones that were later identified as belonging to a hominid species that 'save for an accident of evolution', as one recent commentator puts it, 'might still be around to challenge our human sense of uniqueness'.[25] The performance has the feel of a research presentation. Filling the far wall of a deep and otherwise empty black box studio there are video projections, images of half a dozen middle-aged Norwegians (i.e. Baktruppen) showing us their stuff, examining material under a microscope, holding up specimen jars (Gisle's hazel leaves, Trine's mud and water samples, Jørgen's urine sample and so on), as if a case were being made for these objects' inclusion in some putative 'set of things worth considering'. As with the JRT shows, the things to be taken into account here are mundane enough (during one sequence one of the male performers explores masturbation), and not without beauty (a harp performance of the 'oldest known tune'). Neither mundanity nor beauty, however, are what is at stake so much as an open-ended process of investigation, pitched somewhere between amateur enthusiasm and academic analysis, into whatever might *matter* – a process that is free to go anywhere except, it appears, on to the stage.

A video 'trailer' for the show on the company's website might have persuaded us that things would be otherwise, showing various members of Baktruppen in frocks and tuxes 'making an entrance', showbiz style, down some steps through a spangly curtain. As it is, though, these same performers are – and remain, throughout the show – camped under the risers where the spectators are sat. Down there they put together their investigations as if hidden from the world, as if the passages between themselves and the 'outside' still need to be thoroughly tested. These tests involve making the most of what comes to hand ('I am trying to find out if my sperm act like me. I don't know anybody like me. I'm the one. Hello! I'm not the other. Hello?'), and – where there is nothing to hand, other than what has been written in books – speculating upon possibilities ('The Neanderthals were living side by side with common people for more than 30,000 years. Still authorities claim they didn't mix. It is impossible to live 30,000 years without fucking').[26] Results, meanwhile, are disseminated by throwing out from under the risers eggs inscribed with slogans, gobbets of ill wisdom such as 'Defining the Neanderthals, we explain who we are', 'Way back in time we find the biggest, banging news', 'Sperm must die if culture shall live', and 'He examined himself in a niggermirror, and caught one in the eye'. Little texts that read (when we see them held up to the video camera before ejection) like satirical graffiti scratched upon the walls of the cave where the anthropological machine is fed and watered. That, or the verses of a found poem cut up out of its operating manual.

The effect is a theatre that is not so much hyper-real as hyper-familiar. The video images show close-ups – a mouth that fills the screen, a fingertip upon a dial, the dome of a head looming across and out of the frame – so blown up it seems we don't take in what we see so much as we make approaches, our gazes creeping up on the blind side of the strange flesh, inching towards an encounter. Coming to terms so to speak with the *Homo*, that creature of sheer resemblance that the eighteenth-century taxonomist Linnaeus defined in the early editions of his work (until he devised the species-defining term *homo sapiens*) by no other characteristic than an obligation to recognise itself.[27] This is a task, however, whose terms are still

Figure 1.1   Baktruppen, *Homo Egg Egg*, Photograph: Carlo E. Prelz.

being worked through in the dialogue taking place beneath us, which opens with an acknowledgement of *our* proximity, but only as a part of what needs to be taken into account:

> Hello, who are you? Are you there?
> Hello, it's me, Baktruppen, we're right down beneath.
> Is there a difference between them up there and us down here?
> They are looking at us.
> We can't see you.
> We are like the Neanderthals.
> Is there no difference between Homo Sapiens Neanderthalensis and the ordinary Homo Sapiens Sapiens?
> That's an open question, you don't have to answer yet. You never know how prehistoric you are, and why.

A full-on 'scientific' questioning, then. As grown up, as significant, as that. And also something altogether theatrical. As childish, as 'trivial', as that. Baktruppen are playing a game with us. Or, they are just playing a game. 'Good evening,' someone says. 'This is a rerun. What has happened?' What has happened, as in the JRT performances discussed above (although by different means), is a regression, a return to the serious play of pretend. Down there, Baktruppen are cutting patches to fix up a new world out of the cloth of the old one. They make an echo chamber in which to sound out futures from a hole under the stairs and an ancient cousin from a pile of old bones. They make up an 'us' from the human – and human-resembling – and also non-human – stuff that claims attention at the edges of 'our' world, where even the *pre*historic dead might still have something to say. It is as if, in all three of the performances discussed in this chapter, a vacancy were opened between the performers' self-*presentation* (that takes place, for example, at the end of an evening when the seven members of Baktruppen come on stage for the first and last time to take a bow) and the event of *representation* that is effected by way of the distorting mirror of the video screens in *Homo Egg Egg* (and *By Gorky*), or through the JRT ensemble's bag of mimetic 'tricks'. This is not to say that nothing that happens here is 'real', or for that matter that the human is out of account. Rather, 'what happens' happens as a sort of testing of the real that has to do with a *feeling out* of the proximate, the other stuff that is also *here*, a recognition if you like of neighbours, whose other worlds – be they over our heads or under our feet or right beside us in the same room – overlap and (potentially) interact with our own.

I have written of returns in contemporary European performance: in particular, variations upon a return to a certain anthropological concern – and its theatrical rendering (for example, in the sociological realism of the naturalist stage, the racist pantomimes of the ethnology exhibitions, or what was once the high drama of palaeontology and its quest for evolutionary ancestors) a concern that went alongside the unfolding of industrial modernity towards and around the turn of the nineteenth century. A key figure of this concern was borrowed from the *fin-de-siècle* theatre in the shape of an altogether theatrical gesture, an immense and universalising claim ('Only man exists, the rest is the work of his hands and his brain') upon an image of humanity that was in itself nothing more than a passing movement and a boast, a shape we don't see and a sound we never get to hear for ourselves – unless, that is, we see it and hear it here or there, among inhabitants of the 'lower depths', whose first claim upon 'us' is the fact of their proximity, their *being here also*, which is where all of *our* questions could begin.

As it happens, such a figure turns up again in the most up-to-the-moment of texts, a book that has contributed greatly to the thinking of this essay. In his 2004 volume *Politics of Nature*, Bruno Latour writes of 'the way burning brands trace shapes in the darkness of the night only through the rapid motion to which we subject them'.[28] In Latour's figure, however, it is no longer 'mankind' that is traced in these shapes but a conception of the *polis* – i.e. a conception of contemporaneity as a space of political decision – that involves humans and non-humans in a 'collective' of ever-complexifying associations with each other. This or that collective would of necessity be provisional, perpetually redefining itself and redrawing its borders, refusing any temptation to claim for itself a state of 'nature' (as if reality were all used up in such a claim); nor on the other hand treating nature as a dumping ground for scientific 'facts' against which human 'values' should be established (as if there were no other realities worth becoming sensitive to). As such, rather than the pursuit of modernity's ambitious drive towards clarity and simplification and abstraction, any 'end of history' scenario will be put aside in the anticipation of a future that 'will attach us with tighter bonds to more numerous crowds of *aliens* who have become full-fledged members of the collective that is in the process of being formed'.[29]

In the contemporary work discussed in this chapter we have seen something of theatre's part in the establishment of such a politics, not least in the donation of a mimetic technology (a whole laboratory of pretend) towards a critical and historically informed engagement with the ways in which the human animal has been 'made up', and 'makes up', with the others – not least the whispering dead – whose worlds impinge on ours. At the same time, as much in the crowded mimesis of the JRT as in Baktruppen's vacant scenography, there is a sense of something that remains undelivered, something that grieves even as it dreams, which may have to do with the fact that in the vicinity of all these images are actual humans: the ones who make – or inhabit – the gestures, the ones who look and listen and learn, and the ones who stand at the side waiting. At the conclusion of *By Gorky*, as in the original play, an actor hangs himself. The production ends, then, with a speech that functions as a contemporary coda to Gorky's drama. A woman describes an imaginary flight in a fantastic aeroplane that will never land, and a vision, reflected in 'the sky in others' eyes', of humanity's 'true, rescued image'. 'After this wondrous world of images', however, there 'remains only the afterlife of the screen', its 'glassy, transparent non-corporeality', and the longing of 'infinite loneliness'. After the reality shows, as it were, the desert of the real. Except with this proviso: in this afterlife of the image 'the same longing . . . repeats immeasurably many times'.[30] There are others there. They are *that* close. We need to know them better.

Notes

1   JRT is a state theatre company with an ensemble of about fifteen actors, which, as Hermanis has described it, 'somehow manages to be inbetween the idea of a big theatre factory making a product called theatre or independent companies struggling to survive. We are more like a studio and can afford to rehearse a play for half or even one year, which is very exceptional in Latvia'. A. Tudeer, 'In a strange club of theatre freaks', interview with Alvis Hermanis, *Baltic Circle Festival Newsletter*, 2003. http://www.q-teatteri.fi/baltic_circle/newsletter/mon 241103/strange.html, last accessed 25 August 2004.

2   See the JRT website, http://www.jrt.lv/, last accessed 25 August 2004.

3   NTIL are producers of the biannual Homo Novus festival of international contemporary theatre. See http://www.theatre.lv.

4   H. Bey, 'Waiting for the Revolution', *The Temporary Autonomous Zone, Ontological Anarchy, Poetic Terrorism*, http://www.t0.or.at/hakimbey/taz/taz.htm, last accessed

25 August 2004; H. Bey, *Immediatism*, Edinburgh and San Francisco: AK Press, 1994, p. 5.

5 M. Gorky, *The Lower Depths and Other Plays*, trans. Alexander Bakshy with Paul S. Nathan, New Haven and London: Yale University Press, 1959, p. 68.

6 Gorky, *The Lower Depths*, pp. 23, 30, 39, 29.

7 See C. Stanislavski, *My Life in Art*, trans. J. J. Robbins, Harmondsworth: Penguin, 1967, pp. 362–70.

8 I recommend a visit to Riga's Museum of Occupation.

9 The list is Mary Midgley's from *Beast and Man: The Roots of Human Nature*, London and New York: Routledge, 2002, p. 198.

10 Midgley, *Beast and Man*, p. 198.

11 P. Virilio, *Art and Fear*, trans. J. Rose, London and New York: Continuum, 2004, p. 29. For a 'heroic' reading of the early twentieth-century avant-gardes, see P. Bürger, *Theory of the Avant-Garde*, trans. M. Shaw, Minneapolis: University of Minnesota Press, 1984. For an account of later returns to the avant-garde project in art see H. Foster, *The Return of the Real*, Cambridge, MA: MIT Press, 1996.

12 M. Heidegger, *The Fundamental Concepts of Metaphysics: World, Finitude, Solitude*, trans. W. McNeill and N. Walker, Bloomington: Indiana University Press, 1995, p. 195. For an extended commentary on the Heidegger text, see G. Agamben, *The Open: Man and Animal*, trans. Kevin Attell, Stanford: Stanford University Press, 2004.

13 S. Žižek, *The Fragile Absolute, or Why is the Christian Legacy Worth Fighting For?*, London and New York: Verso, 2001, pp. 82–92.

14 The phrase is Heidegger's, cited by Žižek, *The Fragile Absolute*, p. 87.

15 Žižek, *The Fragile Absolute*, pp. 90–1. Žižek acknowledges that his formulations here owe much to Walter Benjamin.

16 For a classic (early) Marxian statement of the theme, see the section 'Alienated Labour' in K. Marx, *Economic and Philosophic Manuscripts* (1844).

17 Agamben, *The Open*, p. 77.

18 Tudeer, 'In a strange club of theatre freaks'.

19 JRT prospectus.

20 B. Kirschenblatt-Gimblett, 'Objects of Ethnography', in I. Karp and S. D. Levine, eds. *Exhibiting Cultures*, Washington and London: Smithsonian Institution Press, 1991, pp. 386–443 (p. 415).

21 J. R. Goodall, *Performance and Evolution in the Age of Darwin: Out of the Natural Order*, London and New York: Routledge, 2002. See pp. 82–3.

22 Baktruppen website, http://www.baktruppen.org, last accessed 25 August 2004. I saw *Homo Egg Egg* at Kaaitheatre, Brussels, in late November 2002.

23 Agamben, *The Open*, pp. 37–8.

24 In the early 1990s, Baktruppen changed their name to that of the eponymous hero of Ibsen's epic *Peer Gynt*. They produced several versions of a show titled *Per, You're Lying. Yes!* which reversed the claim of theatrical illusion articulated in the opening exchange of Ibsen's text. Baktruppen don't deny the pretence. They affirm it.

25 F. Fernández-Armesto, *So You Think You're Human? A Brief History of Humankind*, Oxford: Oxford University Press, 2004, p. 132.

26 *Homo Egg Egg* text, Baktruppen website.

27 Agamben, *The Open*, pp. 25–7.

28 B. Latour, *Politics of Nature: How to Bring the Sciences into Democracy*, trans. Catherine Porter, Cambridge, MA and London: Harvard University Press, 2004, pp. 147–8.

29 Latour, *Politics of Nature*, p. 191.

30 English translation of *By Gorky* performance text distributed at the theatre.

Chapter 2

Investigating the entrails
Post-operatic music theatre in Europe

Nicholas Till

It is almost forty years since Adorno declared that that opera was an eviscerated art form that didn't know that it had died.[1] Some stiffs just won't take no telling. But for me at least, despite my professional and academic engagement with the form, opera is the encounter that never happens; *can* never happen, probably, despite its sociocultural visibility and its scandalous consumption of resources. This essay is about European artists working in music theatre today for whom, like me, the aesthetic, institutional and ideological baggage of opera render it essentially moribund; artists who know that the significant developments of twentieth-century music and theatre fundamentally negate the nineteenth-century dramaturgies and metaphysics that continue to underpin most operatic practice, but whose continued engagement with the relation between music and theatre inevitably treads warily around, sometimes through and beyond, opera. Hence: a post-operatic music theatre.

Many innovations in this area are paralleled in American forms of music theatre inspired by John Cage, performance art or minimalism (Robert Ashley, Robert Wilson, Meredith Monk, Laurie Anderson). But I want to suggest that, whereas new American music theatre is essentially innocent, European artists are always profoundly aware of the burden of history, and it is for this reason that the operatic continues to haunt the imagination of so many European musicians and theatre artists. Moreover, it is clear that the works that claim this terrain with the greatest urgency have emerged primarily from within German and Italian theatre. My guess is that this should be understood as a need by artists from these countries to re-engage history. And for these artists, to engage history demands an engagement with the forms of its representation. In Italy and Germany that has meant dealing with the operatic.

In Bertolucci's film *The Spider's Stratagem* of 1970 a young man returns to his family village twenty years after the Second World War to recover the truth about the assassination of his father during the fascist era. He finds that his father is honoured as an anti-fascist hero, and manages to track down and question three of his father's former associates. 'What was our anti-fascism based on?' replies one. 'We fancied conspiracies . . . *Ernani* [hums theme from Verdi's opera] . . . you know, conspirators. Or Samuel and Tom in [Verdi's] *Un ballo in maschera*. We saw ourselves as such characters, but we understood nothing'. Bertolucci suggests here the way in which opera – or perhaps what I would prefer to call the 'operatic' – has shaped the imagination of modern Italian politics. This link between opera and Italian politics goes back to the Risorgimento, the mid-nineteenth-century movement for the liberation and unification of Italy. For most of the seventeenth and eighteenth centuries, opera was the predominant form of drama in Italy, but in 1833 Giuseppe Mazzini, ideologue of the Risorgimento, also identified opera as the art form most likely to unite Italy because of its ability to transcend the divisions of language in the peninsula, its representation through the operatic chorus of an idealised national community beyond region or class, and its powers of heroic arousal.[2] Verdi became the exemplary composer of the new romantic nationalism, his name daubed on walls as an acronym for the political slogan of the Risorgimento: 'Vittorio Emmanuele Re D'Italia'. The great choral lament of Hebrew slaves in captivity in Verdi's opera *Nabucco* became the signature tune of the movement. The recurrent themes of nineteenth-century Italian romantic opera – loyalty, conspiracy, revenge – colour Italian politics to this day, the result of what the historian Paul Ginsborg describes as a social structure based on familial allegiance and networks of patronage.[3]

There are many similarities between modern Italian history and its German counterpart. Both countries underwent political unification during the nineteenth century, and in both cases there is an evident connection between the necessity to forge a supra-geographical and supra-historical national consciousness and the subsequent emergence of fascism, an ideology that (amongst other things) is based upon the elimination of difference. And in Germany, as in Italy, opera developed during the nineteenth century as a key contributor to this process. Until the later eighteenth century opera meant in Germany, as everywhere else in Europe other than France, Italian opera. The move to create a German-language opera emerged as an aspect of a developing German cultural identity in the later eighteenth century, and was, from the time of Mozart, combined with an interest in Greek tragedy as a precursor for the ideal of a communal national theatre in Germany, which became central to Wagner's construction of a myth of origin for his own operatic works. In Wagner's hands a reformed German music drama (already anti-operatic) was to offer a new mythology for a German national identity based on narratives of renunciation, sacrifice, purification and redemption, themes that had since the early nineteenth century enjoyed an insidious potency within German cultural thought.

It is in those European countries where history has been thus mythologised through opera that artists have found themselves forced to confront the operatic: Italy, where history is either melodrama or *opera buffa* – the latter farcical, cynical, cruel; Germany, where history is mythologised as sacrificial tragedy. Fascism and Nazism swept these narratives to their inevitable outcome in the Second World War, and in each instance the postwar political and cultural life of these countries has been over-determined by a coming-to-terms with those events. A common part of that process in both countries was the experience of a violently polarised repoliticisation in the early 1970s, culminating in state crises in both Italy and Germany in 1977–8.

The problematic of opera during the postwar period has to be understood in this context, and it may best be considered in relation to other cultural forms. The immediate reaction to the rubble of European civilisation after 1945 was that this *Stunde Null*, or 'Zero Hour', offered a moment to start anew, to reinvent a culture that had so palpably failed in its mission to civilise. More immediately pressing was the need to reject those aspects of culture that had been compromised and degraded by fascism and Nazism. In Germany the literary Gruppe 47 promoted writing based on plain language, refusing the windy abstractions of literary German that were believed to have contributed to the rhetoric of Nazism. German theatre underwent a comparable purging of the expressionist acting styles that had been appropriated by Goebbels to such malign effect. In Italy the neo-realism of postwar cinema offered an antidote to the glossy bombast of fascist films; more *rappel à l'ordinaire* than *rappel à l'ordre*. In both Germany and Italy, filmmakers and theatre artists in general avoided dealing directly with the fascist and Nazi eras until after the events of 1968, whose energies were in Germany, as one historian suggests, 'specifically addressed to the generation responsible for Nazism'.[4] Fascism was confronted in Italian films like Visconti's *The Damned* (1969) and Bertolucci's *The Conformist* (1970), and even more extensively (if more obliquely) in what came to be known as the German New Cinema, in which the recovery of history, memory, identity and even myth become prevalent themes in the films of Kluge, Wenders, Herzog, Fassbinder and Syberberg in the 1970s. These offered a corrective to the official ideology that postwar reconstruction had depended upon a forgetting – even denial – of the events of Nazism. The effect of amnesia – the morphine that the sinister doctor supplies to both the victims and beneficiaries of Nazism in Fassbinder's *Veronica Voss*, or the tragedy of Herzog's Kaspar Hauser, a fully grown man without memory or history – is a recurrent theme of the new German cinema of the 1970s, as is the search for a lost childhood home or absent parents (Wenders' *Alice in the Cities*, *Kings of the Road*), or the return of the undead to haunt the present (Herzog's *Nosferatu*).

Some sort of related periodisation may be found in the trajectory of the postwar operatic in Germany and Italy, in which I think there may be discerned four distinct tendencies:

1   A rejection of opera as an impossibly compromised art form, because
of both its historical affiliations and its rhetorical forms. This is the
immediate response of postwar modernist composers, whose ambition
is to effect a radical purging of Western art music. 'I wanted to make
an experiment that set out from the "degree zero of writing,"' said
Pierre Boulez, the chief ideologue of postwar modernism. 'For me this
was an essay in Cartesian doubt: I wanted to question everything, to
make a *tabula rasa* of the whole musical inheritance and begin again
at degree zero'.[5] Even Schönberg, previously revered as the founder
of musical modernism, must be rejected for the lingering elements of
romantic expressionism in his music: 'c'est du Verdi sériale' was the
appalled response of one of Stockhausen's associates on first examining Schönberg's serial opera *Moses und Aron*.[6] In operatic production
the equivalent to this new puritanism is the move by Wagner's
grandson Wieland Wagner at Bayreuth to abstract Wagner, stripping
his operas of any dodgy historical and mythological associations.

2   An effort to reclaim opera for liberal humanism without questioning
its basic theatrical or musical forms. In operatic production this
response is represented by the neo-realism of Visconti in Italy or the
socialist humanism of Felsenstein in East Germany. By the 1960s leftist
modernists such as the Italian Luigi Nono, or in Germany Berndt
Aloys Zimmermann, are attempting a more radical reclamation of
opera for both the Left and modernism. At the same time composers
with more oblique political positions such as Luciano Berio, György
Ligeti or Mauricio Kagel approach opera through modernist parody
or deconstruction.

3   The development in the 1960s of forms of non-operatic music theatre
that explore the rituals of musical performance, or new relationships
between music and space or image. I'm thinking here of the followers
of Cage in the Fluxus movement, the 'instrumental theatre' of Kagel
or Vinko Globokar, the multimedia works of Stockhausen or Dieter
Schnebel. Where these works differ from my more recent examples
of post-operatic music theatre is in their modernist abstraction: a search
for the 'essential' properties of sound, space and performance that,
like so much early performance art, sets itself in deliberate opposition
to the apparatus of theatrical representation and illusion or, indeed,
the operatic.

4   Diversion of the operatic into other media – most obviously film.
Thomas Elsaesser has noted that in Italy, when directors such as
Bertolucci, Fellini and Visconti came to deal with the fascist era, they
broke with the dominant mode of realism for 'a subjectively slanted,
melodramatically or operatically spectacular representation of history'.[7]
This turn to the operatic is even more marked in Germany, where
filmmakers of the 1970s engaged the problematic of fascism by

re-engaging those dangerous aspects of German culture that had been repressed in the immediate postwar period, evident in the expressionist/melodramatic/operatic elements in the work of Kluge, Schroeter, Herzog, Fassbinder and, above all Syberberg. Syberberg's quasi-Wagnerian epic *Hitler, a Film from Germany* (1977) is described by film historian Anton Kaes as 'the rebirth of . . . film from the spirit of music and theater'.[8] For Syberberg film becomes the essential medium for the remythologisation of German history, necessary because postwar cultural prohibitions had denied the aesthetic materials with which Germans might have been able to engage in the therapeutic task of acknowledging and mourning for their past. In *Hitler*, which Syberberg describes as an act of 'Trauerarbeit', he charges his subject:

> You took away our sunsets, sunsets by Caspar David Friedrich. You are to blame that we can no longer look at a field of grain without thinking of you. . . . The words 'magic' and 'myth' and 'serving' and 'ruling', 'Führer', 'authority', are ruined, are gone, exiled to eternal time. And we are snuffed out. Nothing more will grow here.[9]

Writing about German cinema of the 1970s Wim Wenders once said: 'I speak for everyone who, in recent years, after a long barren period, has started producing sounds and images again, in a country that has a profound mistrust of sounds and images about itself'.[10] At some point one has to re-engage with history, and with the sounds and images of its telling. For artists this entails a rejection of the deliberate amnesia and abstraction of high modernism. Boulez, for instance, has argued that 'strong, expanding civilisations have no memory; they reject, they forget the past'.[11] But by the mid-1970s in both Italy and Germany the repression of historical memory had erupted in political violence. As Heiner Müller argued, 'In order to get rid of the nightmare of history, you have first to acknowledge its existence. You have to know about history, otherwise it comes back in the old-fashioned way, as nightmare, Hamlet's ghost . . . .Very important aspects of our history have been repressed for too long'.[12] An aspect of this revaluation involves the role played by music in shaping the mythical and historical imagination – all the more powerful because it is often subliminal. For Syberberg, music in German history can only mean Wagner, to whom he has returned obsessively. But from the late 1970s there is a more general critical re-engagement with the historical genealogies of music in Germany and Italy; expanded musical and theatrical practices that renegotiate the repressed forms and energies of the operatic.

Composer and theatre artist Heiner Goebbels offers a useful starting point for an analysis of such approaches. Born in 1952, Goebbels studied sociology and music in Frankfurt from 1972, where he encountered the critical theory of the Frankfurt School and became associated with the leftist grouping called the Frankfurter Spontis, one of a number of post-1968 movements who combined a critique of West German consumerist capitalism with a determination to make Germany face its Nazi past.

Herzog has said that his generation 'had no fathers, only grandfathers'.[13] Goebbels located just such a grandfather figure in the composer Hanns Eisler, renegade pupil of Schönberg, friend and collaborator of Brecht and committed socialist. Through Eisler Goebbels felt able 'to connect to a German musical history of resistance'.[14] Of particular importance was Eisler's dialectical understanding of the relationship between music and society, encapsulated in the phrase 'Fortschritt und Zurücknahme' ('Progress and Recuperation'). Goebbels himself explains: 'If you want to develop one element you have to accept the convention of another to be able to communicate', and, in opposition to dogmas of postwar modernism, Goebbels believes strongly in the necessity of engaging with existing musical forms and sounds. 'I mistrust the idea that it is possible to be entirely original. We are all full of memories, full of history, full of taste which is not ours; which comes from the past'. This is not, for Goebbels, a mark of weakness. Nor is it a capitulation to po-mo pick'n'mix assemblage; Goebbels always engages with the social and historical meanings of the musical gestures he draws on. Indeed, certain forms or sounds may carry too much baggage; a part of his difficulty in setting German words to music is because sung German 'always has a reference back, a connotation', the reason why Goebbels uses predominantly spoken texts in his works. When singing is incorporated it almost invariably enters as an autonomous significr of otherness: the Sufi-derived keening of Sussan Deyhim in the radio *Hörstuck SHADOW/Landscape with Argonauts*; West African song in the music-theatre piece *Ou bien le debarquement désastreux*; the laid-back Brazilian tropicalismo of Arto Lindsay in the 'staged concert-piece' *The Man in the Elevator*, based on Heiner Müller's narrative of bureaucratic entrapment. In each case song opens a window into transcendence of the 'here and now' in familiar operatic fashion, but that transcendence is problematised as an effect of certain kinds of colonial, orientalist or primitivist fantasies that serve to push such desires to a safe distance.

Goebbels eventually found that he could deal with the problematic relationship of music and language after encountering the strident declamation of German new wave bands such as Einstürzende Neubauten, who employed language as a sound medium rather than as a vehicle of expressive communication. Alongside his work with the art-rock band Cassiber throughout the 1980s, Goebbels made radio dramas in which he wove found sound, documentary material, literary texts and vernacular musics into complex montages. Eventually, in the early 1990s Goebbels started to make theatre works which extended his methods to include space, light and image; works that reflect in some way on European history and culture.

Film historian Thomas Elsaesser notes a prevalent 'angst' in German films of the 1970s, suggesting that directors 'situate history between apocalypse and tabula rasa'.[15] There is a similar sense of angst in Goebbels's work, most obvious in his sustained engagement with texts by Heiner Müller, whose bleak dramatic monologues are invariably located under the shadow of 'an unknown catastrophe', or in 'a landscape beyond death'.[16] Much of Goebbels's edgy music sounds like the soundtrack to some lost film noir of modern European history, and Goebbels himself acknowledges that his outlook is coloured by the need 'to face German history', most evident in his best-known theatre work *Black on White* of 1996, written for the contemporary music group Ensemble Modern. The formal structure of *Black on White* hangs upon Edgar Allan Poe's tale *Shadow*, which recounts the dread of a group of ancient Egyptians awaiting the imminent destruction of their decaying civilisation. At the heart of the piece is a scene where the whole ensemble repeat obsessively the line 'a dead weight hung upon us', which is immediately followed by distant florid voices taken from recordings of prewar Jewish cantors calling the Kaddish (the most 'operatic' voices in Goebbels's oeuvre and, from within the heart of Europe, undeniably 'other') around which Goebbels's players weave a threnody at first angry and then consolatory; *Trauerarbeit* for the dead weight of a past from which the future begs to be released.

Goebbels's work extends the instrumental theatre of Cage, Kagel or Fluxus artists through a much more concrete theatrical imagination. In *Black on White* the musicians of the Ensemble Modern are let loose from

Figure 2.1   Heiner Goebbels and the Ensemble Modern, *Black on White*. Photograph: Wonge Bergmann.

the theatre musician's subterranean refuge in the orchestra pit, emerging to construct a musical community making and remaking itself collectively, starting from the basic elements of space, sound, gesture and language, reaching for identity and meaning through the exploration of shared fragments of musical and literary memory. *Black on White* was in part a memorial to the recently dead Heiner Müller, whose voice we hear reading from *Shadow*, a parable about the posthumous survival of the writer. *Black on White* celebrates the power of inscription to memorialise but also acknowledges the melancholy ephemerality of music; one of Goebbels's most telling images is a lament for piccolo and the tuned whistle of a boiling kettle whose wheezy notes (sounding like the emphysemic voice of Müller himself) dissolve in a smudge of steam, fading away as the kettle boils dry.

Goebbels dislikes the *Gesamtkunstwerk* principles of opera or modernist music theatre: 'I try not to match words and people, words and pictures, music and words in an illustrative way. Distance on stage keeps our senses awake and curious, and actualizes our longings and desires for the matches'. But he is also alert to the immediate physicality and playfulness of musical performance, especially in the possibilities afforded by improvisation from his free-jazz background as a metonym for non-hierarchical forms of social organisation. And, as if offering recompense for his refusal of the figurative vocal fireworks of traditional operatic performance, Goebbels takes particular delight in actual pyrotechnics, which offer a kind of substitute for the combustive and explosive energies of the operatic. Despite the fact that he provocatively titled *Landscape with Distant Relatives* of 2002 an 'opera', a title earned perhaps only for its scale and length, of all contemporary composers Goebbels has pushed the theatrical possibilities of non-operatic music theatre furthest.

Paradoxically, some of the more direct investigations of post-operatic lyricism – with singing as a primary medium of theatrical communication – have come from theatre artists rather than composers. Admittedly the Swiss theatre director Christoph Marthaler trained originally as a musician. But, in contrast to Goebbels, Marthaler prefers to rework existing musical texts. *Murx*! (full title *Murx den Europäer! Murx ihn! Murx ihn! Murx ihn ab: ein patriotischer Abend*, roughly translatable as 'Screw the European! Screw him! Screw him! Go screw him: a patriotic evening'[17]), made for the Volksbühne in East Berlin in 1993, is a haunting (and often painfully hilarious) meditation on the intractable problems of German history and cultural memory after reunification. A group of institutionalised misfits incarcerated in some kind of bleak, featureless 'home' find moments of fragile communality working their way through a repertory of songs relating to different moments of German national identity, from the first benign envisionings of Germany as a peacefully united entity after the devastation of the Thirty Years' War in the seventeenth century, via heroic calls for national insurrection against the French during the Napoleonic period, to the Prozac pop songs dispensed by the purveyors of organised happiness in both the former East and West. Wagner makes a kitsch appearance absurdly vamped up amidst a cocktail-piano medley, a commodified signifier of transcendence during which the inmates all raise their heads to gaze futilely at the ceiling. The piece ends with a sequence in which proscribed verses from the national anthems of both the FGR and former GDR surface as troubling spectral presences.

Murx! was created at a time of uncertainty about the political and cultural identity of a newly reunited Germany. The location is significant, since Berlin is the site where Europe has repeatedly had to confront the problem of what to remember and what to forget. The city is a palimpsest where layers of history rub their dreams and failures against each other. Its empty spaces often speak louder than its monuments, although many of these are empty too, abandoned shells that contain uncomfortable memories that no one can quite bring themselves to erase. In a sense the whole of the eastern part of the city, where the Volksbühne is located, is just such an empty space. Drained of history and memory after the Second World War in the name of a future that never came, it is now a place where the wipe-easy dynamic of commercial redevelopment snags against inadmissible nostalgias for a past that never was. In *Murx!* the occupants of Marthaler's 'home' are stranded in the stasis of a continuous present: the hands of the clock on the wall are stopped at an impossible time. Marthaler's inmates are the left-over victims of what the East German writer Martin Ahrends called 'the great waiting', who have now been inserted forcibly into the equally flattened present of capitalist *posthistoire*. Into the routines of the present erupt the repressed of history – forbidden memories of nation dimly recalled. The piece asks: How can a people live without history or memory? But how can they live with *those* histories and *those* memories? When these people sing it is without volition or solidarity, as if they are being sung through by songs that colonise their minds. Towards the end of the performance is a sequence in which faint voices emerge from the ovens of a huge boiler when it is opened to be stoked, songs that evoke the vanished Heimat of the GDR, recently consigned without compunction to the flames. This is followed by the Nazi *Horst Wessel* song, escaping from a tinkly musical watch that is peremptorily silenced by being snapped shut (if only history could be so easily silenced, the gesture says). At the close of the piece the inmates hum wistfully 'that tune' from Haydn's *Emperor* quartet, miming the graceful bowing of a string quartet – as if this somehow effaces its political connotations. But everybody knows the forbidden words that accompany the tune, which is finally whistled softly as the lights fade. For what imagined Germany could the eyes of many in the audience be seen brimful with tears when the houselights go up?

Marthaler's decision to theatricalise communal singing does for postnational and post-collective societies what the operatic chorus once did for the nascent nationalisms of the nineteenth century, and he has continued to explore his distinctive form of 'choral theatre' in a series of works.[18] But if German theatre artists like Goebbels and Marthaler are preoccupied with the mythologising of German culture and history through music, the post-operatic in Italy seems to be more concerned with the rhetorical *forms* of the operatic, reviving Antonio Gramsci's critique of the relationship between the operatic forms of Italian culture and the rhetorical forms of fascism.

Voyage au bout de la nuit (1998) is an adaptation by the Italian theatre company Socìetas Raffaello Sanzio (SRS) of Céline's bitter saga of the interwar descent into fascism in which passages from Céline's novel are declaimed in a kind of reinvented operatic recitative for four female vocalists. Céline's prose conveys the tension between the formulaic banality of everyday speech and the fierce distortions of linguistic propriety brought about by the frustrated energies of those imprisoned within such language. The singers torment Céline's text, wrenching it between choric generality and grotesque expressive intensity. On two screens are projected images that similarly bound the fragile space of bourgeois autonomy: newsreel footage from the traumatic world events described by Céline, brutally objective documents of mechanised modernity set alongside images of flayed animal bodies. In this adaptation Céline is put to work to subvert the shibboleths of subjectivity sustained by conventional operatic representation, his own savage dissection of the 'effluvia' of speech production mocking the familiar operatic equation of voice and ideality.

The turn to the operatic in the work of Socìetas Raffaello Sanzio seemed to follow logically from the preoccupations of their previous work, in which engagement with the disaster of twentieth-century history had already pushed them to the borders of the operatic – to those places where the relationship between opera and pathology becomes obvious. In *Giulio Cesare*, as in *Voyage au bout de la nuit*, Socìetas Raffaello Sanzio effected a radical challenge to the delusions of interiority and transcendence that underlie the expressive forms of nineteenth-century (and most modernist) opera, revealing both the 'carnal sexuality'[19] that underlies the production of the spoken or sung word[20] and the externally imposed, 'symbolic' frameworks that permit language to be meaningful only within an economy that ensures that the subject is always thereby alienated from himself or herself. The narrating female chorus in *Voyage* occupies a discursive space where collectivity is nothing more than a narcissistic identification of sameness against difference, which finally gives way to the regimented clatter of a mechanical goose-stepping machine.

Post-operatic theatre artists and musicians in Italy seem to be especially sensitive to the dangerously regressive illusion of omnipotent self-presence and emotional persuasion that the traditional operatic voice promises. Like many contemporary composers Giorgio Battistelli has repeatedly returned to melodrama, in its original meaning of 'dramatic texts spoken over music', to enable him to tap the energies of the operatic without succumbing to its delusions. *Experimentum Mundi* (originally created in 1981) is a theatrical concert-piece in which Diderot's descriptions of pre-industrial crafts from the *Encyclopédie* are recited against the sounds arising from the co-ordinated labour of an on-stage orchestra of cobblers, smiths, tanners, coopers. The word *opera* means nothing more than 'work', and *Experimentum Mundi* is a celebration of precisely that: the usually concealed labour of operatic production, and also offers a critique of the fetishisation of virtuosity in opera. But it is an elegy for the imminent passing of music itself as a mode of bodily and social production as well.

A more fundamental address to the operatic voice is offered by Salvatore Sciarrino, although his pared-down theatre is very different from Battistelli's occasional flirtations with kitsch excess or the hysterical theatricality of SRS. Sciarrino is a self-taught composer who positions himself in conscious opposition to the structural complexity and a historical abstraction of most postwar modernist music. 'The problem of vocality is central to my recent production', Sciarrino has said,[21] and in a series of theatre works written since the mid-1980s Sciarrino has probed and reprobed this most evidently worrisome constituent of the operatic. In *Lohengrin* (1984), an 'invisible action' based on a scabrous parody of Wagner by the late nineteenth-century French poet Jules Laforgue, all of the roles in the drama are presented by the female singer who represents Elsa. The form of the monodrama has been a favourite of modernist composers since Schönberg's expressionist masterpiece *Erwartung*, offering opportunities for extended vocal techniques to convey extreme psychological conditions. But in Sciarrino's monologues expression is never achieved. 'Elsa' is seated amidst a small group of musicians. She has a story to tell about a knight called Lohengrin, but her utterances emerge like those of a medium ventrilo-quised by conflicting spirit voices. The boundaries of inside and outside that conventionally secure subjectivity are further troubled, since she also seems to be possessed by the jostling pathetic fallacies of Laforgue's ironic narrative: the sounds of doves cooing, gusts of wind, bells ringing. Close-miked, the performer battles with the Célinian sludge of vocal production that classical singing seeks to expunge: gulps, teeth chattering, saliva squelchings, lip pops. Clearly striving for sustained melodic expression, the joined-up singing that in operatic terms signifies self-presence, all she attains is to end up trapped inside the melodic loop of a Big Ben carillon. Many of Sciarrino's characters seem to be thus confined within the space of pre-linguistic vocality, employing infantile croonings and babblings, or the religious glossolalia of Santa Maria de'Pazzi in *L'infinito nero* of 1998, to fend off the symbolic order. In *Perseo e Andromeda* (1990), based on another parody of the operatic by Laforgue, the self-absorption of Andromeda, who prefers to remain on the island which shapes her existence, is conveyed through electronic sounds that construct an acoustic landscape, a barren island of clicks and howling winds, an anamorphic projection of the plosives, sibilants and glottals by which speech cuts across the otherwise seamless flows of breath striven for in operatic singing.

Luci miei traditrici (1998) appears more like opera as we know it than any of the works hitherto discussed. But Sciarrino here inverts every assumption of the operatic. His secretive, furtive musical style is figured in his choice of a baroque drama of forbidden passion and illicit eavesdropping. The opera is constructed as series of duets, in which the narcissistic sublation of difference of the conventional operatic duet is constantly punctured by the voice of the interloper. Rather than riding on the orchestra, it is the voices that create the dramatic impetus, the musical instruments offering a sexuo-somatic aura of quickened pulses and heartbeats, sharp intakes of breath, fluttering stomachs; acoustic amplification of the bodily symptoms of passion. The vocal style alternates between urgent recitative and the artifice of an almost Rossinian bel canto; tense mutterings suddenly flower extravagantly (the Italian word for vocal embellishments is indeed *fioritura*) and then tail away; impulses towards lyric expression that can no longer quite sustain themselves. The operatic expires for shortness of breath.

Corpses stink. Goebbels, Marthaler, Socìetas Raffaello Sanzio, Battistelli and Sciarrino have all followed the stink to its source to uncover something nasty lurking in the gilded temples of European culture. They have galvanised the entrails of opera, employing theatre to expose the suppressed social and discursive of music and deploying the materiality of musical production to challenge the smooth representational economies of theatre. Their works are clearly anti-operatic; and yet they also confront the operatic, reactivating its once troubling energies while sifting out its ideological metaphysics so that these can be laid to rest.

Notes

1 T. Adorno, *Aesthetic Theory*, Minneapolis: University of Minnesota Press, 1997, p. 18.
2 G. Mazzini, 'The Philosophy of Music' (1833), in *The Life and Writings of Joseph Mazzini*, 6 vols, London: Smith, Elder & Co, vol. 4, 1867. See also 'On Historical Drama' (1830), and 'On Italian Literature since 1830' (1837), vol. 2 (1865).
3 P. Ginsborg, *A History of Contemporary Italy: Society and Politics, 1943–1988*, London: Penguin, 1990, pp. 2–3, 243, 412–18.
4 Eric L. Santner, *Stranded Objects: Mourning, Memory, and Film in Postwar Germany*, Ithaca: Cornell University Press, 1990, p. xii.
5 Quoted in Michael Kurz, *Stockhausen: A Biography*, London: Faber & Faber, 1992, p. 33.
6 Kurz, *Stockhausen*, p. 37.
7 T. Elsaesser, *Fassbinder's Germany: History, Identity, Subject*, Amsterdam: Amsterdam University Press, 1996, p. 138.
8 A. Kaes, *From Hitler to Heimat: The Return of History as Film*, Cambridge, MA: Harvard, 1989, p. 45.

9 Quoted in Kaes, *From Hitler to Heimat*, p. 64. During the 1970s the controversial paintings of Anselm Kiefer also effected a problematised re-engagement with German history and myth – including reworkings of Friedrich's blasted fields and apocalyptic sunsets. See A. Huyssen, 'Anselm Kiefer: The Terror of History, The Temptation of Myth', *October* 48, Spring 1989, pp. 25–45.

10 W. Wenders, *On Film: Essays and Conversations*, London: Faber & Faber, 2001, p. 100.

11 P. Boulez: *Conversations with Celestine Deliege*, London: Eulenberg Books, 1976, p. 33.

12 H. Müller, *Germania*, ed. Sylvère Lotringer, trans. Bernard and Caroline Schütze, New York: Semiotexte, 1990, p. 24.

13 Quoted in T. Elsaesser, *New German Cinema: A History*, London: BFI/Macmillan, 1989, p. 91.

14 All quotes taken from conversation with author, London, November 2002.

15 Elsaesser, *New German Cinema*, p. 217.

16 H. Müller, *Theatremachine*, London and Boston: Faber & Faber, 1995, pp. 55, 133.

17 But also, perhaps we hear, '*Marx* the European'?.

18 In particular, *Stunde Null* (Deutsches Schauspielhaus, Hamburg), made for the 1995 commemorations of the end of the Second World War, whose title is a reference to the 'zero-hour' ideology of postwar Germany; *The Unanswered Question* (Basel, 1997), which used the format for a satire upon media appropriations of people's private dreams; *Die schöne Müllerin* (Zurich, 2002), based on Schubert's song cycle of that title, which examines the relationship between romanticism and subsequent Germany history; and *Groundings* (Zurich, 2003) a farce about the collapse of Swissair.

19 R. Castellucci, C. Guidi, C. Castellucci, *Epopea della polvere: il teatro della Società Raffaello Sanzio 1992–1999*, Milan: Ubulibri, 2001, p. 207.

20 In the opening scene of the play, while Shakespeare's Commoner – renamed '. . . 'Vskij' after the great exponent of actorly interiority – speaks his lines, an endoscope reveals the flesh-and-blood mechanisms of vocal production.

21 In R. Fearn, *Italian Opera Since 1945*, London: Routledge, 1997, p. 213.

Chapter 3

Encountering memory

Acco Theatre Center's *Arbeit macht frei MiToitland Europa*

Heike Roms

I

Friday, 23 July 1993, Internationales Sommertheater Festival Hamburg, Germany:

> A memory: a narrow corridor, the smell of wet wood and rotting jute. We are herded together, lined up on wooden benches, heads bent beneath rows of hanging shoes. A face appears in the dim light before us. Through broken glass and barbed wire, a voice begins to ask questions: 'When did you first hear about the Holocaust? What did your father do in World War II?' Israeli actors opposite a German audience, the children of the victims questioning the children of the murderers. Interrogation, interview, dialogue?[1]

The Acco Theatre Center's[2] five-hour-long theatrical tour de force, *Arbeit macht frei MiToitland Europa* (or *Work liberates from the deathland of Europe*), premiered in the northern Israeli city of Acco in 1991 and remained in the company's repertoire for more than seven years. Its importance derived from the bold and self-critical manner in which the performance portrayed the memory of the Holocaust as one of the formative forces in Israeli consciousness, whilst challenging its use in justifying the denial of the right to freedom and self-determination to the Palestinians.

It is important to stress that *Arbeit* was not a piece about the historical Holocaust – rather it explored how the memory of this event continues to impact on life in the present. It proposed that this memory is not exclusively owned by those who experienced the Holocaust directly, or their families, but by all whose current lives are affected by its legacy, including *Mizrahi*[3] Jews and Palestinians. In this, the Theatre Center reflected its own members' biographies: the four core members of the company at the time were director David Maayan, a *Maghrebi*-Jewish Israeli of Moroccan descent with no direct family connection to the Shoah; actor Smadar Yaaron, daughter of a Jewish-Czech Holocaust survivor; actor Moni Yosef, the son of Iraqi Jewish immigrants who was brought up in a village founded by Hungarian survivors; and actor Haled Abu Ali, a Palestinian Israeli who admits to not having heard of the Holocaust until he was in his late twenties.[4] The company utilised their very different autobiographical connections with the Holocaust as the starting point for an investigation into its collective presence.

Between 1992 and 1996, the Acco Theatre Center also brought the work to the *toitland* of German-speaking Europe (under the title *Arbeit macht frei vom Toitland Europa*), where it initiated a related debate about the role that the commemoration of the Holocaust has played in the constitution of postwar collective German identity. The German performances initially met with disapproval from the Israeli establishment, who feared that Jewish self-criticism of the kind portrayed could be used to reduce the German sense of responsibility for the genocide and that the performance's strong liberatory gestus would create a false sense of absolution. The direct encounter described above between Israeli performers and a German audience in a conversation about their personal histories, placed midway through the five-hour-long performance, encapsulated this concern. I have revisited this scene many times, actually and imaginatively: first as a member of the audience at a performance in Hamburg in 1993, a young German of the Third Generation whose grandfathers both died as a result of fighting for Nazi Germany; two years later as one of the performers on the other side of the broken window, during a month-long visit of *Arbeit* to the German city of Recklinghausen, which I accompanied as production manager; and then as a writer.

Arbeit underwent substantial alterations at each of its locations, taking into account local historical and political differences. Judging by Freddie Rokem's detailed analyses of the Israeli version of the performance,[5] the piece was there structured around two main characters, a Jewish survivor of the death camps (played by Yaaron) and a Palestinian Israeli (played by Abu Ali), whose changing relationships to the memory of the Holocaust were constructed to mirror each other. At a pivotal moment in the performance the survivor handed over to the Palestinian to explain the workings of the Treblinka extermination camp, thus challenging the Jewish sense of ownership over this memory. The German version of *Arbeit* explored another mirror image, the encounter between Jewish Israelis and Germans of the postwar generation, who are both divided and united by the history they share – an encounter which, according to the company, 'created a new reality'.

What I am about to attempt is an account of *Arbeit* as I first saw it in Hamburg in July 1993, which aims to focus on the implications of this shift of emphasis and is intended as an additional reading to the ones made of the widely discussed Israeli performances. Much analysis of theatre is predicated on a desire to revisit our primary encounter with a particular performance and recapture some of the 'shock' it first caused us through fascination, insight or incomprehension. I find it impossible, however, to separate my initial impressions of the performance from my subsequent efforts to engage with it as a spectator, collaborator or scholarly commentator. As Dominick LaCapra notes, 'no memory is purely primary. It has always already been affected by elements not deriving from the experience itself'.[6] *Arbeit* made the impossibility of primary memory the centre of its investigation: it forced us to recognise who we are when we arrive at this encounter, and how such a meeting continues to resonate in the further practices it provokes, including the practice of writing. What follows is therefore a retrospective reconstruction of experience on the basis of knowledge gained of the work since, pieces of which have helped me to fill in what I had forgotten or what I simply failed to see, yet which I still am unable to claim will add up to a full representation of all that the performance was.

2

In Hamburg, *Arbeit* begins its excursion into the past where many such journeys begin: on a sightseeing trip. Our small party of thirty spectators is asked to mount a coach in which a colourful video commercial for the medieval crusader town of Acco serves as the first of a number of different modes for representing history that will be worked through in the course of the performance. It also helps us to acknowledge the work's relocation from Israel to the *toitland* of Europe. Here, the memory of the Holocaust is above all preserved in its 'trauma sites',[7] in the remains of ghettos and camps that have since been turned into museums and memorials. The trip suggests that the first encounter with this memory in contemporary Germany, where these sites have long become visitor attractions, is through the eyes of the tourist. Yet the trip is also invested with a different meaning, which is to gain prominence during the course of the performance. The meeting point where we were asked to wait for the coach was chosen carefully: in each of the German-speaking locations the spectators were instructed to gather at spots from where deportations of Jewish citizens to the ghettos and camps departed. We retraced their journeys – often unwittingly.

As the video ends, a sign comes into view. We have arrived at KZ Neuengamme, a former concentration camp in the outskirts of Hamburg, now a museum. At a memorial stone outside, a ceremony is held in commemoration of the victims of the Holocaust in the presence of two visitors from Israel, who are introduced to us as a survivor of the camps, Zelma Greenwald (Yaaron) and her son Menashe (Moni Yosef). This scene was specifically devised for the performances in Germany. Speeches, songs, the placing of wreaths, a minute of silence – the whole performance of atonement at the heart of German memorial culture is played out. It mirrors a scene later in the piece in which the actors parody a children's commemorative ceremony in Israel. Both are shown to have developed into empty rituals. But, whereas the latter will clearly be characterised as satirical – with adult actors impersonating children, exaggerating their mishaps – the mocking overtones of the former are subtler, thus inviting us to consider it as real. It may indeed be difficult to distinguish between a genuine commemorative ceremony and its theatrical re-enactment when thus placed within the context of an authentic memorial site.

A similar blurring between the realities of an act of memory and its re-enactment is at work in the scene that follows. We are invited to accompany the two Israeli visitors on a guided tour round the exhibition that is attached to the former work camp. Zelma introduces herself as the director of a Holocaust museum in Israel. She wears her hair in the style of the 1930s and is dressed in an old-fashioned suit and thickly soled orthopaedic shoes. She speaks a mixture of Yiddish, German, English and Hebrew in the typical accent of the central European, locating her both in the past and the present, Europe and Israel. With the authority of the survivor, Zelma interrupts our young German guide and her carefully chosen didactic phrases with provocative comments. She envies the 'beauty' of the authentic relics available in the 'deathland' – 'Excuse my excitement. But in Israel we do not have this variety of evidence. We are very far from the centre of the black hole. We only have one pair of pyjamas on display, only one item'[8] – and admires the immaculate working of the Auschwitz death machine – 'The cherry on the cake'.[9] Some of her more sacrilegious comments are hard to tolerate, as when she draws parallels between the 'Übermenschen' ideology of the Nazis and the Jewish belief in being the Chosen People. We don't know how to react. Should we be moved by the exhibition or feel provoked by her presentation; follow quietly, or intervene and protest? We remain silent – not surprising, perhaps, for a contemporary German audience who finds itself confronted with a survivor's narrative (even if it is one thus theatricalised). Whatever our reaction, we realise our complicity in this act of theatre that situates us as '"naïve" listeners'[10] who have to be guided and have to be told, yet who are being constantly challenged to respond with our knowledge.

Every statement in this scene is cited from authentic documents, collected by the company during three years of research. The museum scene contains the central elements of the performance like a nucleus from which the next four hours of *Arbeit* will be developed: its main themes are presented (the mechanics of intolerance and oppression; the enigma of survival; the teleological link between the Holocaust and the Israeli state), and its leit-motifs are played out for the first time (hunger and food; nationalist music). The performance carefully choreographs the audience's movement through the exhibition, directing our gaze toward specific objects which will later reappear in the performance. These include a torture table, on which, so the guide explains, naked Jewish inmates were whipped before being rushed to the gas chambers, while camp guards were looking on smoking and drinking beer.

As Rokem has argued in his insightful reading of this scene in the Israeli version, the museum section 'creates a strong unification between the first-person testimony of the survivor and the objective documentation in the museum'[11] – or between what we may term the 'witness' and the 'archive'.[12] Importantly, the 'witness' here is a mode of remembering rather than a real person. This is what Rokem has identified as one of the central themes of *Arbeit*. By transforming herself into the character of Zelma, a witness of the Holocaust, and by making this transformation transparent, the actress Yaaron, herself the child of a survivor, attempts to become 'a witness able to testify for the survivors, the real witnesses'.[13] This form of testimony by proxy has become central to Holocaust memory and yet is its most problematic aspect: with the gradual disappearance of the eye-witness generation, the responsibility for remembering must transfer to what LaCapra calls 'secondary witnesses',[14] which challenges the primacy and authenticity of the survivors' experience on which Holocaust memory is traditionally built. It is this 'transference'[15] of memory that the contemporary proliferation of museums, monuments and memorials is also attempting to effect. Yet it risks what James E. Young, in his critical study of Holocaust memorial culture, criticises as a displacement of memory-work by the 'fetishization of artefacts' in the archival practice of Holocaust museums.

In postwar Germany, this problematic of the memorial that threatens to replace the need for personal memory-work is of particular urgency: the abundance of historical artefacts left in the 'deathland' is in stark contrast to the almost total absence of Holocaust survivors in the country. Yet if, as historian Harold Kaplan has argued, a 'true memorial to the Holocaust gives first an approximate, a distant sharing with the experience of the victims',[16] memory culture in Germany raises the ethical question of whether such an identification with the victims may divert us from our responsibility to accept the guilt of the perpetrators that is our own legacy. As a result, German museums and memorials of the Holocaust have for a long time relentlessly focused on the representation of the annihilation of Jews (only the recently opened Jewish Museum in Berlin locates the event in a historical narrative that includes Jewish life in Germany before and after the genocide and uses individuals' stories to personalise their deaths). Zelma's living presence among the preserved remains of her murdered people displayed in the German camp museum reminds us of this dilemma.

3

The second part of *Arbeit* is set in a reclaimed quasi-industrial space. Although it is not a conventional theatre, it is nonetheless clearly marked as a theatricalised space, and it is here that for the first time our tickets are inspected before we can enter as if the performance were only really beginning now. We are guided through a vault illuminated only by the flicker of a torch. Roaring Nazi songs and speeches can be heard. An image appears out of the darkness: a wooden watchtower, and in front of it a leather armchair, from which Zelma slowly rises. She unwraps a bandage and reveals a number across her forearm, the sign of the camp survivor. She drops headlong on the floor, where, in the light of a projection showing documentary footage of the Holocaust, she is touching the mark as if both to caress and to erase it. In the scene that follows we are to be presented with a video which shows how the actor Smadar Yaaron Maayan had the number (19277) tattooed on her arm. (What we are not told is that the figures represent the date of the death of Yaaron's father, himself a survivor of the camps.) As Rokem points out, the transference of testimony is here physicalised as a lasting inscription on the body that is 'passed down' from the generation of the survivors to that of their children.[17] This direct, material way in which Yaaron thus claims the number for herself presents a potent provocation, as she herself has pointed out: '[E]specially for this generation it's terrible, it's a blasphem [sic!]. . . . And it's forbidden to do. It's not written anywhere but nobody dares to do such a thing.'[18] The blasphemy consists in her disrespect for the division that the Holocaust has effected between the survivors, defined by the uniqueness of their experience, and those who weren't there, and in her insistence that the Holocaust has left its mark on both.

We are led into a small 'memorial garden', surrounded by barbed-wire fences. In its centre stands a miniature concentration camp of cardboard barracks encircled by a steaming toy train. Four of the adult actors, dressed as children, perform a parody of a school memorial for the annual Yom Hashoah, the Israeli Holocaust Remembrance Day. Led by Zelma, the children sing out of tune into microphones that hang far too high over their heads. The words of nationalist poems are spoken with the wrong emphasis or lost in electronic feedback. A glance at a monitor in the corner of the room, which shows original footage of a school's memorial celebration, reveals that the caricature of a ritual bereft of its content for the children who perform it is not far from reality. Now we are allowed to recognise the satirical overtones of this re-enactment and take up a position of ironic distance that was not available before. This momentary distance is deceptive, however: at the end of the ceremony, we are asked to rise for a minute of silence – and find ourselves standing first for the Israeli, and then for the German, national anthem.

A curtain rises and reveals a replica of the gate at Auschwitz with its infamous inscription, 'Arbeit macht frei'. Behind it stands a labyrinthine wooden construction, a kind of model camp barracks, filled with iconic Holocaust objects such as shoes, suitcases and clothes. We enter this 'camp' through the gate, where Zelma is waiting to 'select'[19] us: to the right, to the left, into a narrow and dark corridor, where the actors are waiting behind broken windows to interview us about our personal pasts. The questions are simple: Where and when did we first hear about the Holocaust? Do we have a family connection with it? The theatrical situation – with its clear distinction between those of us who watch and those who act on our behalf – is momentarily suspended, and we are asked to contribute something of our own personal memory to the work. This forces us to articulate the point where our personal stories connect with the traumatic narrative of our collective past. The company has remarked upon the reluctance and even open hostility that this scene occasionally provoked in its Israeli audience (particularly in those who found themselves questioned by Haled Abu Ali, the Palestinian actor); in Germany, however, the answers came willingly and fluently, as if the German audience had eagerly awaited this occasion to confess to the Israeli actors. Yet, in a moment of the greatest intimacy between spectators and performers, the interview scene also made painfully obvious their separateness – Jews were facing Germans on different sides of a broken window, and their conversations revolved around their historical roles of victims and perpetrators. By marking them both as equally implicated in the trauma of the Shoah, however, there emerged the possibility of an affinity between positions that are historically separated by irreconcilable difference.

The interview scene presents a point of transition between the institutionalised forms of public commemoration which the performance has so far portrayed and the often suppressed pain of personal memory that is to be explored in its remainder – a rite of passage into the inner world of the set and the deeper levels of individual recollection. We are invited into a small and cramped chamber under a low ceiling, furnished with a grand piano and family photographs on the one hand, and old suitcases and scattered pieces of clothing on the other: at the same time a living room in modern Israel and a room in the wartime ghettos of Eastern Europe. We are seated surrounding the piano on which Zelma gives a virtuoso musical lecture on the similarities between the nationalist sentiments expressed in fascist and Zionist music. The provocative peak of her lesson is her passionate rendition of the so-called 'Horst-Wessel-Lied', regarded as the unofficial anthem of the Nazi state: 'This song is really arousing. . . . Doctor, doctor, I fell in love with a monster'.[20] The 'apparently bizarre empathy with the German culture, including its fascist traits' that Israeli scholar Kaynar has identified for what he terms the 'Iconic Phase' of Israeli theatre in the early 1990s and which he interprets as a 'means to spite the parents' generation'[21] also has a strong effect on us German spectators. One German critic refers to the scene as reaching 'the pain threshold'.[22]

The scene changes into a neighbourhood tumult. Neighbours competing over who suffered most in the camps, a son made to re-enact his mother's traumatic experiences – painful images of a post-Holocaust Israeli child-hood are set against the depictions of a new discrimination in the form of the humiliation of the Arab servant. The pace of the sequence grows ever faster, the mood ever more hysterical, until it erupts into an absurd choreography, with characters appearing heads down through trapdoors in the ceiling or fighting over scraps of food, and Zelma sliding back and forth across her piano, cabbage leaves stuffed into her clothes. The grotesque nature of these scenes makes them disturbing and difficult to watch, even more so as the somatic experience of being in such a claus-trophobic environment is quite overwhelming. We are made to 'get closer' to the experience of trauma in a very literal sense.

The mayhem ends abruptly when the ceiling falls in and we find our-selves sitting at a table laid for dinner. In place of a cloth, the table is cov-ered in photographs and documents referring to the Holocaust. Our host is Menashe, the distraught son of Zelma, who was seen re-enacting the trauma of the selection for his mother only moments before, now grown into a reserve officer in the paratroops, who intimidates his guests with a torrent of racist and chauvinist jokes. Yosef uses the information given to him dur-ing the interview scene and addresses some of us directly by name, inviting us to join in. 'Don't compare,' he barks at his wife (played by Yaaron), chal-lenging her liberal views when she contradicts his insistence on the unique-ness of the Holocaust with a list of other historical and contemporary atrocities. The argument is accompanied by music, which grows louder and louder as the verbal abuse increases, until it stops suddenly at a point when the volume has become almost unbearable, leaving us to finish our meal in embarrassed and uncomfortable silence. When the table is again lifted and cleared, Zelma returns to her piano and invites us to join her in singing Hebrew and German children's songs. We, who have moments before heard her lecture on chauvinist music, find ourselves singing along to songs with a strong nationalist sentiment. Haled appears to serve us coffee and baklava, speaking to us about his life as a Palestinian in Israel, finishing his story with a near-verbatim quotation of Shylock's famous appeal for accep-tance from Shakespeare's *The Merchant of Venice*. Haled is interrupted by a group of demonstrators, who force their way into the room, shouting inter-changeable political phrases: 'Arabs go home! With blood we liberate Palestine! Who are we? Jews! What are we? Intelligent! The world is against us. We don't care! Israeli people live! PLO-Israel no!'[23]

4

A siren, then a sudden silence. The table rattles down once more. On it lies Zelma, now an almost naked skeleton of skin and bones – the embod-iment of a *Muselmann*,[24] the starved, 'living dead' body that has become the most recognisable symbol of the death camps. She lies on her back with her head tilted backwards and slowly takes out a piece of bread that has been hidden inside her vagina. Earlier, during the tour of the museum, Zelma had called attention to a photo of a *Muselmann* and remarked: 'you can see how the stomach sticks to the back, but really, where he or she hide a piece of food in his body . . . . The creativity of these people . . . this is one of the climaxes of that era . . . . I would give a fortune for only once for a moment to hear this creature . . . what does it sound like . . . for that I would give millions'.[25] The material corporeality of the *Muselmann* with which Yaaron confronts us here provides us with an answer to Zelma's question about the enigma of survival. Primo Levi, himself a survivor of the camps, who devoted his life to bearing witness to his experience, has called the *Muselmänner*, and not the survivors, the true witnesses to the experience of the Holocaust: 'They are the rule, we are the exception. . . . We speak in their stead, by proxy'.[26]

By staging the 'submerged' (Levi) and mute memory of the Holocaust that is figured in the body of the *Muselmann* on to the scene of her own body, Yaaron proposes that to bear witness in the name of the *Muselmann*, the true witness, is here not just to speak in his proxy, nor to inscribe his traumatic memory merely *on* the body (as in the case of the number tattoo), but to realise this memory in a transgressive act of incorporation *in* the body, from which it is being externalised. Historian LaCapra, in his study of history and memory after Auschwitz, has identified 'inscription' and 'incorporation' as the two modes in which memory is articulated and suggests that only by interacting and counteracting the two can a trans-ference of witnessing take place.[27] Herein lies the answer which *Arbeit* proposes for Zelma's question: the true key to the 'survival' of the *Muselmann*; that is, to the continuing remembrance of his painful, trau-matic experience, is to re-present this Holocaust 'body in pain' and at the same time make transparent its creation in performance.

The *Muselmann* is offered to us spectators for consumption on the metaphorical dinner table right in our midst, in a manner that makes it impossible to divert our gazes from it. And yet, the hyper-visibility of this image and its key position in the work's dramaturgy is in stark contrast to its near invisibility in the available accounts of the performance. It is striking that only one commentator (Rokem), to whose interpretation I am hugely indebted, has acknowledged the importance of the scene for an understanding of *Arbeit*. Although most articles describe the performance in detail, the *Muselmann* image is either only mentioned in passing,[28] or missing altogether from the analysis.[29] This omission is particularly striking in the German reviews of the performance. In my first essay on the work, I too failed to understand this image, generalising it 'as an image as unex-pected and disturbing as a long forgotten memory',[30] a failure that became the central target of a critique by Rokem.[31] This failing may be partly explained with the dramaturgy of the piece, which relies on the audience to make connections (here between the *Muselmann* image and the museum scene) across a considerable length of performance time and across different performance spaces. But it is more likely to be taken as evidence for our difficulty in actually 'seeing' the image and recognising its full meaning, which confronts us in a direct and physical manner with a corporeal manifestation of the traumatic memory of the Shoah, a difficulty that seemed particularly evident in the case of the German audience.

The table is pulled up again, and from beneath appears Haled, singing a song of mourning. A disembodied voice orders us to climb through trapdoors in the ceiling into a room above the chamber, from where the image of the *Muselmann* had descended – and enter the 'hell' of the Israeli subconscious, which is presented as part death camp, part discotheque. A deafening cacophony of national songs and watchtowers emitting spinning lights envelops the performers, who are engaged in painful forms of self-punishment: images of bulimia, aggressive and reactionary militarism, a young woman trapped in a glass cage filled with Zionist writings, and in their midst Zelma/the *Muselmann*, hanging upside down by one leg over the remains of a broken piano, whacking herself with a whip. The cacophony slowly merges into one recognisable melody (that of a nationalist Zionist song), during which the *Muselmann* descends from her suspension, climbs over the gate, walks to a microphone, and joins in the singing. This is one of the most painful lessons that *Arbeit* proposes: that the sound of survival that Zelma was so eager to hear has turned into a nationalist roar.

Our own passivity and silence (only temporarily suspended in the interview scene), usually regarded as one of the privileges of modern theatre, has becomes increasingly difficult to bear as we have found ourselves being ascribed a variety of roles in which our attitudes have been tested and interventions provoked. Now, at the far end of the room, Haled Abu Ali is dancing naked on a table which is an exact replica of the torture device explained in the museum scene. The area is marked as 'smokers' corner', and beer bottles surround him. We are invited to smoke and drink – to open the bottles, we have to use an opener which hangs around Abu Ali's neck. Meanwhile he is hitting himself with a truncheon, inviting us to do the same – and indeed one man accepts the invitation, climbs on to the table, takes over the truncheon and beats Abu Ali with it. He thus transforms himself into a portrayal of the beer-drinking, smoking, torturing camp guard. But none of us interferes to stop him, thus becoming complicit in his act – yet if we had, we too would finally transgress the barrier that seemingly protects the 'innocence' of our watching. *Arbeit* demonstrates that no such innocence exists: no matter how we react, we inevitably become complicit in the actions we witness.

By offering us the bodies of the performers as physical materialisations of an Israeli collective consciousness that can thus be touched, metaphorically and literally, the performance involves us too in its attempt to reclaim the subjectivity of Holocaust trauma, including us in its process of transferring witnessing. There is an obviously cathartic element to this process, one that is portrayed in the final scene as an act of symbolic and physical purgation. But it is an uneasy process – one that subjects us spectators to aggression, anxiety and somatic distress, rather than transcendence, and one that was resisted repeatedly by members of the audience.

Finally, Zelma/*Muselmann* opens the gate for us to leave. The last image that we manage to glimpse is that of the *Muselmann* rocking the Palestinian in her arms in a *pietà*, the Christian symbol of deliverance – an image that in its emphasis on the shared experiences of victimhood (beyond a simplistic comparison) proposes the possibility of a more ethical form of Jewish and Arab co-existence in Israel/Palestine. As we are leaving the space, the deafening noise comes to an end. All that remains is the sound of Abu Ali's weeping, a sound which finally takes us out of Europe and into the camps in Gaza, while reminding us that these are also a European, and particularly a German legacy.

5

Upon leaving we are handed a sheet of programme notes, which includes an enigmatic paragraph, printed without spaces between the words:

> CompilingWrittenDocumentsFictionNewspaperCuttingsImagesChaim RumkowskyLettersPhilosophyViewingOfNumerousVideosISurvivedT heSelectionDocumentaryFilmsMoviesAboutTheHolocaustEscapeFro mSobiborStatementsDocumentationWitnessesAndSurvivorsChoiceOf MusicTheMusicContainsEverythingVisitToMemorialsCursedIsTheGr oundOfEuropeAttendingCommemorationCeremoniesMyGodMyGod ItWillNeverEndDeclaimingAndMemorizingWorkMaterials(Arbeitsma terialien)[32]SeeAboveConstructionOfTheSetEventsLaboratorySiteOfEx terminationGhettoRollCallCorridorsWatchtowersLetTheirNameBeBl ottedOutATerribleWomanSpoiltBratGatePitsMovementsTheAudienc eIsAskedToEnterInTheOrchardNextToTheTroughIHaveNoOtherCo untryIWasBornHereIsraeliHellThreeYearsWeSpentInTheLivingDeat hMachineAndWereHappy.Laugh![33]

The paragraph, densely woven from references to the Holocaust, the Bible, traditional Jewish culture and contemporary Israeli politics, alludes to the complex thematic concerns of the piece, most importantly the link that is drawn between the Holocaust – including examples of both Jewish collaboration (Chaim Rumkowsky) and Jewish heroism (Escape from Sobibor) – and the contemporary state of 'Israeli hell'. The list also invites us to consider the making of the piece, the long period of research, followed by the creation of set and characters, and the staging for an audience. The performance is thus framed not merely as resulting from, but as continually reiterating the process of its own making – the double sense of 'work' in the context of theatre (and art-making in general) that is brought to mind here, referring to both the process of labour and its product, is also provoked repeatedly during the piece itself, where it is connected to the more sinister historical abuse of the term. Historical time and theatrical time become superimposed: the 'three years we spent in the living death machine' may refer to both the devising period and the years between 1942 and 1945, the period of the Nazi death camps. The death-bringing labour regime of the camps (and their cynical motto of 'Arbeit macht frei' – 'work liberates') is thus provocatively linked to the potentially liberating work of theatre, ending in the imperative 'laugh!' As the subtitle of the performance proposed, 'We opened the gate. We opened it wide. It was hell and this was the work'.[34]

But why choose this 'work', which is nearly fifteen years old at the time of writing, as an example for a 'contemporary theatre in Europe'? Much has changed since *Arbeit*'s premiere in 1991: the short period of liberalisation in Israel came to a brutal end in 2000, when a new wave of violence has made the peace process ever more improbable; unified Germany finds itself struggling with its Nazi past between the desire to 'move on', the spectre of a new right-wing extremism, and a public commemoration culture that stages itself more prominently than ever (see recent high-profile projects such as the Jewish Museum and the Memorial to the Murdered Jews of Europe in Berlin). *Arbeit*'s continuing relevance to me lies in its challenge to what makes a 'contemporary theatre in Europe': it questions the notion of 'contemporaneity' by exploring the continuing presence of the past in the 'now-time' of memory; it critically evokes the cultural and historical legacy of what we call 'Europe'; and it addresses the philosophical and political questions that are raised by both of these concerns – questions circulating around the representation of history and memory – as ones that are already the work of the theatre. Acco Theatre Center is possibly the last representative of a particular tradition of experimental theatre making in Europe, a tradition that has included Grotowski and Kantor (whose work is directly referenced in *Arbeit*), and that must be understood as a theatrical contemplation 'in performance' of the 'deathland' that was twentieth-century Europe.

Notes

1   H. Roms, 'Time and Time Again: *Arbeit macht frei vom Toitland Europa*', *Performance Research* 1, 1, pp. 59–62, (p. 59).
2   The transliteration of the company's name and those of the performers from Hebrew to English causes some variations of spelling in the literature. I have chosen the spelling the company itself uses in its publicity, but I will retain other spellings in quoted materials.

3 Jews whose families immigrated to Israel from Middle Eastern countries were given the name *Mizrahim* ('the Eastern ones').

4 A. Tlalim, *Don't Touch My Holocaust (Al Tigu Li BaShoah)*, video, 140 minutes, colour, Hebrew and German with English subtitles, Israel: Set Productions, 1994.

5 F. Rokem, 'On the Fantastic in Holocaust Performances', in C. Schumacher, ed., *Staging the Holocaust: The Shoah in Drama and Performance*, Cambridge: Cambridge University Press, 1998, pp. 40–52; F. Rokem, *Performing History: Theatrical Representations of the Past in Contemporary Theatre*, Iowa City: University of Iowa Press, 2000.

6 D. LaCapra, *History and Memory after Auschwitz*, Ithaca and London: Cornell University Press, 1998, p. 21.

7 LaCapra, *History and Memory*, p. 10.

8 V. von Flemming, '*Sarajevo*' und '*Theaterzentrum Akko*': *Politisches Theater beim Internationalen Sommertheater Festival Hamburg*, video, 54 minutes, colour, English and German; first broadcast 23 August 1993, Germany: Norddeutscher Rundfunk. My translation from the German.

9 A. Veiel, *Balagan*, video, 94 minutes, colour, Hebrew, English and German, Germany: JOURNAL–FILM Klaus Volkenborn KG, 1993.

10 Rokem, 'On the Fantastic in Holocaust Performances', p. 49.

11 Rokem, 'On the Fantastic in Holocaust Performances', p. 49.

12 See G. Agamben, *Remnants of Auschwitz: The Witness and the Archive*, trans. D. Heller-Roazen, Cambridge, MA/London: Zone Books, 1999.

13 Rokem, 'On the Fantastic in Holocaust Performances', p. 51.

14 LaCapra, *History and Memory*, p. 21.

15 LaCapra, *History and Memory*, p. 11.

16 H. Kaplan, *Conscience and Memory: Meditations in a Museum of the Holocaust*, Chicago: University of Chicago Press, 1994, p. 9.

17 Rokem, 'On the Fantastic in Holocaust Performances', p. 51.

18 Yaaron in Veiel, *Balagan*.

19 'Selektion(en) "Selections(s)": Nazi term for the process by which members of a transport were chosen: some, generally a small number, for slave labour; the rest, usually the vast majority, being sent to the gas chambers', A. J. and H. Edelheit, *History of the Holocaust: A Handbook and Dictionary*, Boulder, San Francisco and Oxford: Westview Press, 1994, pp. 424–5.

20 Recklinghausen 22 June 95

21 G. Kaynar, '"What's Wrong With The Usual Description of The Extermination?!" National-Socialism and The Holocaust as a Self-Image Metaphor in Israeli Drama: The Aesthetic Conversion of a National Tragedy into Reality-Convention', in H.P. Bayerdörfer, ed., *Theatralia Judaica (II): Nach der Shoah – Israelisch-deutsche Theaterbeziehungen seit 1949*, Tübingen: Max Niemeyer Verlag, 1996, pp. 200–16 (p. 214).

22 W. Jens, 'Balagan – Anläßlich der Friedensfilmpreisverleihung', unpublished laudation, Berlin, 21 February 1994. My translation from the German. The quote is taken from the laudation for the German Peace Film Award 1994, which was awarded to *Balagan*, Andres Veiel's documentary about *Arbeit*.

23 Veiel, *Balagan*.

24 'Muselman – "muslim": Concentration camp slang term referring to an inmate on the verge of death from starvation, exhaustion, and despair. It appears that the term originated with the similarities between a concentration camp victim and the image of a Muslim prostrating himself in prayer', Edelheit and Edelheit, *History of the Holocaust*, p. 377. For an account of the history of the term, see Agamben, *Remnants of Auschwitz*, pp. 44–5. The implications of the term for *Arbeit*

and its investigation of the communality of Jewish and Muslim victimhood are complex.

25 Tlalim, *Don't Touch My Holocaust*.
26 P. Levi, *The Drowned and the Saved*, trans. R. Rosenthal, London: Abacus, 1989, pp. 63–4.
27 LaCapra, *History and Memory*, p. 45.
28 R. Rovit, 'Emerging from the Ashes: The Akko Theatre Center Opens the Gates to Auschwitz', *The Drama Review (TDR)* 37, 2 (T138), 1993, pp. 161–73.
29 R. Schechner, 'Believed-in Theatre', *Performance Research* 2, 2, 1997, pp. 76–91; D. Urian, 'Arbeit macht frei in [sic] Toitland Europa', *Theatre Forum*, 3, Spring 1993, pp. 60–6.
30 Roms, 'Time and Time Again', p. 61.
31 Rokem, *Performing History*, p. 60.
32 'Arbeitsmaterialien' or 'Work materials'. 'Nazi term applying to categories of Jews, in ghettos or camps, capable of doing productive work for the SS or for German private industry. Those designated thus were permitted a brief reprieve before being murdered', Edelheit and Edelheit, *History of the Holocaust*, p. 189.
33 Acco Theatre Center, 'Values for the Next Millennium', unpublished project notes, Acco, 1994 (my translation from the German).
34 Acco Theatre Center, 'Values for the Next Millennium'.

Chapter 4

On the border as theatrical space

Appearance, dis-location and the production of the refugee

Sophie Nield

Outward journey

My first proper encounter with mainland Europe, aside from family holidays as a child, was when I went round it by rail as a student in 1988. Somehow, Britain didn't really count to us as 'Europe' proper, and it was only when we had crossed the channel and boarded the first of those many trains at Calais that we felt really 'abroad'. You don't know what it feels like to live on an island until you leave it. My memories of that trip are of an unprecedented sense of huge expanses of land – we could have gone all the way to China without having to cross water again. We also encountered the novelty of the land border – waiting in a dusty Spanish town to cross into France, being woken in the middle of the night by an irate East German guard halfway to the strange island that was West Berlin, and then coming back on a night train that had started its journey in Moscow.

This encounter with borders and trains, with the idea and the reality of Europe and its edges, with that sense of vast amounts of land being used and shaped and invented by the people we met moving around it – travellers, students, migrants, workers – is, I suppose, the one which begins this journey.

My work has been about the construction of theatrical spaces by events in public, rather than more conventionally understood theatre events and spaces. I want to focus in this essay on the particular experience of the refugee – addressing the 'theatricality' of the border, and how it, and the encounters it stages, 'produce' the individual who attempts to cross. The essay will use key concepts from these important European thinkers: Giorgio Agamben on the refugee as border-concept; Hannah Arendt on the problem of equating the human with the citizen when the human is not a citizen; Etienne Balibar on how the subject is made to 'appear' at the border. It will concern itself with space, appearance and dis-location.

Europe, like anywhere, is a place that is determined by histories of particular movements. I mean this initially in the literal sense, as spatial changes and redefinitions cause political and social realities to take shape. The borders of modern Europe are constructed out of the experience of pogroms, enforced evacuations, and continuing displacements arising from post-colonial inequality and poverty, twentieth-century fascism and war. Between 1850 and 1920, for example, some thirty million people left the continent for North and South America, with millions more moving between various European states.[1] As a consequence of different speeds and processes of industrialisation, many workers moved in great numbers from Poland and Ukraine into France, Germany and the UK, while Italians and Slavs moved into France, Switzerland and Austria. Meanwhile, several hundred thousand Jews from Eastern Europe were forced to flee 'pogroms', anti-Semitism and economic hardship for the great metropolitan centres of Berlin, Paris, London, Vienna and Prague. The word pogrom entered into common currency following the outbreak of violence against Russian Jewry that followed the assassination of the Tsar in 1881, and which triggered a westward migration lasting well into the twentieth century. It was this movement of people that led to the first formal legislation concerning the regulation of migration into the UK, with the introduction of the 1905 Aliens Act.

The great cataclysm that was the Second World War saw fifteen million people displaced from their homes, and by the close of the war an estimated thirty million were on the move. The United Nations Relief and Rehabilitation Administration was established in 1943, and in 1945 the organisation assisted with the repatriation of some five million people. As well as those who had been forced into exile during the war, including those Jews who had fled or survived the Holocaust, the redrawing of the boundaries of the formerly occupied territories at the conference at Yalta in 1945 led to the movement of large numbers of people between Czechoslovakia, Poland, Hungary and other Eastern European states.[2] A further million displaced persons, who did not wish to return to their countries of origin, were resettled between 1948 and 1951 with the assistance of the International Refugee Organisation, established in 1947. Many of these organisations, concerned with the treatment and management of refugees and migration, were forged in face of postwar displacement, to assist and aid the hundreds of thousands of people who found themselves in places where they shouldn't have been, or didn't want to be, or unable to go to places they needed to be in. New international agreements were also pioneered, such as the Universal Declaration of Human Rights (1948), the European Convention on Human Rights (1950) and UNHCR Refugees Convention (1951). Since 1951, migration from outside Europe has increased and, as Robin Cohen notes, 'Fortress Europe confronts immigrants and asylum seekers trying to enter western European countries'. Despite the apparent ease with which the war-torn economies of Europe absorbed the displaced of the Second World War, Cohen observes that there was an undercurrent of racism in the selection of immigrants which has only gathered pace and force with more recent Turkish, African, Caribbean and post-colonial migration.[3]

It is no surprise that these literal, physical movements become a part of the cultural imaginary, influencing the ways in which we conceptualise and describe the continent. The work of novelists such as W. G. Sebald and Anne Michaels; of memoirists and thinkers such as Primo Levi and Walter Benjamin; of many of the performance makers represented elsewhere in this volume, and of films concerned with migration, post-colonial and postwar experience – all speak to the profound influence of journeys, displacements and the experience of difference on contemporary European cultural production. But, while all of these instances are deeply connected to the ways we move, or fail to move, across the continent, and to the experiences of the displaced and those seeking refuge, I argue that the space of Europe itself is also being forged as a theatrical imaginary through the ways in which people try to cross it. These migrations are, of course, 'real'; the people whose lives are disrupted or altered are not actors. How, then, is this 'theatre'?

This essay is not about conventional theatre events. You will not read about theatres, plays or actors. What this essay represents is one of the ways in which our discipline is undergoing a strategic broadening, and is beginning to address and encompass many different kinds of event. In a way, it starts from another perspective. Instead of asking what events in the public arena have in common with the theatre, it asks: What are we talking about, really talking about, when we talk about the theatre?

And, having identified some of those things, can we use those ideas to help us to talk about other things, such as identity, politics, experience? The question is, how can we use a particular frame of reference – in this case, a theatrical frame of reference – through which to look at the world around us in new and useful ways?

This strategic broadening has already been happening in the adjacent field of performance studies. We have seen over the past two decades the expansion of performance as a viable concept in social and political analysis. There is, however, a frustration here, which lies with the attendant limitations that have been imposed on the term 'theatrical'. This has consequences for the interpretation of the theatrical itself, as it becomes tied to a 'theatre' which is limited discursively in crucial ways[4] and the properties of 'theatre' find themselves over-restricted to conventional theatre practice (the acting of a play in a theatre). These restrictions are extended into cultural analysis as the 'theatrical', which comes to mean 'having properties *like* the theatre' and indicating such concerns as pre-scripting, rehearsal, illusion, a self-conscious 'acting', decorative elements and an organisation of appearances. I think that a means must be found to root the identification of these events as 'theatrical' in more than a surface likeness to 'theatre', and in more than metaphorical terms. The 'theatrical' must be seen as having a set of qualities, practices and forms of spatialisation which may certainly be present in, but are by no means limited to, the practices of theatre. In this way, the strategic 'return' to the theatre and the theatrical can be seen as a means of saying useful things about social practices, and providing us with useful means of interpreting (and learning to act in) our world.

I don't propose, then, that the actions of refugees, or the management of borders by nation states, are 'theatrical' because people are acting or pretending there (though they may well be), or that the border is rolled up and taken away to a props room when the show is over (though I will return to the migration of borders shortly).

I mean, rather, that some of the ways in which identity, space and appearance work together in the encounter at the border are similar to the ways they work together in the theatre. I am therefore expanding the idea of the 'theatrical' to imply the production of a space in which 'appearance' of a particular kind becomes possible; indeed, a space which is organised in such a way as to compel certain kinds of appearance. A place which does not exist (Elsinore, Narnia, Lyra's Oxford) is made 'present' through the theatrical event, whether through design and realisation, or through being described in language, like the locations for Shakespeare's plays. The theatre's production of space demands a particular kind of suspension of disbelief which I think remains constant to it, despite its taking on different aspects and configurations that change with the particular historical context. For example, the relationship of audience or character to 'fictional' space is by no means the same in late nineteenth-century realism as it is in Restoration comedy or contemporary dance. Nevertheless, there is a relationship between the space of the fiction, the space of the stage and the space of the audience which requires all three somehow to be present and absent in different combinations – producing something which I think can be identified as a peculiarly 'theatrical' configuration of space. This space, doubling or trebling itself in this way, and being constituted through the moment of performance or event, is reciprocally inhabited by 'fictional', yet clearly present, people, who are only functional as long as the event, or play, or encounter, lasts. The theatre is the place where these people appear – it is the only place where they can appear. The question of who exactly is present – actor, performer, character; material body or representational figure – carries precisely the sense of ambivalence that I think is reproduced in the experience of the border-crosser. The opening lines of that most iconic of theatre pieces, *Hamlet*, is, after all, 'Who's there?' The presentation of 'character' requires a figure to operate simultaneously as both what they are (the material physical body of the performer) and also what they are representing themselves to be (their 'role' within the performance). This is 'theatrical' appearance.

The border, like the theatre, is a place where you have to appear. The border, and the border-dweller or refugee, I argue, both 'appear' at the moment at which they come into conjunction. This encounter, too, requires the production of a space in which identity can be doubled; in which it is possible, indeed necessary, to be present in more than one way; in which one must simultaneously be present and be represented. The issue is not whether a person is there. A person is clearly there. The issue is precisely 'who is there?' – whether the person who is there *is* who they *represent* themselves to be, and is, in fact, the legal/juridical object that the legal/ juridical mechanisms require them to be in order to assign the rights and freedoms that are being claimed. This representation may take the form of documentation (passports, permits to travel, proofs of nationality, photographs); verbal accounts of reasons for travel; narratives of suffering or oppression, which have caused a person to be in flight. It may, in other words, be more, or less, 'performative', but nevertheless this strange double exposure would seem to me, in any event, to echo the simultaneous presence of actor and character. As you move from one state to another, you 'play' yourself, and hope you are convincing. As W. B. Worthen notes in discussing the work of Judith Butler, 'the performance of identity is never sovereign; it is always an elaborate process of citation'. This, he says, is particularly so at a border.[5] And if the double exposure fails, if you are not able to represent yourself effectively, presence itself breaks down, and appearance fails. I will return below to this idea of the 'non-person', and how failure to broach the border causes people to disappear, both legally and performatively.

In these ways, then, the relationship of the border encounter to the theatre is not one of the imitative to the authentic, of the 'fake' to the real, but rather is contained in a series of shared concerns around space, appearance, disappearance and representation. It is a theatrical moment, the moment at which 'you' are produced. These appearances, too, are witnessed, by observers, inspectors, judges – audiences.

Border crossing

I will expand on some of these thoughts in the following section, as I look more closely at the space of Europe and the philosophical, and practical, question of the border. I am going to look particularly at the work of Etienne Balibar and Giorgio Agamben – who are writing not as theatre scholars, but as philosophers and political economists – to show how the ideas of presence, appearance and representation, which I am claiming as theatrical ideas, seem to permeate discussion of borders and migration.

Balibar suggests that borders themselves are a European invention, citing the first division of the world made by Pope Alexander VI between the Spanish and the Portuguese at Torsedillas in 1494 (and immediately contested by the English and the French), right up to the division of Africa at the Conference of Berlin in 1895.[6] With the recent expansion of the European Union to encompass Poland, Estonia and other former Eastern bloc countries, and with Russia apparently considering an application to join, the entity of 'Europe' as it is imagined here clearly transcends its conventional geographical boundaries. This is not merely a mapping of a conveniently titled economic entity on to an almost congruent set of national parameters. Not only do the economic variegations of Europe and its constituents derive from very particular moments in the imperial, colonial and other pasts of the continent, but contemporary movements, which impact upon national boundaries, derive their momentum from economic causes. Migrants from Estonia to Britain, for example, are not just crossing a geographically coherent clump of land – they are positioned within the economic inequity deriving from post-colonial, postwar and post-cold war realities. In the context of this movement, borders serve several functions. As well as marking the limits of a nation's territory and hence rule of law, rights, control and so on, they serve to construct the national imaginary, by making and unmaking the 'other', who is of course, as Balibar points out, often already a part of the European imaginary.

In part, these anxieties are played out as part of a national(ist) politics internal to the continent and the economic community. When in 1995 'Schengenland' came into existence – the agreement under the terms of the Maastricht Treaty to suspend border controls between France, Germany, Spain, Portugal, Greece, Italy, Austria and the Benelux countries – the UK did not choose to participate. David Cesarani and Mary Fulbrook note also that the arrangement was only permitted at the price of 'massively strengthened external controls'.[7]

For Europe, too, as it is imagined, is defined by its outer edges. The phrase 'Fortress Europe' has had currency in public discourse since the cold war, and, after the collapse of the Eastern bloc in the late 1980s, was supplemented with perorations on who, or what, would be next to assail the 'Gates of Europe'. The point of a border is as much to determine who is outside as who is inside. Cesarani and Fulbrook continue (though writing before the inclusion of some of the eastern states into the EU):

> the paradoxical effect of European unity, and the greater interna-tionalism of the Europeans (within Europe) has been a strengthening of Eurocentrism, a sort of higher xenophobia directed against Muslims and the modern version of the Mongol hordes – east Europeans attempting to escape the economic rubble of communism.[8]

More recent political developments (not least the so-called 'war on terror' and its attendant consequences) have all conspired to make the question of Europe's borders and the movement of people into and through the continent a particularly pressing one. These anxieties lead, of course, to increases in the mechanisms of regulation governing migration. Yet these mechanisms are not neutral instruments; they contribute to the construction of both identity and space – to the production of theatrical space and the theatricalised encounter.

'You do not,' notes Balibar, 'cross the border between France and Switzerland, or between Switzerland and Italy, the same way when you have a "European" passport as when you have a passport from the former Yugoslavia'.[9] Today's borders, Balibar writes, are designed 'not merely to give individuals from different social classes different experiences of the law, civil administration, the police and elementary rights . . . but actively to *differentiate* between individuals in terms of social class'. While appearing to be stable, and the same for everyone, rather, they 'conceal differentiation, by pretending to treat everyone the same, to recognise national equality, while actually constructing and performing difference, hence reinforcing the connection of citizenship, identity and nationality'. In other words, while pretending to be neutral, to merely administer the passage (or lack of passage) of the individual through a juridical/political obstacle, the border and the individual's experience of the border are constitutive of their social selves. His argument that the border 'constructs and performs' difference applies not only to the identification and delimiting of the feared 'other', but of the citizen, the subject himself or herself. Borders construct the outsider, but – crucially for the theatrical imaginary – they also construct the nation and the idea of 'belonging'.

There is a major potential difficulty here, however, which is what happens to the person for whom the mechanism fails – who cannot demonstrate belonging. Giorgio Agamben cites a thought of Hannah Arendt's, as she notes that one of the key documents of European freedom has at its very outset a profound inconsistency.[10] The founding statement of the French Revolution from 1789, the Declaration of the Rights of Man and of the Citizen, she argues, accidentally seems to enshrine the rights of the person as they are consolidated and produced as the rights of the citizen – of, literally, the member of a nation-state. This of course produces a significant problem at the time of Arendt's observation – the wake of the Second World War and the unprecedented numbers of stateless and displaced persons in Europe. The consequences for Agamben remain significant into the contemporary moment, as they are played out in the experience of those attempting for whatever reason to pass across borders and between boundaries of those nation-states. He observes that 'the rights of "man" prove to be completely unprotected at the very point it becomes impossible to categorise them as the rights of a citizen of the state'.[11] The refugee, the stateless person, is already part-way to becoming a person without rights.

For Balibar, this becomes an issue of the ability of the refugee to appear, to make themselves present in the way that the encounter with the border demands. He explicitly identifies those in search of refuge as 'people who are individually or collectively engaged in a process of negotiation of their presence and their mode of presence (that is, their political, economic, cultural, religious and other rights) with one or more states'. Failure to negotiate this mode of appearing, or to inhabit the space of the border properly, causes a sort of spatial disjuncture, a stasis. The refugee becomes a non-person, a border-dweller. Balibar says that for the poor person from a poor country, '[the border] is a place he runs up against repeatedly, passing and repassing through it as and when he is expelled, or allowed to rejoin his family, so that it becomes, in the end, the place where he resides'.[12] And in fact the new borders of Europe are fringed with refugee camps: non-places for non-people, holes in the fabric of the union of nation states.

The consequences of these breakdowns in presence and encounter apply also to the borders themselves. As Balibar observes, 'Nothing is less like a material thing than a border, even though it is officially "the same" whichever way you cross it'.[13] The discourse surrounding borders and their policing speaks to the profound anxiety that meets the recognition that the supposedly concrete and visible entity, the border itself, is vulnerable. The prevalence of terms such as 'porous' and 'permeable' in describing borders, and the threats of 'flooding', 'swamping' and 'overrunning' all reflect a particular spatial imaginary.

These also suggest to me that this patchwork of superimpositions, mistakes and gaps speaks more of the imagined and performed space of Europe than any coherent 'map' of boundary lines and nations. Various sources, in fact, point to the physical migration of the borders of the nation-states of Europe themselves. Migreurop describe themselves as a 'collective initiative of militants (individuals, NGOs, academics, from France, Italy, Belgium) to reflect, inform and act on (and against) camps of foreigners in European States; migration and asylum policy; new projects of "externalisation"'. They report the literal shifting of borders, understood as instruments of regulation and restriction, away from the locations of borders understood as the limit of national territory. They note that:

> European proposals increasingly mention the possibility of detaining asylum seekers in camps located outside the European Union. This 'externalisation' or 'subcontracting' applies not only to asylum, but also to the protection of borders. The aim is to make them more and more impenetrable, pushing them beyond their physical materialisation'.[14]

An article in the *Observer* of 15 June 2003 points to this as an element of UK border control proposals, reporting that 'asylum seekers arriving in Britain will be shipped to an "offshore" camp in Croatia as part of a radical move to process all asylum claims outside European borders'.[15] Citing a letter from the Prime Minister, Tony Blair, the story mentions plans to create a 'buffer zone' beyond the external borders of Europe, by building camps in, for example, Russia, Belarus, Romania, Bulgaria, Ukraine and Albania. The camps are to be run by the International Organisation for Migration, a screening system approved, according to the *Observer*, by UNHCR. Longer-term plans include 'regional protection areas' in, for example, Kenya and Pakistan. (Leigh Daynes, spokesperson for the Refugee Council asks in the same piece for urgent assurance that these centres 'will be compliant with the European Convention on Human Rights and the 1951 Refugee Convention'.)

Migreurop also cites the franchising out of borders, and the forcing of third countries to cooperate in the fight against illegal immigration, noting that 'the European Union finances the control of Moroccan borders in order to fight illegal immigration into Europe. It is a way of transforming this country into a "European border watchdog"'.

These practices and proposals are not without critics. The BBC reported on 30 September 2004 that Spain had raised objections to proposals made by Germany for 'transit' camps, in which asylum seekers would be processed in centres outside the European bloc.[16] The proposal was for processing centres in countries such as Libya and Tunisia, where asylum seekers would go first. Spain said that 'care must be taken to ensure Europe does not "allow itself any moral backward steps"'. The UN refugee agency and Amnesty International also raised reservations as to whether such a system could guarantee people's basic human rights.

What this would all seem to suggest is that, like the refugee, the border is not quite 'there'. Rather, it 'appears', or is produced, wherever the encounter, the narrative or story of movement takes place. It is the site at which identity (or its lack) is staged, enacted and performed. The border itself appears in the bureaucratic production of it, and we, as identities or selves ('characters'), are made to appear and disappear at the border. And this dis-location, this permanent temporariness, is what the migrant ends up inhabiting. Balibar observes of refugees that they become themselves a form of border, dwelling in 'an extraordinarily viscous spatio-temporal zone, almost a home . . . in which to live a life which is a waiting-to-live, a non-life'.[17] Agamben, too, says of the refugee that (he or she) 'should be considered for what he [or she] is, that is, nothing less than a border concept that radically calls into question the principle of the nation-state'.[18]

In this way, then, the refugee makes all our citizenships compromised, makes all our locatedness compromised – exposes the 'theatrical', performative, tentative, provisional nature of our locatedness. We are, ultimately, held in tension between here and there as the theatre holds us in tension between here and there. We are able to move only in so far as we are able to appear at the margins, at the borders, only in so far as we are able to accurately represent ourselves to the audiences we encounter there.

Return journey

In 1990, shortly after I made my rail trip around the Continent, construction workers drilled through the last piece of rock and joined the two halves of the Channel Tunnel together, linking Britain to mainland Europe for the first time in 8,000 years. When *Eurostar* began operation a few years later, it was not only possible to travel to the Continent by train, but a way had opened up for people to get into Britain by land, one which has vexed commentators, political parties and immigration officials ever since.

In the months before the closure in 2002 of the last mainland refugee camp before the English Channel, at Sangatte in northern France, I watched several news reports which featured Kurdish, Eastern European and other prospective immigrants to Britain play a deadly serious game of cat and mouse with immigration controls and the border guards. As darkness fell, many people, some with children, shivering in coats and woollen hats, would walk the three kilometres to congregate on the roads and waste ground near to the *Eurostar* freight terminal. There they would attempt to scale the razor wire and stow away on one of the slow trains moving through the night towards the Channel Tunnel. On 3 March 2001, the BBC reported that nine people had been found clinging underneath the *Eurostar*. Passengers on the 399 kph train heard a frantic banging during the three-hour journey, and alerted train staff. A three-year-old girl was crammed into the tiny space with the adults. The nine, who claimed asylum and had come from Romania, were arrested at Waterloo. In August of the same year, forty-four people were stopped after walking eleven kilometres along the Channel Tunnel from the Coquelles terminal on an unlit metre-wide walkway next to the tracks. The tunnel is sixty kilometres long.

I was struck initially by the dramatic and performative qualities of what was taking place – groups of people, waiting by day and hiding by night, trying to do the impossible, and hang underneath a train as it made its journey under the sea and into the south of England – possibly even to London, which sounded in their descriptions like some latterday Dick Whittington fable – streets paved with employment, houses for all, safety from persecution, the chance of a new life.

But as I considered it, it occurred to me that these encounters were about theatrical space and appearance, too. These people running through the dark, hiding in ditches, crossing Europe in the boots of cars, under trains, are all trying to be invisible, to avoid appearing in the way that the encounter of the border and the nation-state tries to insist that they appear. If they can disappear from view, resist the visibility and the definition, which the mechanism of the border imposes, and the necessity to demonstrate insiderness, belonging, citizenship, then movement may once again become possible for them. This same disappearance is of course what is being mobilised in the illegal and vicious trafficking of people across borders, not least those women trafficked into invisible slavery in the sex industry.

This essay started with a trip on a 'real' train; it closes with a theatrical train, in the East End of London, palimpsest of European and now post-colonial migration. In the autumn of 2004, Marisa Carnesky's *Ghost Train* was installed behind Brick Lane.[19] In this city of migrants, the East End has a particularly rich and varied history, having provided refuge to Huguenot weavers in the late sixteenth and early seventeenth centuries, Eastern European Jews in the nineteenth and early twentieth centuries, and more recently the Bangladeshi community. The show, a 'dark ride across haunted borders', used ingenious Victorian theatre tricks built by the illusionist Paul Kieve, and presented images of women refugees in various predicaments and situations to the audience, who were seated in the wooden train that circled the ride.

The performance conjures a moment before post-colonial migration, it does not feature the community in whose streets it is located; rather it materialises the first wave of migrants fleeing pogroms and displacement a hundred years ago, the women of 1881, of 1905. As the train circles the track with the passengers on board strapped into their seats, women in nineteenth-century clothing reach out to us, detach their own limbs to more easily climb out of their cages, sink slowly and silently through the floor, escape their bonds, ask us for help, enter and exit through a series of incomprehensible doors. They use all the means of theatrical appearance at their disposal to enjoin us to admit them, to release them from the theatrical space and into the world. They want to board the train. We, the witnesses, the audience, the judges, cannot help them; we cannot validate their appearance and grant them the refuge which they are pleading for us to provide. So, as the train pulls up, and just before we are disgorged back into Banglatown, we look back into the mechanism of the ghost train. The tracks, structures and machines of appearance are mysteriously gone, the space is open, waiting. All the migrant, refugee, border-crossing women we have seen during the course of the ride are there. They look back at us, they dance, they signal to us across the space. The music ends. And then, as if by magic, they all instantly, and completely, disappear.

Notes

1 For a full treatment of these issues, see R. Cohen, ed., *The Cambridge Survey of World Migration*, Cambridge: Cambridge University Press, 1995, particularly Colin Holmes, 'Jewish Economic and Refugee Migrations', pp. 148–53; D. Kay, 'The Resettlement of Displaced Persons in Europe, 1946–1951', pp. 156–8; H. Fassmann and R. Munz, 'European East–West migration 1945–1992', pp. 470–80; Section 9, 'Labour Migration to Western Europe after 1945', pp. 271–316.

2 The Yalta conference between Roosevelt, Churchill and Stalin took place on 11 February 1945, and covered, among other matters, the plans for the dismemberment and occupation of Germany at the close of the war. See http://www.fordham.edu/halsall/mod/1945YALTA.html for a full version of the report.

3 Cohen, *Cambridge Survey*, 1995, p. 271.

4 As Herbert Blau notes: 'We are aware of theatrical behaviour outside the theatre ... What we characterise as theatrical seems to be measured by some generally accepted behavioural norm, though it should be clear that no behaviour is theatrical/dramatic except so far as we have an image of theatre in the mind' (*Take Up the Bodies: Theater at the Vanishing Point*, Chicago and London: University of Illinois Press, 1982, p. 9). Jill Dolan notes that 'performative metaphors get extended into many cultural avenues through cultural studies, but rarely is theatrical performance a site of such extension. If the practices of everyday life and media textuality appear multiple, contradictory and open, theatre performances are positioned by other scholars [as] simple, closed ... 'known' and coherent' ('Geographies of Learning: Theatre Studies, Performance and the "Performative"', *Theatre Journal* 45, 4, 1993, pp. 417–41).

5 J. Butler, *Bodies that Matter: On the Discursive Limits of 'Sex'*, New York: Routledge, 1993, p. 2, cited in W. B. Worthen, 'Bordering Space', in E. Fuchs and U. Chaudhuri, eds., *Land/Scape/Theater*, Michigan: Michigan University Press, 2002, pp. 280–300.

6 E. Balibar, *Politics and the Other Scene*, London: Verso, 2002, p. 93.

7 D. Cesarani, and M. Fulbrook, eds., *Citizenship, Nationality and Migration in Europe*, London: Routledge, 1996, p. 3.

8 Cesarani and Fulbrook, *Citizenship*, p. 3.

9 Balibar, *Politics*, p. 75.

10 G. Agamben, *Homo Sacer: Sovereign Power and Bare Life*, Stanford: Stanford University Press, 1998, p. 126.

11 Agamben, *Homo Sacer*, p. 130.

12 Balibar, *Politics*, p. 83.

13 Balibar, *Politics*, p. 81.

14 See http://www.migreurop.org/IMG/pdf/camps–en.pdf.

15 'Secret Balkan camp for UK asylum seekers', M. Bright, P. Harris and D. Hipkins, *Observer*, 15 June 2003.

16 'Concerns over EU "transit camps"', http://newsvote.bbc.co.uk.

17 Balibar, *Politics*, p. 83.

18 Agamben, *Homo Sacer*, p.134.

19 http://www.carneskysghosttrain.net.

Chapter 5

Foreign bodies

Performing physical and psychological harm at the Mladi Levi festival, August 2003

Sarah Gorman

Mladi Levi, an annual international festival organised by Ljubljana-based promoter Bunker, works to bring together artists, audience members and promoters in order to facilitate an annual celebration of experimental theatre and dance. The promoters attempt to forge a culture of dialogue and exchange by housing artists in budget accommodation and funding an extended stay in the city. In her introduction to the festival, artistic director Nevenka Koprivšek writes,

> As we arrange the program, we try to avoid a single theme for fear of conforming to a mould. Yet in the blessed moment when all the performances come together in some sort of logical rhythm, all of a sudden we feel that we want to be driven by a hope. An invisible thread, a thought, a curiosity and a desire for new experience. . . . We hope that we might catch a glimpse of ourselves in the reflection of someone who sees differently, if only for a short moment.[1]

Travelling to this festival, I was interested to consider how my own viewing conventions might be disrupted by my dislocation out of one very familiar environment and into one that would be literally 'foreign'. Considering myself to be, for what is it worth, 'adept' at reading experimental theatre on British soil, I was intrigued by the challenge offered by this work, and considered the extent to which it might take me out of my comfort zone and call upon me to rethink my reading strategies.

The scrutiny of my 'reading' or 'subject' position prompted me to address my existing understanding of myself as European. Inevitably, my presuppositions about Europe are reinforced by Western European ideology. It is important to bear in mind the fact that I am travelling from Western Europe to address work presented in the recently defined 'Central' Europe[2] and that even my own sense of identity as 'European' should not be taken for granted. Zdenka Badovinac has pointed out that '[t]he idea of the united Europe rests primarily on the Western definition of being European, and it has been politically and economically institutionalized in the

European Union, which is now cautiously opening its doors to new members from the East'.[3] Over the past thirty years, the work of Central and Eastern European artists has emerged in a very different context to that of the West. In Yugoslavia, under Tito's comparatively liberal model of communism, art was a crucial tool for promoting and realising the ideal of 'self-managing socialism'.[4] In addition, the enduring absence of an art market in both communist and post-communist Yugoslav society, and the constant sense of being 'other' to the dominant art practices of the West, has resulted in an art practice comparatively impervious to the recuperative politics of market forces.[5]

In addition to addressing the socio-geographical complexities of Europe, I must also address the way in which I have become accustomed to 'reading' performance, and the debt my deconstructive practice has to the field of performance studies as a discrete disciplinary field being developed in North America and the United Kingdom. Over the course of the last ten years I have become accustomed to approaching performance in order to read for signs of 'deconstructive' practice.[6] The uncertainties I acknowledge, and use to position my culturally specific reading position, owe much to the work of a body of artists and academics working without reference to Eastern Europe. In addition, I must remind myself of my position as someone fluent in English, the language adopted for use in Dood Paard and Conservas' translations of their work. The grammatical slippages in Dood Paard's unrehearsed improvisations and the faltering, outdated superlatives used by Conservas will inevitably signify, for me, 'mistakes', and will reinforce my sense of the work as 'other' or 'strange'. In recognising these slippages as 'mistakes', I inevitably accrue a sense of authority and mastery over the dominant language.

The project of this chapter, then, must be to scrutinise the meanings I forged from the three theatre pieces I witnessed in Ljubljana within the context of the Mladi Levi festival. Before going on to relay my experience of each of the shows, I will set out to explore the contexts of viewing lent by the festival: the city of Ljubljana and the country of Slovenia. The 2003 festival saw companies from Madagascar, Kenya, Great Britain, South Africa, Russia, Austria, Turkey, Spain, France, Poland, Slovenia, The Netherlands, Italy, Portugal and Norway. The festival customarily takes place in August each year and, as such, in 2003, nine months before Slovenia's accession into the European Union.

Although part of former Yugoslavia, Slovenia's status as a 'Balkan' country, and its Slavic heritage, has long been contested. In their 1991 book *Ljubljana, Ljubljana*, Erjavac and Gržinić note that, as part of the 1980s social upheaval, many Slovenians argued that they were descended from Venetians not from Slavs and so had little or nothing in common with Serbs and other Yugoslav ethnic groups.[7] Slovenia is perhaps reluctant, then, to identify as part of 'Eastern Europe', and its status as the first ex-Yugoslav country to be accepted into the European Union may be a welcome opportunity to reinforce the perceived cultural differences between Slovenia and the other Balkan countries. When discussing Slovenia and Yugoslavia, a number of authors define it as 'Central' rather than 'Eastern' Europe.[8] Ben Aris has noted that '[Slovenia] is lumped with eastern Europe, but Austria, immediately above it, has borders that extend further east than any part of the tiny republic of 1.9 million people'.[9]

Slovenia's independence, won in 1991 after a ten-day war with Yugoslavia,[10] represented the culmination of an increasing and long-fermenting desire to be recognised as an independent country. On 1 May 2004, Slovenia gained accession to the European Union, as one of ten new members. Its status as the only former Yugoslav country to enter was thought to be partially attributable to the healthy export trade set into motion under Tito.[11] Although Slovenia enjoys a healthy tourist industry and Ljubljana is celebrated as a liberal-minded city, with a large student population, ethnic rivalries continue to influence public and political life. Slovenians recently voted on whether to permit a mosque to be built in Ljubljana and whether or not to restore rights to 'The Erased', a group of Serbian, Bosnian and Muslim immigrants who refused Slovenian citizenship in 1991.[12]

These ongoing manifestations of nationalistic sentiment provide a stimulating context in which to respond to the work of international theatre makers. Given that the festival in question took place nine months before European Union accession, it might be possible to consider the artistic policy of the festival as part of an ongoing project to align Ljubljana with other 'mainland' European capitals.

To take the shows in order of viewing, I saw Uninvited Guests' piece *Offline* at the Plesni teater. Uninvited Guests are a British/German company founded in 1998. The company[13] are interested in exploring what they have described as a 'confessional mode' of performance, and in considering the integration of new technology into contemporary patterns of social intercourse. The company publicity for *Offline* from spring 2003 states that:

> we're interested in the ways people are using the web as a site for confessing, for making the most private lives public; their loves, their loneliness, their fetishistic desires and sexual misdemeanours. . . . It is as though the performers have arranged to meet online and have only encountered each other before now in virtual contexts. *Offline* is their first 'real' encounter and they don't know what to say, how to interact at this new, lo-fi social event.

My interest in watching this piece was framed by the fact that I was already familiar with the piece, having seen it in the United Kingdom in two different modes of performance. I was interested to see what new 'meanings' might emerge when viewing it as part of the festival.

The first element that struck me when watching this show in the context of Ljubljana related to the temperature outside. The temperatures were around 30 degrees Celsius, and the Mladi Levi audience were appropriately attired in summer dresses, shorts and T-shirts. As the performers stood watching the audience filter into the auditorium, I was struck by the comparatively heavy materials of the performers' clothing, having been designed to lend warmth rather than allow skin to breathe. Richard and Jessica H. were both dressed in corduroy; Jessica M. sported an acrylic blouse with an interwoven shimmering silver thread. Jessica H.'s trousers had obvious creases where they had only recently been packed in her suitcase, and each performer wore socks and shoes rather than sandals.

In addition, the carpet upon which the performers were standing signified for me in a wholly different way from previous encounters. In Bristol and London the carpet appeared incidental, barely contributing to the meaning of the show. However, in Ljubljana it appeared to point towards the soft furnishings of a 'foreign' country, a country with cooler temperatures, where wall-to-wall carpets presented a way of militating against the cold. I suddenly found myself recalling the experience of sitting on the carpets in my parents' house, and remembering how the nylon fibres would often make my naked legs sore when I sat down for too long. Jessica

Figure 5.1   Uninvited Guests, *Offline*. Photograph: Thomas Hall.

M.'s noisy activity with the many scattered audiotapes reinforced this potential signification of the carpet for me, as the sound of the clunking and ejecting of tapes suddenly reminded me of my own teenage tapes, pirated from Radio 1 chart and request shows. The carpet in this version of *Offline* suddenly made England seem very different to Ljubljana; indeed, almost akin to a 'foreign' place. I suddenly got an unexpected glimpse of my home country as a cold, potentially inhospitable place.

In contrast to the recognisable, familiar signs of 'home' witnessed in *Offline*, I found Conservas' *7 Dust Show*[14] a comparative mystery. The piece was presented at Mladinsko Theatre, situated in the grounds of a university building. A raised platform had been constructed at one end of a thirty-metre-long subterranean cavern, the curved walls of the cavern rose to a height of approximately fifteen metres, giving a sense of overhead enclosure. As they filtered in, the audience were progressively seated at a number of small round tables, laid out as if for a cabaret or stand-up comedy event. A male performer held his tray aloft and took orders for drinks (which never arrived); a nervous female performer, who had introduced herself as 'Judit', fidgeted at the side of the stage area. She wore a tight red PVC dress and had 'Conservas' stamped or tattooed on to her leg.

Over the course of the two-hour performance, the audience are presented with a number of different scenes. They appeared to invoke images from Western popular culture, performers variously mimicking hapless game-show participants and roles of TV pollsters garnering votes for erotic dancers and politicians. The audience, for the most part, appeared to be addressed as a fictional audience for a TV game show, in turns flattered and rebuked for their temerity. Other slightly incongruous sections of the show were more akin to examples of performance or body art. One of the opening images of the show revealed the muscular torso of a naked woman illuminated by a white spotlight; as part of another section, a female performer inserted a torch into her vagina and attempted to 'write' by gyrating her hips over a light-sensitive screen.

Further scenes included the image of a row of three women operating self-feeding 'machines' and the image of a game-show couple perched nervously at the side of the stage. They became increasingly troubled as the female member of the party began to dribble effervescent white saliva. Later in the piece, an extended fight took place between a male and female performer, with the female performer appearing to sustain the more significant injuries. The female performer in question later nailed the male performer's lapels to a table. A further section, towards the end of the show, saw graphic pornography projected on to the screen.

On my return to England, I learn that the company are 'yet another company from "the Catalonian theatre basin"'[15] and that the 'Seven dust is a show about the alienation of labour'.[16] Promotional material found on a festival website provides the following commentary:

In a sequence of scenes quoting the various tropes of dance, theatre, TV and media, *Seven Dust* asks us to review our commonplace thoughts on the mass media. We are presented with couples stultified in their marital bliss, troubling reports of sexual violence, our surprising complacency at market research intrusion, the nauseatingly cheap eroticism of TV quiz shows. Somehow, negotiating responses to scenes of amusement, modesty and impudence, we realise that the funniest scenes captivate.[17]

Watching this show, and contemplating its effect made me realise that any practised certitude or confidence about my ability to 'read' even the most 'open' and 'indeterminate' of theatre texts had been shaken by the shift in context from Britain to Slovenia. I found myself incapable of making any useful connection between the various scenes, and reluctant to fall back on my intuition as to what the show might be 'about'. I had reflected upon the use of English as the generic language during this piece, and on the ways that the mistranslations and mispronunciations had affected my reception of some of the scenes. However, I was not sure how this might contribute to its overall effect. I had also found myself feeling uncomfortable, as if ethically compromised, by being invited to watch explicit pornographic footage of heterosexual intercourse and the performance of the violent exchange between the male and female performer. I was also mildly shocked by the reference to 'disability' on the questionnaire we had been given as we entered. One of the questions asked, 'Which of the following disabilities would you prefer to have as a means of getting a good job: a/colour-blind; b/near-sighted; c/schizophrenic; d/woman; e/for fuck's sake a cripple! f/other'[18]. Although irony was readily identifiable in these questions, my sense of unease remained about equating this literature with the kind of humour experienced in Britain as a backlash to New Labour's celebration of political correctness.

The statement that this show was 'about' the alienation of labour was both reassuring and unsettling. On the one hand it gave me a starting point from which to recall key images of the show. On the other, it seemed wholly reductive, as the presence of soft and explicit sexual violence had remained with me as the most potent and threatening image on stage. I began to consider the possibility of 'sexual labour' being a key idea in the show and about the currency of sexual promise as it has been used in advertising across the developed Western world. What surprised me the most, however, was a sense of the images somehow extending beyond the boundaries of my own cultural experience. I partly attribute this to the different attitudes British and Spanish people have to the representation of gender and sexuality, although my awareness of what this might be is restricted to viewing the films of Pedro Almodóvar and performances by La Fura dels Baus. I was also aware that, until 1977, the Spanish government exercised rigorous censorship, and that adultery, homosexuality and the sale of contraception were not decriminalised until 1978. In addition, divorce and abortion were only legalised as recently as 1981 and 1984,[19] factors which may go some way to contextualising the sexually explicit images as signs of sexual 'freedom'.

This performance, perhaps more than any of the other performances at the festival, prompted me to consider my viewing position as an 'outsider'. In my bid to be open to different cultural signs and images, I became confused and uneasy about my seemingly conservative response to the pornography, and the use of irony in relation to violence against women and people with disabilities. Although this performance took place in English, it was clear to me that it could not 'translate' easily across cultural boundaries. The generic conventions of this piece appear to be in line with those of La Fura dels Baus and La Cubana, contemporary experimental Catalan theatre companies that have enjoyed significant success across Spain in the last twenty years. Maria Delgado identifies both of these companies as part of the experimental theatre scene that emerged after Franco's death in 1975.[20]

Conservas would certainly appear to be working in a similar vein to both La Cubana and La Fura dels Baus. They represent another Catalan company working in both Castilian and Catalan dialects in order to promote an anti-intellectual and multi-disciplinary vision of contemporary Spain. Their use of sexual imagery is more akin to that of La Fura dels Baus, although their intention in including explicit images of sexual activity appears to blur the boundaries between body art and popular culture. Simona Levi, the founder of Conservas, is Italian rather than Spanish, having been born in Turin, and her artistic agenda in setting up Conservas' performance space in Barcelona is to provide a space in which to programme theatre work that would not customarily find its way on to the traditional theatre circuit.[21]

The final piece witnessed as part of Mladi Levi, was, by contrast again, comparatively 'accessible'. Dood Paard, a Dutch performance company performed their show, *40,000 Sublime and Beautiful Thoughts* in the Železniški Musej (the Railway Museum),[22] a venue transformed into a theatre space especially for the festival each year. In their publicity material for the event the company acknowledge the fact that much of their material was taken from Austrian author Peter Handke's 1966 piece *Selbstbezichtigung (Self-Accusation)*, and that it would be performed in English, with no translation.

The set consisted of a large projection screen mounted approximately three metres from the first row of the seating bank. Before it, approximately thirty upturned beer crates were arranged in a random pattern, creating the effect of a kind of plastic Giant's Causeway. To the right of the screen sat the DJ at his turntable. Behind the screen a collection of Turkish carpets had been rolled out, providing an alternative performance area behind the screen.

Figure 5.2   Kuno Bakker in Dood Paard, *40,000 Sublime and Beautiful Thoughts.*
Photograph: Sanne Peper.

The projection screen featured a series of alternating captions juxta-posed against contemporary newspaper photographs. Headlines such as 'Fun with Fascism', 'I Survived the Moscow Theatre Siege' and 'Avoid the Middle of the Road' were placed alongside photographs of Dutch celebrities, members of the British royal family and Roy Orbison. The line 'How Long is it Since you Last Had Ice-Cream?' alternates with 'Fun with Fascism' against a backdrop of a beautiful couple simulating erotic activity in a familiar Häagen-Dazs advert. The heading 'Finding a Deep Quiet Within Yourself' is superimposed onto footage that appears to show an extreme close-up of the surface of one of the performers' skin.

Towards the end of a prolonged introductory section, the DJ mixed a deep masculine voice repeating the word *echt* into the more ambient music he had been playing previously. A male performer with a shaved head entered from behind the screen, and appeared to stumble as he climbed on to the makeshift stage of beer crates. He began to recite lines from the beginning of Handke's piece, 'I came into the world. I became. I was begotten. I originated. I grew. I was born. I was entered on the birth register. I grew older'. The performer speaks in a muted, faltering tone, apparently relaying these ideas with great solemnity. His speech continued for approximately fifteen minutes, becoming increasingly convoluted, as he described, in a clipped and clinical fashion, his entry into the socialised world.

The piece takes the form of a list of regulations and codes of behaviour apparently internalized by the speaker. As the list continues, it appears to take the form of a protracted confession, the speaker(s) account for their conception, their birth, their entry into language and the social system into which they have been born. Handke described this piece as one of his *Sprechstücke* (or *Speaking Pieces*[23]), as a way of marking its difference from more traditional plays. In the introduction to his work, he identifies it as having been written for 'one male and one female speaker'. Hern suggests that Handke does not wish the performers to be called 'actors' at all, but rather 'speakers'.[24] Dood Paard is faithful to Handke's anti-illusionary intentions, appearing to present the performers 'as themselves' on stage. Two male performers and one female performer share the confessions, occasionally completing lines for each other, or completing sentences together. There is no attempt to 'act out' or animate the text; sections are differentiated by inflection and rhythm alone.

In common with *Seven Dust Show*, *40,000 Sublime and Beautiful Thoughts* was organised according to a non-linear structure, and punctuated by sections apparently improvised and pre-rehearsed. Dood Paard's show had an added layer of difficulty to consider, in that they are a Dutch company performing a piece by an Austro-Slovenian[25] playwright in English. The figure of Handke suggests further layers of complexity that might also be addressed. Handke was born to a Slovenian mother and German father. Many of Handke's novels and plays contain memories of his youth in Slovenia.[26] In his 1991 book *The Dreamer's Farewell from the Ninth Land* Handke spoke out against the separation of Slovenia from Yugoslavia[27] and was lambasted by the international press for the articles, books and plays he wrote criticising the representation of Bosnian Serbs by the Western media.[28] Although Handke is notorious in Slovenia, it is difficult to say how the incorporation of his 1966 work *Selbstbezichtigung* might have affected the local audience's reception of the show.

In contrast to the Conservas piece, I found *40,000 Sublime and Beautiful Thoughts* somehow familiar. The confessional mode was reminiscent of the work of British companies such as Forced Entertainment and desperate optimists, and the presence of the DJ at the side of the stage appeared to be a subtle indicator of the amalgamation of popular cultural forms into much experimental European theatre work (as found in the work of Jérôme Bel and Blast Theory). I also felt that I could 'read' potential meaning or cultural relevance in the piece by considering how the Handke text had been used in juxtaposition with the freer, more celebratory sections of *40,000 Sublime and Beautiful Thoughts*. It appeared that, although I had no greater understanding of Dutch or German culture, I had recourse to an expertise in experimental theatre practice which enabled me to 'make sense' of this piece, in a way that I did not feel to be true in the case of Conservas.

Reflecting upon the relative ease and difficulty of reading work in this 'foreign' context, I began to wonder whether, rather than being an artistic style specific to a geographical region, it might represent a currency of ideas within a particular artistic community, potentially that of a certain type of small-scale European experimental theatre. I cannot identify exactly where these boundary lines might be drawn, but I thought that Conservas' work probably lay somewhere just beyond these boundaries, so that some of the techniques in their work were familiar, yet others caused confusion. I might crudely distinguish between the work of Uninvited Guests, Dood Paard and Conservas, by naming the former two companies as indicative of a Northern European experimental theatre culture and Conservas as representative of a Southern European sensibility.

In questioning what might mark the work of Conservas as 'outside' the Northern European experimental theatre community, I attempted to identify the differences between the different bodies of work. First, the issue of gender and sexuality had been placed centre stage in *Seven Dust Show*, whereas it went unremarked in *Offline* and *40,000 Thoughts*. Second, *Seven Dust* had been a much more active or vital show in that performers executed a range of different gestures, activities and rituals, whereas the Northern European work had largely comprised the conspicuous performance of restraint and self-control.

Both Uninvited Guests' and Dood Paard's performances included a confessional element, and I began to wonder about the possibility of considering the work I had designated as 'Northern European' as using confession to address the 'harm' the internalisation of ideology might have upon a member of Northern European society. The more transgressive confessions within this work made explicit each speaker's sophisticated understanding of his or her appropriate demeanour according to a mutually agreed sense of social propriety. The need to 'confess' could perhaps be interpreted as a means of drawing attention to an otherwise naturalised form of societal constraint. By contrast, Conservas' work would appear to be preoccupied with issues of sexual predation and commodification. This could be seen to be representative of a sexualised genre of Southern European experimental theatre, sharing features with other established Spanish companies such as La Fura dels Baus and La Cubana. In contrast to the subtle verbal repetition of societal interpellation, Conservas appear to be showing newly liberated, sexualised bodies on stage. However, an unresolved sense of uncertainty exists between the exposure of the female bodies as liberated or objectified. The female characters are shown to be available as 'prizes' and their sexual favours described in terms of commodity consumption.

If it is possible to recognise an over arching discourse of 'harm' in each of the three pieces, then, the 'harm' the Conservas performers simulate takes place at the hands of a member of the opposite sex, or as a result of enforced consumption of trite capitalist game-show culture. The Northern European representation of 'harm' appears internalised, meditative, asexual and subtly subversive. It works with an awareness of how societal constraint might be self-policing. By contrast the Southern European work appears to concomitantly celebrate sexual freedom and critique the sexualised language of late capitalist culture.

The differences I have suggested between Northern and Southern European models of theatre work have emerged as a potentially reductive binary contrast, the Northern European work as internalised, 'cognitive' material, and the Southern work as being characterised by a visceral 'bodily' excess. Inevitably, there are problems with this approach, not least because societal influence is never entirely physical or psychological. However, one issue that becomes particularly pertinent when considering how this work might signify in Slovenia emerges through the consideration of the body and the proximity of 'harm'. In *Body and the East*, Zdenka Badovinac writes about the contrasting experiences of 'harm' between performance artists in Eastern and Western Europe, reminding the Western reader that, despite the expansion of the European Union, there is little commonality of experience across the different member states. In characterising the changing climate of Eastern/Central Europe she writes of the

> shock experienced in face of the transition to new reality, and the direct threat of war to our bodies – for the war in the Balkans was actually directed against the body, it employed the most primitive means, i.e. knives and raping – have reminded us that we are captives of our physical existence.[29]

In speaking of a 'direct threat . . . to our bodies', Badovinac underscores a crucial difference between ex-Yugoslav countries and other members of the EU, for the majority of whom civil war is a distant memory. The internalised confessions of Uninvited Guests and Dood Paard suggest that these companies are preoccupied by psychological constraint, whereas the explicit nature of sexual images in Conservas' work could be understood to be fighting against a drive to contain libidinal freedom. Both positions presuppose a position of fundamental physical 'safety' from which to speak, and as such could be understood to be as similarly 'foreign' to Slovenian spectators.

Although Slovenian independence was won with comparative ease, Slovenia still came under direct attack by the Yugoslav army, with a resultant loss of lives.[30] In addition, close ties to other Balkan families and enforced migration between the countries meant that Slovenia experienced the conflicts in Bosnia and Croatia at close proximity. Badovinac's recent

memories of 'direct [bodily] threat' may appear incongruous in the context of contemporary Ljubljana, but they draw attention to sentiments that endure, just beneath the surface of the collective Slovenian sensibility.

Handke's publications and public statements about the war in Yugoslavia also serve as a reminder of the ideological gulf represented by the Western European interpretation. Handke himself became labelled 'pro-Serb' when he took issue with what he considered to be an over-simplistic apportioning of the blame for wartime atrocities on the Bosnian Serbs.[31] However, as Bernard Reinhardt points out, a close reading of his work suggests that he sought to present a balanced, rather than a biased, view:

> There is . . . nothing in Handke's public statements to indicate that he is a supporter of the Serbian nationalist Slobodan Milosevic, or his pol-itics. Anyone who has followed his writings over recent years can see this clearly. His latest play about the war in Yugoslavia – *Die Fahrt im Einbaum oder Das Stück zum Film vom Krieg* (Journey in a Canoe, or the play about the film of the war) – which premiered in June at the Vienna Burgtheater, likewise contains no trace of pro-Serbian sentiment.[32]

Ultimately, Handke's presence at the Mladi Levi festival appeared inci-dental rather than deliberate. Dood Paard did not foreground Handke's Slovenian heritage, and his identity as an 'Austrian' author went uncon-tested. However, the fact of his engagement with the Balkan conflict does bring an accidental layer of signification to any consideration of the recep-tion of the work in a Slovenian context. It works to foreground the role the Western media play in representing Eastern and Central Europe, and hints at enduring misconceptions about the atrocities committed by the distinct ethnic groups involved. Handke's presence creates an accidental fissure, in the appearance of the otherwise stable, cosmopolitan Slovenia.

The difficulty I had in reading the work of Conservas increased my sense of distance from the culture it represented. However, it did not ulti-mately prevent my extrapolating an overarching preoccupation with physical and psychological control in the work. It struck me that the discon-certing motifs of physical and cognitive harm also mapped on to a sense of an internalised policing and self-control in the work of Uninvited Guests and Dood Paard. Inevitably this reading of the work is partial and the product of my own cultural position. Indeed, I doubt that I would have arrived at such a conclusion had I not considered the work in the context of Slovenia. In light of these circumstances, this reading must be acknow-ledged as a kind of fortuitous accident. It might be possible to imagine that I had discovered a fundamental preoccupation shared by three very different European companies; however, the most important factor in this discovery is to remember that it only became visible in a country where the assumption of physical safety has only recently been assured.

Koprivšek suggested in her introduction to the festival, '[w]e hope that we might catch a glimpse of ourselves in the reflection of someone who sees differently'.[33] However, I would argue that the images we get back and those we make of 'others' are not, and can never be, mirrored directly back. Instead, the images we receive are the result of multiple refractions, distorted as a result of our self-conscious, but necessary, reflection upon the nature of cultural difference. The easy companionship between member states that EU membership implies is dependent upon the invisibility of cultural difference and, as Badovinac reminds us, is predicated upon a generic Western European sensibility. Festivals such as Mladi Levi can work to foster a sense of cultural inclusion for the host country, but any considered response to international work such as that presented by Dood Paard, Uninvited Guests and Conservas must attest to the difficulty, rather than the ease, with which these countries communicate.

Notes

1 Promotional copy in Mladi Levi festival brochure, summer 2003.
2 A. Erjavac and M. Gržinić, *Ljubljana, Ljubljana: The 80s in Slovene Art*, trans. M. Majcen and M. Mlačnik, Ljubljana: Založba Mladinska Knjiga, 1991.
3 Z. Badovinac, ed., *Body and the East: From the 1960s to the Present*, Ljubljana: Moderna Galerija, 1998, p. 9.
4 Erjavac and Gržinić, *Ljubljana, Ljubljana*, p. 12.
5 Badovinac, *Body and the East*, p. 15.
6 'Deconstruction' as defined by Jacques Derrida in works such as *Writing and Difference* (1981) and *Of Grammatology* (1974).
7 Erjavac and Gržinić, *Ljubljana, Ljubljana*, p. 13.
8 D. Bisenic, 'Peter Handke: Lies about Central Europe Broke up Yugoslavia', independent pamphlet, representing a collection of articles by Bisenic published in Belgrade daily *Nasa Borba*, 5–8 March 1996, pp. 3–15.
9 B. Aris, 'Standing Alone', *Guardian*, 28 April 2004, available online, http://www.guardian.co.uk/eu/story/0,7369,1197494,00.html, accessed 27 April 2004.
10 Mirjam Kotar's 'Chronology of Attainment of Independence of Republic of Slovenia' includes the following entry about the war for independence: '26 June–5 July 1991: The "Ten Day War" – fighting between the Yugoslav People's Army and Slovenian forces. Yugoslav People's Army Neutralized', in D. Fink Hafner and J. R. Robbins, eds., *Making a New Nation: The Formation of Slovenia*, 1997, p. 306.
11 Aris, 'Standing Alone'.
12 Reluctant to lose their indigenous identity, these citizens refused to accept a Slovenian passport, and as a result their names were removed from the national register. Only 4 per cent of the electorate supported the Constitutional Court ruling in April that the rights of the disenfranchised should be restored. See E. Brcic, 'Slovenians Restore "Erased" People Rights', *Guardian*, 4 April 2004, available online, http://www.guardian.co.uk/worldlatest/story/0,1280,-3940065,00.html?=ticker, accessed 4 April 2004.
13 The performers for *Offline* included Richard Dufty, Jessica Hoffman, Thomas Keller and Jessica Marlowe. The piece was directed by Paul Clarke.
14 The performers included Judit Saula, Agnes Mateus, Xisco Segura and Mireira Serra. The piece was directed by Conservas founder Simona Levi. This performance took place at 8 pm on Saturday 23 August, at the Mladinsko Theatre, Ljubljana.

15 Theatre Festival MALTA, http://www.malta–festival.pl/en/historia/13/gwiazdy/3/.

16 Simone Levi in *Mira Vista* #3, festival brochure for Mira Vista L'Autra Espagne Festival, Toulouse, spring 2004, available online, http://www.mira-toulouse.com/pdf/Mira-journal3.pdf, accessed 2 February 2005.

17 Promotional copy on Mira Vista festival website, spring 2004, available online at http://www.mira-toulouse.com/theatrecabaret/Levi.html.

18 Conservas questionnaire, August 2003.

19 M. Delgado, *Other Spanish Theatres: Erasure and Inscription on the Twentieth-Century Spanish Stage*, Manchester: Manchester University Press, 2003, p. 225.

20 Delgado, *Other Spanish Theatres*, p. 225.

21 Barcelona *Metropolis* newsletter, 2002.

22 The performance took place on 26 August and the performers included Manja Topper, Gillis Biesheuvel and Kuno Bakker. The piece also featured live mixing by DJ Steve Green.

23 Hern suggests that the term '*Sprechstücke*' is possibly analogous with Brecht's '*Lehrstücke*'. See N. Hern, *Peter Handke: Theatre and Anti-Theatre*, London: Oswald Wolff, *Modern German Authors: Texts and Contexts* vol. 5, 1971, p. 18.

24 Hern, *Peter Handke*, p. 18.

25 Peter Handke's identity as a 'Central European' is complex. He is thought to currently live in Paris, but comes from Carinthia in Austria. He was born in Griffen in 1942 to a Slovene mother and a German father. At the time of his birth, 'Austria was known as Ostmark, a southeastern province of the Third Reich' and Carinthia was home to a 'once-sizable Slovenian minority'. In addition, 'Griffen . . . went from being "Slovenian" to being "German" in the years after Handke's birth', J. S. Marcus, 'Apocalypse Now', *New York Review of Books*, 47, 14, September 2000, available online, http://www.nybooks.com/articles.13838, accessed 4 April 2004.

26 Marcus, 'Apocalypse Now'.

27 B. Reinhardt, 'The Austrian writer Peter Handke, European public opinion, and the war in Yugoslavia', World Socialist website, 1999, available online, http://www.wsws.org/articles/1999/aug1999/hand-a11.shtml, accessed 5 July 2003.

28 A collection of interviews with Slovenian newspaper *Nasa Borba* (March–August 1996) suggests that Handke had published essays and letters in the German national press from 1991 to 1996. In 1997, Handke published his best-known works associated with his engagement with the Yugoslav war, including *A Journey to the Rivers: Justice for Serbia* (1997, Viking Press) and *The Journey in the Dugout Canoe, or The Piece about the Film about the War* (1999, Suhrkamp).

29 Badovinac, *Body and the East*, p. 17.

30 Kotar, 'Chronology of Attainment', p. 306.

31 Bisenic, Peter Handke.

32 Reinhardt, 'The Austrian writer Peter Handke'.

33 Promotional copy in Mladi Levi festival brochure, summer 2003.

Chapter 6

Dying bodies, living corpses

Transition, nationalism and resistance in Croatian theatre

Marin Blažević

In an introductory chapter of his landmark book *Postdramatisches Theater*, Hans-Thies Lehmann warns his reader against 'the mistaken judgement that the theatrical phenomena of the 1990s might be caused directly or indirectly by the political eruption around 1989'.[1] However, is it really possible to imagine that the sorts of political, social, economic and cultural transitions referred to here, transitions from one construction of reality to another, did not (directly or indirectly) affect the supposed aesthetic autonomy of theatre, initiating its re-examination, even inspiring innovation?

When it comes to Croatia, we can talk about two waves of transition. The first one occurred in the late 1980s and early 1990s (from communism to post-communism) and the second took place after president Tuđman's death: his biological death, and then his subsequent political death when his party lost the January 2000 elections (from tuđmanism to post-tuđmanism). This essay starts from the assumption that the two-wave and multi-layered transitional process (sometimes modernising and liberal, sometimes retrograde and criminal) has indeed – directly or indirectly – affected at least local 'theatrical phenomena of the 1990s'.

However, aside from some general comments, my intention is not to give a panoramic view of contemporary national theatre and its particular transitional context. Rather, I will mainly focus on the agency of the performing body as the lifeblood of any cultural performance, also including various national(istic) performances and transitional counter-performances.

I

Sociologist and political scientist Vesna Pusić had defined the Croatian post-communist regime (and not only the Croatian one) as a 'dictatorship with a democratic legitimacy', a paradoxical 'political hybrid' that combined a recently established democratic infrastructure and its institutions with a 'political culture inherited from the totalitarian period'.[2] Three factors were crucial for the practice and consolidation of the regime:

First – an efficacious ideological springboard. At the beginning one of transition's main driving forces and later its main obstacle, Croatian nationalism has run the whole gamut of manifestations, interests and functions: from liberal and emancipatory to xenophobic, chauvinistic, offensive and totalitarian.[3]

Second – centralised authority. Political and symbolic capital, increased through the hegemonisation of the *national idea* and *national interest* on the (discursive) battlefield of the newly founded national state, flowed into the hands of its *First president*. The concentration of presidential authority was so high that ultimately he dared to take actions that abolished even the *democratic legitimacy* of the dictatorship.[4]

And third – just like any other regime, the Croatian one also engaged its institutions, media and other apparatuses to construct and display its self-image. Apart from re-producing the usual myths (of ethnogenesis, identity, historical mission and continuity of sovereignty, etc.), the *image of Croatia* also propagated the need for national homogenisation and consensus: for example, over enemies of the state and traitors to the nation; or over the cause of the war recently waged inside and outside the borders of the *homeland*; and, as a consequence, consensus over the need to occasionally suspend the process of democratisation (which had only just begun). Through the various mediatised and theatricalised performances of the *Big Propaganda Text*[5] on the Stages of the Nation (i.e. in the mass media, most of them controlled by the party in power, and through various kinds of festivals, political rituals and spectacles), the *image of Croatia* was soon sanctified and successfully instituted as a multimedia *Super-icon*.

Naturally, this spectacular social, political and cultural project found its proper environment in the theatre.

2

Before attempting an analysis of the features, functions and paradoxes of the performing body in particular socio-political-theatrical situations, let me identify the mechanisms of representation through which theatre and theatre-like performances reflect and reinforce the concept and practice of the kind of dictatorship (or democracy) developed in transitional Croatia.[6]

Throughout the post-communist 1990s, let alone the age of communism, the dominant position in Croatian performing arts was held by a type of theatre that tended to reproduce the nationalistic and authoritarian regime, and do so by means, so to speak, of an indirect agency – that is to say, a set of complex and mostly concealed mechanisms that served to set up and maintain hierarchical relationships between those elements, subjects and bodies that constitute the structure, situation and process of (theatrical) representation.

As a *deep structure* of representational and interpretative intention in dramatic theatre,[7] the *theological stage*[8] establishes the following hierarchy: the writer as the *One* who created and rules the wor(l)d; the director as privileged interpreter and re-creator of *His* wor(l)d on the (theatrical) stage, the invisible representative of the supervisory authorial function whose power is being implanted into the performing bodies; the actor as executor, trapped in the course of a fictional story and a theatrical illusion with an utterly reduced right of speech; and finally the nameless and silent spectators, representatives of the people squeezed together in the dark auditorium.

The logocentric imperative and hierarchical organisation of the *theological stage* would be inefficient, however, were it not for the 'fantasies' and 'therapeutic' effects of realism.[9] As an echo of the 'call for order, a desire for unity, for identity, for security, or popularity', *realism* 'preserves various consciousnesses from doubt'. That is to say, by means of the 'correct rules' and using 'the effects of reality' *realism* stabilises and adjusts the referent 'according to a point of view which endows it with a recognizable meaning'.

I would argue that both mechanisms are intrinsic to any mode of cultural performance that is chained to a normative function and framed by a fortified institution. While the *theological stage* structures the representational situation, distributing authorities and thereby managing semantic capital (various kinds of values, from political to aesthetical), *realism* provides – that is to say, stimulates and simulates – the identification of the truth-like sign and its referent: the dramatic fiction and the so-called referential reality, the author's or the autocrat's Word and the (represented) World; the *Super-icon* and Croatia.

When theatre is entrapped in that kind of role it appears that the only acceptable body is the body that serves only the transmission and representation of a predetermined wor(l)d and cannot be much more than a 'vehicle of signs and itself a sign'.[10] However, even under the pressure of demands for a total *semiotisation* of the performing body, this body produces/embodies much more than just a sign or network of signs, produces much more than a text.[11] If the body really is, according to Hans-Thies Lehmann, an 'emphatic/problematic reality',[12] then certain questions arise. Is it so just because of its sheer materiality, 'the presentness of the body's fleshly presence'?[13] Or it is so also because the body embodies and produces a certain reality? And, if so, is that reality due to the body's acts, its own performance? Or, on the other hand, is it due also to its potential state of total and final inaction, the *end of performance*? What is it, then, that gives the body (at the very least) a double power: to 'interrupt semiosis'[14] and also to cause eruptions of symbolic investments (indeed eruption may also bring on interruption); to cause disturbances in the image and breakdowns of the mechanisms of authority/identification, but also to make the image more affecting and the functioning of the mechanisms more efficacious?

3

In her introduction to the anthology *Performance and Cultural Politics* Elin Diamond argues that one moment is often excluded from explorations of the impact of the correlative notions of *performance* and *performativity* on normative (gender, national, etc.) identities, and that is the moment of 'discrete performances, that *enact* those norms in particular sites with particular effects'. '*A* performance' challenges the idea of de-substantialised (discursively constructed, fictional, culturally determined, performed) identities because it 'both affirms and denies this evacuation of substance'.[15] Let me radicalise this argument.

Always dependent on illocutionary force – that is, the contextual support (say: institution, convention) and the quality (say: intensity, even technique) of the particular performance – the perlocutionary effect of the performative act can also result in the production of a seeming fact: for example, the referential reality of national identity. But, the referential effect of the nation's performance can become, so to speak, more *real* than the auto-referential enactments that the nation and its state are repeatedly arranging (through the *Big Propaganda Text* and the *Super-icon*) for the sake of their own self-identification, absolutisation and naturalisation. In specific circumstances the performative challenge of Jon McKenzie's formula 'perform, or else' – *or else* you might have trouble – can get transformed into an implicit (in the worst cases, even explicit) performative blackmail: perform according to the (national) norm, or you will be excluded. The totalised, even ontologised national norm appears as an effect of nationalistic exclusivity, which is the product of the exclusive performative – the act that excludes. And the extreme nationalistic exclusion will act on the body drastically: the totalising identity politics of nationalism progressively reduces others' bodies, first to suspicious characteristics, then to essentialised hostility and in the terminal stage to the object that has to be eliminated.

The act of elimination takes along the fact of reality. In the very moment of 'live action', in any actual, particular performance of killing, it is somebody's real flesh that is cut up and somebody's real blood that is shed. And, let's not forget, it was somebody's real hand, somebody's gesture that performed (not enacted!) the act of final, total exclusion. That fact is irreversible. Death eliminates doubts about the *substance* (flesh and blood!). Now, a (national) identity has to be ascribed to that reality.

Elimination of *an* other's, enemy's (national) body not only leaves more space and less trouble for the national-body. It is also the cause of the final, more than just referential, in fact even literally tangible, *substantial* difference: between a live and a dead body, the body which will never again be able to act on its own, and the body which is – in the closest possible proximity to unquestionable factuality – becoming aware of the power of signification with no resistance. This may easily – in specific situations occupied by totalitarian normativism – give rise to the hunger for further lethal actions.

Therefore the *theological state*[16] has to produce dead bodies, bodies that are deprived of any agency, bodies which can be made to support a heap of symbolic (national) capital, bodies that can be subjected to various actions of manipulation and marketing, bodies which – due to their inaction – can be rendered harmless to the constructed identity-reality of the nation and its state. Next to war and terror, the most efficacious subjection mechanism is the *theological stage* – of mass media, theatre, political spectacles and rituals – where bodies can be turned into *vehicles* for petrified symbols: signs of unquestionable meaning, extraordinary value and performative force. This is a force that might foment the need for *killing*, whether literally in war (where symbolic capital is made out of dead bodies on both sides), or symbolically on the theatrical or theatre-like stages, where the living bodies of actors can be imprisoned by lifeless symbols and turned into living corpses.

A close interrelatedness between *state* and *stage* is established and maintained by the identification effect of *realism*. Aside from identification, *realism* is entrusted with yet another crucial function within a certain (nationalistic) representational *theology*. Despite the dead bodies all over the *theological state/stage*, *realism* ventures upon a paradoxical effort: to suppress, conceal and deny the killing, dying and death of the body. *Realism* diverts attention from *an* act and *a* fact to the effect. From the act/fact of *massacre* – actual or metaphorical – *realism* preserves only its affective potential, its symbolic and sentimental effects, while throwing corpses in mass (media) graves or drowning still living (and performing) bodies deep in the mass of symbolic capital they are forced to incorporate. *Realism*'s preservational mission is primarily directed against the body, for it is precisely the body that – whether dead or alive – always remains an *emphatic/problematic reality*. It both absorbs and disturbs meaning; it can increase but likewise reduce embodied symbolic capital – even reduce it to ashes. A dead body threatens through the fact of its prior livingness. A live body threatens through its inevitable and, at any moment, possible death. That manifold and paradoxical potential (dare we say *nature*) of the body is what makes it such a threatening reality, threatening to each representational activity, but especially the representational task of fusing the sign and its referent. Naturally, *realism* cannot prevent the body from dying-living, but it is working on the illusion that this is not happening. It can *hide* the corpse and *mask* the performing body in such a way that constructed and represented reality-identity appears compact and completed, therefore more persuasive and terminally *prevented from doubt*.

The *theological state* is driven by permanent reinventions of history, historicising the present, commemorations, even funerals, various cultural performances that transform already committed acts and actual events into a referential reality subjected to and identified with a certain symbolic (preferably historical) quality.

On the two-faced theatrical (*theological*) stage preserved by *realism*, dying is acknowledged only when it is pretended and 'meaningful'. At the same time there is a demand for 'truthfulness' and 'authenticity' as the essence of theatrical 'life', even when the acting is heavily stylised. In effect, *realism* is the representational mechanism responsible for the *metaphorical* death of livingness on the theatrical stage, even if what appears there sometimes really looks like *real* life. All signs on *realism*'s stage should find their *happy* referents as long as any manifestation of threatening body/reality is cleared away or completely controlled; symbols appear as if growing – naturally – together with the body; stages look like states and states like stages, which gives them extraordinary regenerable performative power – the power to restore corpses to (even embodied) symbolic life, and transform live bodies into symbols or real corpses.

And yet, as long as the body is performing (even in the most repressive representational circumstances of totalising *realism*), is it really necessary to eliminate or cover up all of its disturbing non-signifying effects – effects, that is to say, of a body that is factually living-dying-acting on the stage (of the state)?

Take a look at the strategy of representing the body in the military parade on *Statehood Day* in 1995. Uniformed, de-individualised, maximally disciplined bodies are marching in compact groups, their only task being to follow the rhythm of the march, to hold the flag and bear arms, and to face right towards the figure of the *First president*, the *Supreme Commander* saluting from the grandstand. The formations of Tuðman's *Übermarionetten* seem at first to have totally transformed the organic nature (thereby also the emotional and mental potential) of their bodies into the functions of the military machine, achieving the obvious effect: a demonstration of their war-readiness, a readiness to strike fear into the nation's enemies and, on the other hand, to win the immortality that goes to war heroes predestined to defend the nation and liberate the state's territory. However, even these totally controlled bodies are not mere symbols or *vehicles* of symbols. Beneath the military *decorum* and machine-like appearance, there is still a live body performing. For the so-called enemies of the nation and state, that means perhaps a better chance of winning the fight (real bodies are vulnerable). But likewise, for the national side, that flickering appearance of the mortal, fleshy, warm-blooded body is a risk that is worth taking: the mobilisation and manipulation of the nation might be more efficacious when the symbols, images and ideas are not only on show, but already embodied; when the representation and (trans)mission of these symbols is amplified by the 'auratic presence'[17] of the living-dying bodies; when through *kinaesthetic empathy*[18] the inflammatory sense of mortal danger and re-active belligerence are grafted on to the national body; that is, the bodies of the nation's people, the spectators. More than a massive war cry, the military parade was a curtain-raiser for a funeral.

The following performance implements a similar strategy: maximally reducing the potential for disturbances in the process of symbolisation (disturbances that might be brought about by the live body that is *always already* acting towards its death), yet at the same time using and abusing the carefully controlled, shaped and manipulated emphatic potential of livingness. In this case, however, something went wrong!

In 1997, the show *Of Ways of the Cross the Final End* was given on the stage of the Croatian National Theatre in honour of President Tuðman's seventy-fifth birthday. On that evening, laid bare, *theological stage* and *realism* were operating at full blast in order to reproduce, develop, expand without scruple and thereby fortify one of the fundamental national political myths, the myth of the Founder of the National State and Father of the Nation.

Franjo Tuðman – general in the Second World War, political prisoner during the age of communism, now the *First president* and *Supreme Commander*, a historian by vocation and already proclaimed a historical person – was given the privilege of observing and supervising not just the staging of the highlights from the onerous, yet glorious, national history, but also his own theatricalised apotheosis.[19] At one and the same time an actual distanced spectator (sitting in the state box) and a fictional character (sitting on the proscenium and reading from his history book!), the historical historian was enacted on the way to becoming a mythical hero: the *Saviour* of the Croats from the grand historical drama, the *One* who put a *Final End* to *Ways of the Cross*. The National Theatre did not just reflect his ideas and mediate his deeds, but did its utmost to present *Him* with an exceptional kind of *sacrosanct* presence: *His* body-symbol was expanded across the borderline dividing the real stage (where historical fictions are performed) and the reality of the audience. Being here and there, *He* appeared as *Both* (i.e. both sign and referent), and therefore as the *Only One*: the supreme *Sign*, the general *Symbol*, or the (first and final embodiment of the) *Word*. The effect of which – by referring, again and again, to nothing but itself – was to block *semiosis* as the process of producing the *other*, and raise itself to the metaphysics of omnipresence: eternity, immortality.

But, get real! The irony of fate – or, rather, the irony of life – was the fact (at the time a top secret) that the *First* was already dying of cancer. At the same time as the *Supreme* body was approaching its *most* alive (and most *problematic/emphatic*) final moment, its real death, the National Theatre performance was presiding over a fascinatingly paradoxical process: the mummification of the (still) living body.

4

Now, let us move to the *other* side of Croatian theatre where a different paradigm is taking place under the name *new theatre* or (with increasing frequency in recent years) *postdramatic theatre*.[20]

The paradox of a regime defined as *dictatorship with a democratic legitimacy* both guarantees its stability and provides opportunities for subversions. Dictatorship lurks behind the democratic mask, but the mask sometimes has to pretend to be more liberal than it is in order to act more persuasively. During a decade-long cultural and political masquerade, innovative practices have developed in several enclaves and caused significant changes – in terms of aesthetics, politics, ethics, management and organisation – on the performing arts scene. The process has gradually brought about a level of interrelatedness, interdependence and in some cases also co-operation among its protagonists, to the extent that a restoration of the counter-paradigm can be claimed with good reason.[21] During the 1990s, and – as the war was drawing to its close – with much more intensity in the second half of the decade, the *new theatre*, through indirect agency (although also sometimes by means of explicit political actions) played its role in the second *wave* of transition. Here, though, there were significantly different expectations than those the political opposition was willing to fulfil after it was swept into power in January 2000. That second *wave* of transition carried off the *dictatorship* hiding behind the mask of *democracy*, localised chauvinistic nationalism mainly on the fake pop-folk music scene and the mass rallies staged by the nationalistic opposition, and then begun converting the nationalistic myth into the *EU(ro)* myth. Instead of totalitarian nationalism, it imposed the *totalitarian* market interests of the liberal capitalism that began to flourish in the new Croatian millennium. Once again, dramatic theatre and *realism* – not necessarily as a style, but as a representational mechanism – has assumed the leading role in serving the new kind of *theology*; enriched this time by the growing number of musicals being produced in the theatre and by reality shows on the television.

Meanwhile, on the *postdramatic* stage (where a state cannot find its identification model!) various modes of *radical performing* are being explored as ways of (merely) unmasking and redefining, resisting, sometimes also transgressing and (even) exploding the ideological grip of the *theological stage/state* and *realism*.[22] *Radical performances* are inventing different strategies of experimenting with actions that stress the body's vitality and throw light on the paradoxical fact that the living-performing body gains its *liminal* and resistant performative force from its mortality, from its potential (even if this is only a terminal potential) to refuse being an agent in any signifying practice, let alone the signifying politics of the *Super-icon* and *Big Propaganda Text*. Instead of parasitically making symbolic profit from the effects of – denied and covered up, real or metaphoric – death and killing, radical acts of the counter-performances are dealing with the fact of the potential body's death, its paradoxical *living*-because-of-dying *presence*.

However, just as the affectivity of the body's livingness, radiating through the armour of symbols, is incorporated into the strategy of the militaristic spectacle, and just as the nationalistic political spectacle has to beware of this disturbing livingness that constitutes the real mortality of the body-symbol (as at the birthday party of the terminally ill president), the following performances are both aware and wary of the myriad representational functions the body is forced or willing to take on. In these performances the body plays, as it were, in the gap between its own palpable-fleshly presence, its counter-textual *desire, energy, aura*, and on the other hand the cruelty of framing, the troubling absence due to the various culturally encoded performances that are ceaselessly historicising the body, rewriting it, writing *with* and *on it*.

Fragile, a work-in-progress by Borut Šeparović and Montažstroj-Performingunit (1997–9), confronted, among other textual material, the biblical myth of the conversion of Saul and Kazimir Malevich's avant-garde manifesto *Suprematist Mirrors*. Massive, black hardback books, laid down on the stage, marked the performing area, a black square framed with spectators' chairs – a battlefield of identities and bodies.

The only light source in the central section of *Fragile* is a spotlight reflector hanging from a ceiling on a long rope. Holding on to the rope one of the performers daringly takes off and flies through the air as far as the edge of the performing area, threatening to crash against the thunder-struck spectators. Another performer grabs the spotlight, takes a swing and directs the beam at the body parts of the other performers. Then, the reflector is forcefully hurled towards the wall of the stage, above the

Figure 6.1 Montažstroj-Performingunit, *Fragile*, designed by Borut Šeparović.

spectators' heads, and left to swing loosely, to kick and creak, cutting across both space and bodies with its long, blinking beam. Finally, the performers make the spotlight move in circles around the whole performing area, 'carving' the air less than a metre away from the spectators' breathless faces. The risk-taking performance confronts the bodies of spectators and performers and exposes both to the danger of accident. The performer's body may at any moment succumb to its mortal limitations, and not only break through the frame of fiction (rudimentary and fragile in *Fragile* anyway) but abruptly manifest a (potentially fatal) resistance to technique and training.

Furthermore, the play of the bright spotlight beam, which at the same time makes visible and also cuts out parts of these bodies, reveals the complex and ambivalent relation of the performing body to performed identity (whether identity is conceived as coercive or chosen, coherent or disseminated, fictional and fluid or true and solid). Bodies and identities here are mutually attracting and fracturing, transforming and appropriating, deluding and subverting, attacking, defending and manipulating each other. The continuous merging and diverging of the body and identity turns out to be equally disturbing and vague on both sides – neither seem to have enough power to prevail. Identity cannot be fashioned and restored (as, for example, national identity) without the body. *Semiotisation*, the act of marking as a precondition for any identification, no matter how fragile

Figure 6.2   Montažstroj-Performingunit, *Fragile*, designed by Borut Šeparović.

and volatile, drifts the body away from its (more than referential) *reality* – its living-mortality.

The interpretative horizon of *Fragile* keeps warning that during turbulent transitional processes, let alone during wartime, in the backstage of the ritualised demonstrations of bodies-symbols the collision of living bodies with cultural, religious, national or gender identities becomes drastic and traumatic. Identities are not just taken as temporary and fluctuating, but often imposed as concrete and terminal, empowered to either oppress or dismember the bodies they are imposed upon. All that is demanded of a body, sometimes, all it is required to do, is – literally – to stop doing. It is required either to surrender and act for (or as) the symbol, or else it is forced to die and become a symbol itself (a national hero, a casualty, a war criminal, etc.). Against mass media, political spectacles and a national theatre that together were accelerating the decomposition of corpses through the denial of actual death alongside the creation of identity symbols (moreover against endless debates on conversions, illusions and intrusions of identities), *Fragile* raises a question: How to perform a diversion?

Due to the close proximity of the performing bodies both to the spectators and the light source, the relation of identity and body in *Fragile* is already dramatised at the level of a tangible materiality. The beam of the spotlight exposes in flashes the body's fleshiness – almost burning the trembling skin. Nearness, nakedness, focused intensive lightning, but above all the vulnerability – which is to say the mortality – of the *living substance*, as tangible evidence of the body's concreteness, amplifies the presence of the body at a level where all meaning, let alone symbols and identities, dissolve into a magma of sensations and, as Croatian theoretician Branko Gavella would say, *organic experiences*.

The Grand Master of All Scoundrels, directed by Branko Brezovec in 2001, finally unmasked the mythical weave of the dominant political/national *imaginarium*, and, by means of a series of iconoclastic inversions, degenerated the Croatian *Super-icon* and turned it into the *Super-forgery*, a disruptive anti-myth about the eternal, permanent *Croatian Funeral*. Poisoned *Croatian flesh* obediently rides the treadmill into the meat-mincing machine, to be burned in the huge hell-furnace. *Father* and *Saviour* is now exposed as the *Chief Undertaker* behind the lines, a war profiteer, the superintendent of concentration camps and the protector of Mafia-style accumulations of capital in an economic transition gone wrong.[23]

In Brezovec's spectacular attack on the spectators' sensory organs, the relentless crescendo of iconoclastic aggression nears breaking point. The simultaneous eruptions of images, the multiplication of levels of (meta)-fiction, the complex intertextual twists and turns, the dispersion of narrative fragments in the flood of visual and auditory stimulus; a ceaseless spending, merging, dissolving, forcing, amassing and caricaturing of representational and *dis*-representational attractions and styles, functions and genres, as well

Figure 6.3   Zagreb Youth Theatre, *The Grand Master of All Scoundrels*, directed by Branko Brezovec. Photograph: Sandra Vitaljić.

as of ideological and political (op)positions (these being at the same time nostalgically glorified and maliciously discarded into the mass post-modernist grave) – all of this brings the performance to the edge of perceptual, emotional and mental collapse. There approaches a state of stupor, where, due to total saturation, it becomes almost impossible to distinguish sensorial, affective, semantic exuberance from the void.

It is bodies that deliver (and suffer) the *bloodiest* attacks. They greedily move all over the multi-levelled scenery, follow or disobey exhaustingly repetitive choreography. They roll around, running, falling, singing, swinging, thrusting and breaking, barking, screaming, crying and shaking, stretching the limits of endurance to the utmost, expending all available physical energy by any means possible in a paradoxical *auto-iconoclastic* performance.[24] On the one hand, bodies wholeheartedly carry out various (and in this case enormous) tasks of theatrical representation, while on the other maximally heightening the 'inexplicable seething of the *physis*'[25] and bringing their *mortal vitality* to light.

But then, consistent (auto-)iconoclasm demands an even more drastic *dis*-representational effect: here, the barking, gasping and whining presence of live dogs during one of the many climaxes of the performance.

In the grotesque hypertheatricalised world of the *Grand Master*'s spectacle, the dogs' *non-acting* acts confront both spectators and actors with the appearance of a *reality* that is difficult to define. Dogs are not offered as an animal sacrifice, nor are they left to ramble around freely so as to – unintentionally, of course – violate the frames and rules of stage fiction and aesthetic representation. These dogs – military German shepherd dogs trained to discover mines! – are imprisoned in cages. The enormity and uproar of the machinery of the spectacle, the riotous bodies of the actors, but probably also the smell of the fresh flesh the actors are grinding in the machines on the table, affects the dogs' bodies and provokes uncontrolled manifestations of organic reactions (is it a mixture of fear and hunger?). Again, growling, yelping, trembling has a paradoxically double potential. It intensifies the hue and cry of the spectacle, as much as it disrupts the hell-bound hyperillusionary work of the machinery. The dogs' instinctive reflex reactions graft into the machinery wedges of reality, wedges of the real which can neither be prevented nor controlled – unless, that is, the body is put in a cage or put to death.

Although produced a few months earlier than *The Grand Master of All Scoundrels*, choreographic miniature *2* (*Two*) by Nikolina Bujas-Pristaš, co-founder of the theatre-dance-performance group BAD.co, can be interpreted as a radical minimalist response both to the aggressive exuberance of the self-celebrating multimedia Croatian *Super-icon* and the spectacularity of Brezovec's massive suicidal iconoclasm (which ultimately, despite the *dis*-representational and self-destructing procedures, constitutes itself as an eruption of images). Confronted with the violent, simulated and simultaneous totalising (really or potentially totalitarian) *realities*, the dancer-choreographer decided to – literally – close her eyes. And re-search a distinct sensory reality of the particular: her own particular, her own body.

The performer's body moves through the empty space, predominantly dependent on the senses of touch and hearing. However, her performance is not simply about blindness or the substitutability of the senses. Instead, by wilfully blocking one sense she induces the intensification and broadening of the activity of the whole network of her sensory-perceptual systems. The new intensity and extension of sensory experience revives awareness of corporeal complexity and its potentialities, of sensory living-ness and, ultimately, of mortality.

Does the body *see* more when we do not see (or hear, or . . .)? In the invisible space, a space without any bounds except for an empty smooth floor (and probably somewhere, beyond her reach, the black walls of the stage), the performer at one and the same time explores and sets up her *environment*. The most reliable medium is the sensitive surface and breakable extremities of her body: her skin, the tight muscles and bulging bones. The movements she performs appear as experiments with tactility. At times, following the flickering sound of music, she touches the floor, her own

Figure 6.4 Nikolina Bujas-Pristaš and Jelena Vukmirica in BAD.co, 2, choreography by Nikolina Bujas-Pristaš. Photograph: Marko Čaklvoić.

body, the air, even leaves the impression that she is touching the sound her movements make while cutting or gently shaping the surrounding space. Yet, without obstacles, and without the reactions and challenges of an *other*, all that tactile activity goes on in vain, without any ends but those of the body (performing *for/on/with*) itself. The floor remains silent and the sound elapses. Each movement and sound, each sensation of comfort or pain, is blocked in/by the same body, now extremely sensible but still with no image or sense of itself and the space surrounding it, nor of the sensation of difference that would give evidence of its corporeal distinctiveness and its ability to act outside of the (self-referential and self-dramatising) reality it is creating *by/for/of* itself. That is why the choreographer-performer makes another decision: to find, explore, rely on and finally synchronise with another body, its movements and sounds. In this blacked-out tactile world, that is a risky decision in terms of the vulnerability of her body and her responsibility towards the body of the other performer (another female). Both danger (of a fall, an injury, a fracture) and challenge come from a now physically present and approachable (not imaginary, but only image-less) *other*. Yes, you can imagine it with eyes closed or else see its image when you open your eyes, but only a sense of touch undoubtedly proves it is here and real: the other's and, on reflex reaction, your own body.

This kind of fact, this trust and ethics of performance, the choreographer has further researched in *Solo Me*, but this time with the spectator invited to participate in performance through a concrete physical support. He or she is asked to lend a hand in a demanding sequence of movements. What if the muscles of the spectator's hands fail?

Finally, *War Kitchen*, a 1996 work of Damir Bartol Indoš, was performed underground, in the dank cellar of a theatre building in Zagreb, behind an iron fence, as if in a cage. It was probably the most radical response of the performance theatre to the ravages of war. Even so, no articulated word was said. Instead there was a nightmarish, blaring, hardly bearable composition of deranged sounds and frenzied movements, on the verge of cacophony and chaos: the smashing of dishes and scrap metals, the creaking of machines, the beating of drums; the convulsions, contortions, tremor, stumbling, imploring, howling, groaning, screeching, yelling, panting, glowing and sweating of the body in great labour and pain.

More than just a possessed noisy demolition, more than a destruction of language or outbreak of *physis*, the *War Kitchen* was a Grotowski-like ritualised transgressive performance, dramaturgically and rhythmically structured and controlled, in which Indoš continued his search for an alternative way to express his profound emotional and sensory experiences of

Figure 6.5 Damir Bartol Indoš and Zlatko Burić in Kugla, *War Kitchen*, directed by Damir Bartol Indoš.

various traumatic states (caused by war, terrorism, discrimination, devastation of environment, social oppression, mental disorder) and to transmit *healing messages* of his – only seemingly paradoxical – *organic activism*. Over the years Indoš has invented a personal, *hieroglyphic* – some might say autistic – body-trans-language, which has been described by Suzana Marjanić as a

> reduction of the body to the regression prototype of the 'subnormal' body. . . . Indoš uses twistings of fingers, arms and legs as a dominant deformation, which other kinds of deformation arise from: the performer acts as a *deformer*, as one that disfigures, misshapes and deforms the image of the body.[26]

Indoš's psycho-physically shocking – *transluminational* – performances persistently drive his body to its limits, to extreme conditions, total exhaustion, radical actions *on* the body, always on a high-risk dividing line between mind and sub-mind, trance and *deformance* and, to an ultimate extent, between life and death.

In an interview at the turn of the century Indoš talks about the issue of this essay. Let this fragment be its (only temporary) conclusion:

> I have died an infinite number of times. Both in a spiritual, transcendental sense and literally physically: driving a bicycle over the edge of physical endurance, punching my head, bumping into doors and walls, swallowing a bayonet, wrapping a chain around my neck, driving on the roof of the car. In those situations I made a decision to die, but in the very moment when death was so near that I could touch it, I started fighting frantically to stay alive. And I won. Many times I threw myself on the pure concrete and while others were breaking their spines, I remained unhurt. Like Indian chief Crazy Horse I entered the battle believing that I was invulnerable. From losing my mind and from death I was protected by the fire, by the very processes of combustion.

Notes

1 H.-T. Lehmann, *Postdramatisches Theater*, Frankfurt am Main: Verlag der Autoren, 1999, p. 33.
2 V. Pusić, *Demokracije i diktature*, Zagreb: Durieux, 1998, pp. 68–80, 183.
3 Determined by the complex current and historical geopolitical, social and religious circumstances – which are impossible to elaborate profoundly in this introductory part of the essay – the rebirth of Croatian nationalism should be considered in the wider context of the restoration of the national states which took place after the collapse of communism and unitarianist federations such as the USSR, Czechoslovakia and the Socialist Federation of Yugoslavian Republics.

4 Tuđman refused to recognise the results of the 1995 local elections which had brought victory to the opposition parties in the capital. His argument was: 'We cannot allow an oppositional situation in the capital of Croatia – this would disturb the stability of Croatia'. See O. Žunec, *Rat i društvo*, Zagreb: HSD, 1998, p. 145.

5 Ethno-anthropologist Ivo Žanić (*Prevarena povijest*, Zagreb: Durieux, 1998, p. 15) has defined the *Big Propaganda Text* as the 'strategic paradigm' that works to 'secure and motivate the associative *competences* of both speaker and listener, the sender and the recipient of the message'.

6 Ever since its modern revival in the mid-nineteenth century, theatre in Croatia was constantly under pressure from state power, which was until recently regularly authoritarian or even totalitarian and restrained by different hegemonistic ideological formations. At first monarchies (Habsburg, Austro-Hungarian and unitarianist Jugoslavian); then the fascist regime of the so called Independent State of Croatia during and Communist Party regime after the Second World War; and finally *dictatorship with democratic legitimacy* in the last decade of the twentieth century.

7 This term here assumes artistic practice, the normative discourse surrounding it (from criticism to drama and theatre studies) and – on the whole – its institution.

8 Conceptualised by Derrida in 'The Theatre of Cruelty and the Closure of Representation', *Writing and Difference*, trans. Alan Bass, London: Routledge, 2002, p. 296.

9 *Realism*, exposed by Lyotard in 'Answering the Question: What is Postmodernism?', in Ihab and Sally Hassan, eds., *Innovation/Renovation: New Perspectives on the Humanities*, Madison: University of Wisconsin Press, 1983, pp. 331–5, is here conceived not just as a style of representation, but also as a representational mechanism which is moreover operative in the non-aesthetic domain.

10 H.-T. Lehmann, 'Of Post-Dramatic Body Images', *Ballet International/Tanz Aktuell, The Yearbook* 99, 1999, pp. 40–50, 42.

11 Claims for the full *semiotisation* of the performing body are advocated, for example, by Erica Fischer-Lichte. When explaining the notion of *body-text* she makes incredibly totalitarian demands on the body of the actor, who 'must turn everything unsignifying into something signifying. His individual corporeality thus becomes thoroughly transformed into a symbolic order'. E. Fischer-Lichte, *The Semiotics of Theatre*, tr. J. Gaines and D. L. Jones, Bloomington and Indianapolis: Indiana University Press, 1992, p. 187.

12 Lehmann, 'Of Post-Dramatic Body Images', p. 42.

13 Lehmann, *Postdramatisches Theater*, p. 262.

14 Lehmann, *Postdramatisches Theater*, p. 368.

15 She says (E. Diamond, ed., *Performance and Cultural Politics*, New York: Routledge, 1996, p. 5):

> In the sense that the 'I' has no interior secure ego or core identity, 'I' must always enunciate itself: there is only performance of a self, not an external representation of an interior truth. But in the sense that I do my performance in public, for spectators who are interpreting and/or performing with me, there are real effects, meanings solicited or imposed that produce relations in the real.

16 Regarded as a metaphor and paraphrase of the term *theological stage*, here constructed only for the sake of argumentation in this particular essay, the notion of *theological state* encompasses *dictatorship with a democratic legitimacy*. Even so, distinctions have to be made. *Dictatorship with a democratic legitimacy* cannot be simply

equated with the just dictatorship, especially not with the totalitarian one. Despite obstructions and even suspensions of democracy, the *tuđmanistic* regime collapsed after regular democratic elections in 2000. Non-constitutional government bodies and anti-constitutional governmental practice were immediately prevented by the enhanced power of parliament and the election of the new president (after the previous one died). The case is similar with nationalisms. Two nationalisms regarded as totalitarian do not have to terrorise in the same manner and scale, nor, ultimately, leave behind a comparable number of corpses.

17 Lehmann, *Postdramatisches Theater*, p. 163.
18 The phrase is John Martin's, cited in Elizabeth Dempster, *Performance Research* 8, 4, December 2003, p. 46.
19 The analysis of the representational situation which realises the metaphor (also provided by the *realism*) about the actor/character as a representative of the spectator on the theatrical stage would find an unprecedented challenge in the fact that the leading role of Tuđman was played by the director of the performance himself, an actor by profession – Zlatko Vitez, at that time no less than president's special advisor for cultural affairs!
20 To put it simply, the *new theatre* paradigm is born and developed out of aesthetic-political resistance towards the dramatic-literary and mimetic-realist theatre, the material, means, mechanisms, ideological function of such representation and its self-reproductive institution. After the fundamental break-up, which occurred around the turn of the nineteenth and twentieth century, the theatre, only just emancipated (*re-theatricalised*) from literature and drama, found itself faced with the task of a self-reflection, new self-foundation or eventual self-abolishment. Recently Hans-Thies Lehmann noted a 'caesura of media-society' (*Postdramatisches Theater*, pp. 22–4) and launched the notion of *Postdramatisches Theater*. As a kind of paradigm within a paradigm, it developed in the 1970s and it is still actual. The intention of this essay is not argumentation, nor critique or confrontation of the two controversial notions (*new* and *post-*). On this occasion, these terms are used as tools and hints of the aesthetic context.
21 In the recent history of the contemporary Croatian theatre, the *new theatre* already challenged the *theological stage/state*, firstly in the late 1960s and 1970s, and then again in the dawn of the first transition (late 1980s, until 1991). Each time, though, it was marginalised or almost suffocated by various means of cultural-political oppression.
22 In his book *The Radical in Performance* (London and New York: Routledge, 1999, pp. 16–20), Baz Kershaw argues for the notion of *radical performance* which would have the potential of overcoming, among other *challenges*, the 'radical liberalism', 'ethical relativism' and 'promiscuity of the political' in postmodernism, as well as 'old ideas of "political theatre"':

> My response to this challenge is an argument that claims for radical performance a potential to create various kinds of freedom that are not only resistant to dominant ideologies, but also sometimes transgressive, even transcendent, of ideology itself. In other words, the freedom that 'radical performance' invokes is not just freedom from oppression, repression, exploitation – the resistant sense of the radical – but also freedom to reach beyond existing systems of formalised power, freedom to create currently unimaginable forms of association and action: the transgressive or transcendent sense of the radical. What I am interested in centrally, then, is not the ways in which radical performance might represent such freedoms, but rather how radical performance can actually produce such freedoms, or at least a sense of them, for both performers and spectators, as it is happening.

23 The metaphors *Croatian Funeral, Chief Undertaker, Croatian flesh* are taken from the expressionist short story by Miroslav Krleža, 'The Grand Master of All Scoundrels', a pre-text of Brezovec's hypertextual spectacle.

24 Brezovec's hyperbolic and diabolic theatre follows (radicalises, even) Claudia Castellucci's concept of *auto-iconoclasm*, which insists on the artist's 'assault on his own creation'. 'Zamka za uplašene umjetnike', *Frakcija*, 1, 1996, pp. 63–6.

25 Lehmann, *Postdramatisches Theater*, p. 366.

26 S. Marjanić, 'Deformacije/Apstrakcije tijela', *Frakcija*, 17/18, 2000, pp. 10–17 (p. 12).

Chapter 7

Desire amongst the dodgems

Alain Platel and the scene of seduction

Adrian Kear

> We must demand that theatre, to use [Artaud's] image, should affect us
> as music affects snakes, by a shudder that strikes us first in the belly and
> runs through our whole body.[1]

Perhaps it should come as no surprise that, as a psychoanalytic theorist
of performance, André Green should conjure an image of auditory seduction to illustrate his desire for the theatrical encounter to bring about an
experience of bodily captivation. The implication seems to be that the
sensory impact of performance should be equivalent to that of an irre-
sistible embrace, producing nothing less than passionate abandonment in
the face of love's all-consuming presence. The language of theatre operates, in this formulation, as a metonymic extension of the rhetoric of
seduction – a formalised system for the generation of affect and the circulation of emotion. Its overarching ambition and effect is therefore, Green
suggests, to sway the audience with the visceral power of seduction (to
which one might add, ideological persuasion). But the overwhelming
experience of going to the theatre is, for me – amongst others – one of
severe disillusion or disappointment. All too often the actuality of the event
fails to deliver, as though theatre itself cannot live up to the 'idea of theatre'
it seeks to actualise and extend, cannot sustain either its own promise or
the demands and expectations placed upon it. It invariably seems a let-
down. Occasionally – rarely – theatre's capacity to produce the exceptional
is reaffirmed, however, through an encounter with live performance that
is experienced subjectively as a matter of primal importance. Such an
'event' might be figured as an irruption of theatre's potentiality – to interrupt its context, to disrupt social stability, to disturb the spectator's sense
of equanimity – that maintains itself nonetheless within those countless
disheartening, frustrating, head-shaking performances it appears to be set
apart from. This would suggest that the experience of theatre bona fide
is not simply contingent on aesthetic quality but also on the 'chance'
production of affective communicability. To be 'moved' by a piece, to be

shocked, stimulated, exhilarated, amused or horrified is, in effect, to have a 'gut reaction' to it: a visceral as well as intellectual experience 'that strikes us first in the belly then runs through our whole body'.

Although such experiences are infrequent – and intermittent – they serve to reacquaint the spectator with the phenomenal possibilities of theatre, to renew our belief in its enduring matter and import, to reignite our love affair with it. Or at least they begin to. For in reality the immediacy of the theatre experience, the quality of its happening-to-you, necessitates that the analysis of what occurs in that moment follows afterwards, *après coup*. Being struck by the theatre event, or by a fragment of it, strikes me as being an appropriate starting point for interrogating theatre's affective dynamics. Indeed, returning to the scene of a sensate encounter and rein-terpreting from memory an embodied experience of aesthetic 'shudder' might provide a method for extending our understanding of the impact of performance across a range of critical and conceptual registers, not least the psychoanalytic. With this in mind, I'd like to revisit a show I saw several years ago, *Bernadetje* ('Little Bernadette'), which was also my introduction to the Belgian theatre company, Victoria, and the work of the director and choreographer, Alain Platel. This performance was for me 'exemplary' for a number of reasons, not least because watching it made me feel physi-cally sick. I attempt to explain why over the course of what follows, analysing in the process this production's remarkably persuasive investigation and reconfiguration of the logic of theatre as a locus of seduction.

I came across *Bernadetje* almost accidentally, during its brief tour to Britain in October 1997, supported by Artangel and the Centre for Performance Research. Although this piece was in fact the second part of a theatrical tril-ogy – its sister-works being *Moeder en Kind* (1995) and the internationally acclaimed *Allemaal Indiaan* (1999) – there appeared to me to be something singular about the production's impact, form and methodology. Platel, in conjunction with the dramaturg, Arne Sierens, had collaborated with the young people of the Victoria youth theatre company to fashion an event of extraordinary insight and intensity. This is not to say that the show was a thing of great beauty or technical quality, but rather to indicate that it forged a powerful connection, experientially, between what took place inside the theatre and that which conditioned its appearance, culturally. More specif-ically, as I aim to show, *Bernadetje* was exceptional in the way that it linked the traumatic experience of recent cultural history – the revelation of the conspiracy of silence surrounding the Belgian child abuser and murderer, Marc Dutroux – to something like the historical significance of abuse as the silenced experience of childhood's traumatic reality. In so doing, it effec-tively opened up the enduring questions of responsibility, ethics and agency that haunt not only contemporary theatre in Europe, but also European culture, politics and social identity. And, by implicating the audience in this nexus, more importantly, by grounding it in the concrete situation of the theatrical seduction, it went some considerable distance to producing something akin to performative testimony to the historical significance of abuse as the very site and substance of subjectivity.

But this is to anticipate the argument to come somewhat precipitously. Let's return the performance in its materiality as a theatre event, beginning again with its staging in London in 1997 at the (then) recently reopened Roundhouse in Camden. The conversion into a theatre venue of this enormous, cavernous building (a former engine shed famous for being the construction site of Stephenson's first *Rocket*) seemed intended as an audacious provocation to the companies invited to perform there. Its empty shell appeared more suited to housing a rave party than to accommodating theatrical scenery, to the consumption of ecstasy than the construction of dramaturgical intimacy. Yet the contradiction was potentially generative in that it offered the opportunity to conceive of theatre-space outside from the limitations imposed by 'black-box' dimensions and proscenium conventions. A truly site-specific performance might have been able to make interesting use of these alternative possibilities, but *Bernadetje* was remarkable largely for its unique modification of them. Installed within the vast hulk of the Roundhouse was a fully functioning dodgem-car track, whose shiny magnetic surface, rigid steel edges and meshwork electric canopy created a metallic-grey caged environment – both real and fictional – for the show. Lit by fluorescent strip-lights suspended from the gantry, this quasi-formal space-within-a-space echoed

Figure 7.1   Victoria, *Bernadetje*. Photograph: Kurt Van der Elst.

the shape and structure of a studio theatre, albeit a fantastically playful one. Hovering above the back of the stage, and illuminating its recess, was a large neon sign written backwards – 'Lourdes'.

This appeared to attempt to situate the materiality of the stage environment within a nominated diegetic context, to confer the on-stage theatrical activity (which consisted largely of riding the dodgems) with narrative coherence and credibility. The giant caption, placed 'retrospectively', as it were, seemed to signify the stabilisation of the meanings in play in the performance itself – rendering it a 'modern version' of the epiphany story of Bernadette of Lourdes.[2]

Her ecstatic vision was in this case translated into a group of teenagers' obsessive occupation of a fairground attraction, a metaphorical 'place of pilgrimage for young people, a place of awakening adulthood' and site of seduction.[3] The narrative of transformation was at least in part, however, lost in translation – possibly because the Flemish/English was barely audible, let alone comprehensible. The emphasis instead was on the place itself, on the material environment of the dodgem track and the activity contained within it. This consisted of the adolescent actors literally 'playing' in the performance space, driving the dodgems frenetically and performing their enjoyment with a vibrancy and vitality suggestive of an altogether different source of theatrical energy. The performers were clearly not 'acting' in a conventional sense – 'playing characters' – but rather were 'playing themselves'; playing themselves 'playing' (however seriously). Their unadulterated enthusiasm for the tasks undertaken was clear to see – the pleasures taken by the young company in their essentially hermetic expressive repertory reflecting back to the audience the vicarious cause of our own eviscerated entertainment, leaving us both elated and disappointed at not being able to join in. Such preclusion of participation, moreover, appeared central to the construction of an explicitly voyeuristic spectatorial relation, in which the audience became increasingly aware of their own investment in the theatrical occasion. As Platel knowingly remarks, 'you can see [the set] as a dance floor, a centre with its periphery, in which a game of watching and being watched is played out'.[4]

One scene in particular seemed to mark this double movement, rupturing the drama's circular interiority with a direct address to the audience of discomforting familiarity. As the dodgem cars continue to circumnavigate, a young woman writhes enraptured to the sound of Prince's 'Cream'.

One of the boys joins her at the front of the stage, removes his T-shirt, and embraces her violently. The dodgems stop suddenly, as if in protest at this intrusion of up-front sexuality (or the tokens having run out prematurely), and the scene shifts into an even more explicitly sexualising display of adolescent bodies and juvenile exhibitionism. Each of the teenage performers in turn sashays across the stage, from back to front, flashing a piece of their flesh to the audience in a more or less formalised 'catwalk'

Figure 7.2 Victoria, *Bernadetje*. Photograph Kurt Van der Elst.

routine. This is undertaken with such calculated abandon, such intentional insouciance, that it demands to be read as significant.

The clearly coded revealing (and concealing) of these young people's bodies is fairly obviously directed towards the explication of the structural relations of the viewing contract. The activity on stage is designed to reference the spectator's activity off stage, to index, so to speak, their implication in its performance of apparent, if ambiguous, knowingness. The audience would seem to be situated by it as the agents of a disturbingly paedophilic gaze, whose look – like that of the man in dark glasses continuously loitering around the edge of the show – sexualises the performers' activity. In this reading, the sublimated energy of the performance, which might otherwise be seen as a displacement of adolescent sexuality, is offered back to the audience as a new form of sexual activity.[5] The 'catwalk' display thus appears to offer the spectator what he 'really' wants to see – and it is a 'he' quite specifically; the trope works exclusively within a strictly gendered visual economy – but in such a way that it can no longer be looked at innocently. The reversal of expectation makes explicit the scopophilic grounds of the relation, rendering the remainder of the performance so 'charged' that the audience cannot continue to just watch sitting comfortably. It is as if the theatre event introduces the reversal of the process of

sublimation as its critical activity, performing the production of 'new exci-
tation' and 'new energy' as evidence of the traumatising effects of the
imposition of adult sexuality.[6] Perhaps this is one way the show sought 'to
hit the public: from side to side, from the back, and full frontal',[7] making
us conscious of our otherwise unconscious desiring machinery. I for one
was discomforted by the implication – I felt sick to my stomach and incredibly angry at the production – and wanted to resist my interpellation into
its perverse visual economy. But, rather than reject its troubling argumentation, I decided to investigate further the logical dynamics of its intervention.

The burning questions I wanted to address concerned what might be
called the ethics of performance in this theatrical representation. To what
extent were the adolescent actors aware of what it was they were doing?
Did they have ownership of the *mise-en-scène*, or was it subject to a calculated
and controlling directorial strategy? In short, what were the relations of
authorship and agency at play within the compositional process of this
company? Platel maintains that the work emerged directly from collaboration between himself, the dramaturg Sierens and the performers, with
the latter responsible for the generation of material and the former its
selection, editing and arrangement. He suggests that there was considerable input from the young people themselves in making the catwalk scene
from their own experience and expressive resources, 'although I'm not sure
if they're aware of the effect of this showing off on all of the audience'.[8]
But is it reasonable to expect them to be, given that the relations of power
between stage and auditorium are here imbricated in the difference between
childhood and adult matrices of interpretation and intelligibility? Do the
performers need to understand (or be oblivious to) the 'argument' of
the show in order to perform it effectively? As Platel explains, the volatil-
ity of theatre as a signifying practice militates against 'using these elements
very consciously', relying instead upon unconscious representations for
their immediacy and improvisational vitality.[9] But their translation into
performance produces a different order of intentionality, and therefore
demands further interrogation of the questions of representation and
responsibility.

The shift of context from rehearsal room to auditorium automatically
engenders an alteration of inter-subjective relation: theatre doesn't just take
place in front of me; it addresses itself to me in my very subjectivity. As
the psychoanalytic theorist Jacques Lacan writes of what he calls the 'other
scene' of language (its unconscious register), 'the signifier is what represents the subject *for* another signifier'.[10] Although the syntax here is difficult,
the sense is nonetheless clear – signification carries within it a veiled 'content'
or subjective encoding. The spectator of that 'other scene' isn't necessarily the actual spectator but its representation – 'another signifier', if you
like – that is nonetheless addressed by the subject within the circulation
and exchange of signifiers that forms representation's economy. Hence, in

the language of performance, the theatre, 'before signifying something, signifies *for* someone'.[11] The concrete situation of the theatre event thereby draws attention to the material fact of audience, to the others gathered there whom it reaches as address. For sure, the meanings generated within a production might mean more, or other, than they were supposed to – creating an affective supplement or subjective remainder that destabilises any simple conception of theatre as purposive communication – yet at the same time they continue to function in the mode of representation (of something *for* someone). This is not to say that such an effect of intersubjectivity cannot be manipulated or created intentionally, but rather that signification is never a unidirectional transaction or unique responsibility.

In the case of *Bernadetje*, it is tempting to read the disturbing affect of the catwalk scene as an effect of this dynamic ambiguity. With recourse to Lacanian interpretive procedures, we can demonstrate that the performers are simply 'acting-out' a quintessentially *hysterical* theatrical relation. This functions, on the one hand, as a representation of the process of 'imaginary' identification – the identification with an image in which the actors appear desirable to themselves – and, on the other, as a simulation of the structure of 'symbolic' identification, in which the actors identify with the very place from which they are observed, the place from which they appear to themselves as desirable. As Mikkel Borch-Jacobsen explains in his analysis of the performative elements of psychoanalysis, the subjective principle of hysteria is intrinsically theatrical:

> In a word, the hysterics would stage themselves. They would separate themselves from themselves by adopting the point of view of the spectator, of that other *for* whom they played as actresses. Or again, they would put themselves *in representation* in order to better see themselves 'in front' of themselves, from the exterior, through the gaze and speech of recognition of the other – of *all* the others assembled [there].[12]

In this role-playing, then, it is clear that 'imaginary' identification is already anticipated by 'symbolic' identification, and that the image is always formed 'on behalf of a certain gaze in the Other'.[13] That the gaze considered here is gendered and sexualised provides the basis for the parade of gender and sexuality on the catwalk. Its conventions form the theatrical language through which the performers seek to offer 'themselves' to the Other as the objects of its desire – a desire that necessarily exceeds the boundaries of the context of its articulation. The discomfort felt by the audience probably derives from being positioned in this locus of absolute Otherness, as the material embodiment of a primarily 'ecstatic', self-reflexive address. And, as the analysis of hysteria suggests, the transference involved in conflating the Other with the other ('*all* the others') assembled in the audience can have profoundly destabilising effects.

By the same token, however, the function of such 'acting-out' might be seen as a short-circuiting of representation, providing a form and framework for the direct expression of experience or 'passion' that is not motivated by conscious, deliberative consideration.[14] This is confirmed in *Bernadetje*'s subsequent choreography: as the catwalk gyrations continue, the young woman who had been embraced at the outset of the action drives a dodgem round the track manically, watched menacingly from behind the screen of dark glasses of the on-stage 'paedophilic' adult male.

As the scene grows in intensity, he jumps into the car with her, and tries to repeat the passionate embrace that initiated the sequence. She fights him off and the scene comes to a sudden halt with this violent interruption, the dramatic timing of which draws attention to the adult's intrusive misreading of the space of teenage play. This momentary standstill forces a concomitant instant of recognition: the meanings and values imposed by the interpretations of adult spectatorship are not necessarily co-extensive with the 'intentions' of adolescent display. The anticipation and invocation of grown-up desire in the form of the gaze is not the same thing as an invitation to a certain perverse 'grown-up' after all. The onstage adult, for one, superimposes the fantasy with his reality and misrecognises himself as the intended addressee of the catwalk scene, collapsing in the process the distance – the difference – between material and psychic reality. The dramaturgy of his nauseating intervention makes

Figure 7.3 Victoria, *Bernadetje*. Photograph Kurt Van der Elst.

manifest the performance's profoundly *ethical* revelation of the temporal and spatial fissure between adult and childhood frameworks of understanding, a hermeneutic hazard which these adolescent actors are at once trying to illustrate and to navigate, to occupy and eschew.

Their enactment of the circular movement between imaginary and symbolic identification thus appears, in the first instance, to substantiate the abusive process of sexual subjectivation and its associated deflection of the metonymy of desire into the vicissitudes of ideology. However, it is worth remembering that the materiality of performance reminds us of the radical disjunction between utterance and enunciation, between the fact of saying something and the certain 'something' meant by the thing said. The performance of the gap between them is in effect what marks the politics of the 'hysterical' revelation in *Bernadetje*, leaving the audience assessing the space between the performers' articulation of desire and its concomitant encoding in specific movement, speech and gesture. The demand placed upon the spectator is therefore not 'find me desirable!', but an invitation to reject this request because it is a mere refraction of reality, a distortion of the truth. The truth of its 'meaning' rather resides in probing further the problem of desire's perverse translation into 'the metonymy of the discourse of demand',[15] by asking aloud the counterintuitional question, 'What is it you are saying by saying this?'[16]

As the adolescent actors reveal bits of their bodies, it should be increasingly clear that the seeming autonomy and transparency of 'the body' does not itself authorise any simple reading of their gestures as self-referential or self-evidently 'autobiographical'. Rather, their movements might be seen to signify enigmatically – enigmatic being Jean Laplanche's conception, following Lacan, of the signifier that has been divested of its signification 'without thereby losing its power to signify *to*'.[17] The performers' presentation of a clearly mimetic expressive activity further suggests that the catwalk scene points towards, or allegorises, something else in the significatory relays of its address. Enigma and allegory appear closely related, for, as Fredric Jameson has noted in his closely argued study of the theatre-thinking of Bertolt Brecht,

> Allegory consists in the withdrawal of the self-sufficiency of meaning from a given representation. That withdrawal can be marked by a radical insufficiency of the representation itself: gaps, enigmatic emblems, and the like: but more often . . . it takes the form of a small wedge or window alongside a representation that can continue to mean itself and seem coherent.[18]

So, by both existing within yet moving outside of *Bernadetje*'s otherwise hyper-realistic aesthetics, by simultaneously disrupting and drawing attention to its adroit illustration of adult–adolescent relations and dynamics, the mimetic 'interruption' of the catwalk scene at once appears to mark and to mask the materiality and historicity of its signifying practice. One after another, a succession of young people come forward and reveal to the audience a point on their skin (elbow, nipple, lips, thigh, chin . . .), offering it as a 'wedge or window' into the significance of what they are themselves demanding. As has been seen, the mimetic endows the sign with a certain historicity, and its placement on the body appears to ground it in subjective reality. Indeed, it might even possible to speculate what, in the present scene, it is a signifier *of* exactly; but its function is rather, I would suggest, to keep open the possibility of it signifying *to* its own materiality.

The theatrical allegory would here seem to function in relation to its 'other scene' in a way akin to Jameson's description of it as 'a reverse wound, a wound in the text' – or its embodied fabric, the skin – which 'can be staunched or controlled . . . but never quite extinguished as a possibility'.[19] Laplanche would argue that the presence of an enigmatic signifier on the surface of the skin is evidence enough of the scene's index-ical structuring, pointing analysis away from the level of the 'symbolic' and back towards its *material* ontogenesis. The catwalk scene in *Bernadetje* can thereby be seen as a refraction of the relations embedded in the foun-dational scene of seduction. This 'other scene' operates as the traumatic site of the 'implantation' of adult sexuality into the child, of its incorpo-ration into an at least partially sexualised sociality.[20] This 'implantation', Laplanche argues, takes place by 'fixing' signifiers to the psycho-physio-logical 'skin' of the subject – signifiers produced by the adult's necessarily inappropriate 'address' to the child:

> To address someone with no shared interpretive system, in a mainly extra-verbal manner: such is the function of adult messages, of those signifiers which I claim are simultaneously and indissociably enigmatic and sexual, in so far as they are not transparent to themselves, but compromised by the adult's relation to their own unconscious, by unconscious sexual fantasies set in motion by his relation to the child.[21]

In his schematisation, which differs decisively from Lacan, the adult's message forms the first part of the sequence through which the uncon-scious is formed in the subject as the product of material practices and inter-subjective relations. It is a 'message' precisely because it means some-thing to the subject – something more or less 'meant' by the sender – and, equally importantly, because it *represents* someone to an other – 'the subject for another signifier'. Its implantation in the skin of the infant, whose uncon-scious agency as yet remains undifferentiated, leaves it exposed to the child's first active attempts at 'translation'. As translation is impossible without a shared interpretive system, there is a concomitant 'partial failure of translation', which is only resolved by the activation of repression. This system then forms for Laplanche the generalised structure of 'seduction' – message, translation, partial failure of translation–which introduces the unconscious into the infant as 'an alien inside me, and even one put inside me by an alien'.[22] For Laplanche, the theory of seduction 'affirms the priority of the other in the constitution of the human being and of its sexuality. Not the Lacanian Other, but the concrete other: the adult facing the child'.[23]

This returns us, then, to the concrete theatrical situation, to the adult facing the child in the spectatorial relation. My gut reaction at being addressed directly by the 'enigma' of the catwalk scene has its discomfiture confirmed by subsequently coming to understand it as a representational condensation of the dynamics of childhood seduction. Its mimetic quality points to this anteriority, while at the same time being unable to signify it directly. The scene works across the spatial fissure and temporal delay between what is played out before us and the inaccessible 'other scene' buried within it, repeated and replaced by the movement of allegory. The other to which it is addressed is, almost certainly, 'the other of seduction, the adult who seduces the child'[24] rather than the much more vague and fictional Other of Lacanian symbolic determinacy. The scene's affective temporality operates according to the logic of 'deferred action' – Freud's *nachträglichkeit*, which translates as 'afterwardsness' – that ensures that the actual affective *experience* of the traumatic 'other scene' is felt only in the echo of its apparent reoccurrence or repetition on a later, metonymically linked, occasion. In *Bernadetje*, adolescence itself seems to signify the space of developing understanding, during which the matter of what has been 'signified to the subject' is opened through conceptual 'afterwardsness'; the timeframe enabling the retranslation and reinterpretation of the enigmatic message being mapped on to the time of emergent sexuality in such a way that the subject becomes capable of reprocessing the message's 'meaning' and at least partially cracking the code of its intelligibility. 'Growing up' would appear therefore to entail realising on stage what grown-ups do and have done off; but for the adult spectator implicated in the scenic structure of this mimesis of seduction, the 'deferred action' of psychoanalytic understanding offers little comfort or redress. Situated in one moment as the agent of a perversely sexualising gaze, the audience is invoked in the next to bear witness to its traumatic effects. In offering an affective 'renewal of the traumatic, stimulating aspect of the childhood enigma',[25] the choreography of *Bernadetje* simultaneously positions the audience as both object and source of the adult message – as the adult facing the child (in the theatrical reality) and the child faced by the adult (in the stimulated 'memory' of unconscious fantasy). Compromised by their own unconscious's historicity, the audience member is drawn into occupying the three roles in the seduction scene sequentially – adult, child and witness – each played out as the effect of a certain 'afterwardsness'.

In *Bernadetje*, the structure of seduction is at once clarified and condensed by the spatial and temporal organisation of the theatrical scene. However, it also emerges that the catwalk has been watched intently not only by the adults in the audience and the on-stage 'paedophile', but by a small child downstage left, carrying a teddy and wearing a white communion dress. That the scene might function for her primarily as an enigmatic message is made self-evident when she dumps the teddy, takes centre stage from the rest, and is transformed into a miniature 'rave' dancer. With arms and head pumping in ecstatic excess, she herself appears as the embodiment of 'Little Bernadette'. The neon sign spelling 'Lourdes' flashes blue and red above her as she boogies away, energetically performing a bodily translation at the same time as incorporating seduction's core theatrical relation: the scene witnessed is not just 'innocently' observed; it is offered, proffered, presented to the subject, who receives its 'message' as a direct, almost physical address. In other words, it comes loaded with intent. The child translates the meaning of these scenes as best they can, which, given that the adult always 'says' more than they mean, necessarily leaves a residual, untranslated element: the obscure, sexual, enigmatic *content* of the message.[26] So, as the little girl in *Bernadetje* mimetically translates the adolescent movements into the 'new energy' of a further-sublimated *mise-en-scène*, are we to interpret her dance as a similarly precocious display of prodigious sexuality? Perhaps, but not yet, surely; not by seeing through our glasses darkly with an abusive 'adult' gaze; but by recognising that the space and time she's in is incompatible with our own. Without such a distinction, seduction slides into abuse, which may very probably be what the enigmatic signifiers in the body of the theatrical fantasy in fact reference, materially.

This would appear to be the stance adopted by Platel in his choreography; one that that requires the audience 'to think, and to position themselves in relation to what is happening'.[27] In *lets op Bach* ('A Little Something to Bach', 1999), for example, he produces an even more graphic literalisation of the sexual socialisation performed by seduction. A prepubescent teenage girl – a tweenie, you might say – with a bandaged eye and NHS specs sits, downstage right, worshipping a poster of the boyband Westlife. Behind her a sweaty, bald-headed, bare-chested male dancer feels himself up and calls her over. She refuses to budge. He is joined instead by an adult female dancer, who sits herself down on his lap; as they embrace, he looks directly towards the child, making it clear that the scene is given to her to be seen. Later, she replaces the woman on his knee, squirming uncomfortably as the implicit message is literalised as an explicit molestation. She runs away back to the poster shrine, against which she is then pinned by the man's aggression as he implants his violent 'message' in the form of Chinese star-darts thrown around the contours of her skin. The incomprehensibility of the adult's message, its incommensurability with the world of childhood, could not be illustrated more provocatively.

The theatrical literalisation of seduction is, for sure, disturbing to see: but then so is the recognition that abuse is, perhaps, intrinsic to its representational currency. Hence Platel maintains that

> when people feel uncomfortable seeing certain scenes in my performances, then I just have to tell them that I feel uncomfortable myself. And so, for example, when you relate as an adult to how young people look and behave, I can only say I feel uncomfortable too. ... I can describe it, and I understand it more and more, but it's still very upsetting, sometimes. So it's more about putting your demons on stage than about feeling I'm going to give you a lesson in how to watch, how to think...[28]

The ethics of performance in these productions would therefore seem to depend upon our ability to read them *as* representations–albeit representations cross-cut by material relations. When the above scene in *Iets op Bach* triggered a police enquiry in Belgium after complaints from the audience in London, it could not have been altogether surprising, for this show, along with *Bernadetje*, appears to be bearing witness to the culture of abuse that is represented, almost literally, as our shared, complicit, but nonetheless collective responsibility. The after-effects of encountering this in the theatre experience should be then, as Brecht was keen to remind us, a matter of ongoing incredulity.

Acknowledgements

Thanks are due to the Centre for Performance Research and Artangel for the use of their archives. The author gratefully acknowledges the support of the AHRB.

Notes

1 A. Green, *The Tragic Effect: The Oedipus Complex in Tragedy*, trans. Alan Sheridan, Cambridge: Cambridge University Press, 1979, p. 9.
2 'Our Lady of Lourdes', Bernadette Soubirous (1844–1879), is renowned for receiving a series of 'visitations' from the Immaculate Conception in Nevers, France, around the time of her first communion in February 1858. She first appeared to Bernadette on the banks of the River Gave, wearing a pristine white dress, and revealed to her the nearby stream that was the source of the holy spring, telling her to drink from it and bathe in it, too. Bernadette returned to the place every day for a total of seventeen days, she claimed in a letter to a friend, and received instructions from the Virgin to build a chapel at the site of the spring. The shrine of Lourdes, as it became, has since received over two hundred million visitors seeking redemption and curative restoration from its blessed waters. Bernadette – the patron saint of poverty, piety and sickness (as well as shepherds and teenagers), and herself an incomparable beauty – was beatified in 1925 and canonised in 1933: 'The more I am crucified, the more

I rejoice', see http://www.catholic-forum.com/saints for more information.

3 A. Platel, *The Times*, 2 October 1997.

4 A. Platel and A. Sierens, *Bernadetje* press release, 1997.

5 T. Murray, 'Scanning Sublimation: The Digital Pôles of Performance and Psychoanalysis', in P. Campbell and A. Kear, eds., *Psychoanalysis and Performance*, London and New York: Routledge, 2001, pp. 47–59 (p. 50).

6 J. Laplanche, 'The Kent Seminar', in John Fletcher and Martin Stanton, eds., *Jean Laplanche: Seduction, Translation, Drives*, London: ICA, 1992, p. 32.

7 Platel and Sierens, *Bernadetje* press release.

8 Platel, quoted in A. Kear, 'Seduction and Translation: Alain Platel in Conversation', *Performance Research*, 7, 2, 2002, pp. 35–49, (pp. 39–40).

9 Platel, in Kear, 'Seduction and Translation', pp. 40–1.

10 J. Lacan, 'Radiophonie', *Scilicet* 2, 3, 1970, cited in M. Borch-Jacobsen, *The Emotional Tie: Psychoanalysis, Mimesis and Affect*, trans. Douglas Brick and others, Stanford: Stanford University Press, 1993, p. 20 (emphasis added).

11 J. Lacan, *Écrits: A Selection*, trans. Alan Sheridan, London: Routledge, 1977, p. 82.

12 Borch-Jacobsen, *The Emotional Tie*, p. 95.

13 S. Žižek, *The Sublime Object of Ideology*, London: Verso, 1989, p. 106.

14 Borch-Jacobsen, *The Emotional Tie*, p. 144.

15 Lacan, 'The Kent Seminar', p. 293.

16 Žižek, *The Sublime Object of Ideology*, p. 111.

17 J. Laplanche, *New Foundations for Psychoanalysis*, trans. D. Macey, Oxford: Blackwell, 1989, p. 45.

18 F. Jameson, *Brecht and Method*, London: Verso, 1999, p. 122.

19 Jameson, *Brecht and Method*, p. 122.

20 J. Laplanche, *Life and Death in Psychoanalysis*, trans. J. Mehlman, Baltimore and London: Johns Hopkins University Press, 1976, p. 46.

21 J. Laplanche, *Essays on Otherness*, ed. J. Fletcher, London: Routledge, 1999, pp. 79–80.

22 Laplanche, *Essays on Otherness*, p. 65.

23 Laplanche, *Essays on Otherness*, p. 212.

24 Laplanche, *Essays on Otherness*, p. 72.

25 Laplanche, *Essays on Otherness*, p. 224.

26 Laplanche, *Essays on Otherness*, pp. 156–9.

27 Platel, in Kear, 'Seduction and Translation', p. 48.

28 Platel, in Kear, 'Seduction and Translation', p. 48.

Chapter 8

'Constitutive ambiguities'

Writing professional or expert performance practices, and the Théâtre du Soleil, Paris

Susan Melrose

1 Introduction

What *is* in a name – or perhaps I should say, in a signature? I want to draw your attention, in what follows, to a number of curiosities which seem to me to be specific to our attempts, within the disciplines of performance studies or performing arts or theatre studies in the university, to '*write* performance'. Most of us, as far as I have been able to discern, attempt this 'performance writing' – at least where our engagement is with professional performance practices or practitioners – from the perspective of expert spectating.

The term 'perspective', by the way, doesn't tell the whole (analytical) story: spectating is performed according to a particular ground-plan which organises the material event and its various positionings. That ground-plan locates spectators quite precisely with regard to our relationship with or to our chosen object of analysis. Indeed 'objectness' itself tends to result from a particular distance from performance-professional activity; as you are aware, over the years different practitioners and different writers have sought to experiment with this distance itself, without, however, any lasting effect. From that (regulatory) positioning we tend, as spectators, to be able to see *only what we can see*, which means that spectators, within the economy of performance practices and writing production, are required to infer (and thereby participate in the production of) 'the rest'. The processes involved in this complex triggering and inferential activity (these triggers can be defined as 'performance-performative' once they are taken up by spectators) are numerous and some of them are performance-*constitutive*, by which I mean that they are vital to the effective operation of 'the show'[1], to the ways in which a particular practitioner or company of practitioners engages with the economy or economies of performance production.

For the moment, however, let's come back to the delicate question of naming and signature. Have you noticed that some instances of professionally ratified, challenging performance work, but not others, seem to excite an endless stream of more or less ingenious interpretations? Amongst instances of apparently 'inexhaustible' practices and notorious signatures is work by the Théâtre du Soleil, under Ariane Mnouchkine's direction. I am going to characterise this work as *cosmopolitan* rather than 'European' as such, for the apparently simple reason that it plays on and to an international circuit, in terms which seem to ignore and/or transcend national or regional borders. At the same time, however – and here we find one of the constitutive ambiguities of my title – instances of professional, signed practice have also succeeded, at a particular moment, in actualising and illuminating certain aspects of the historical context of their emergence. We return to this question a little later.

The name I have set out above points us to the opposite of the notorious ephemerality[2] of performance – an ephemerality, besides, which has only ever been specific to spectating's experience of a given performance, and not at all appropriate to an understanding of performance practitioners' own 'knowledge engagement' in performance production. It economically signals 'signature' practices (and practitioners) precisely to the extent that 'the work' remains; that it transcends, in some manner or form, the context and circumstances of its own initial emergence. I have written 'in some manner or form' because exactly *how* work survives as shared knowledge, in both the university, in the wider arts communities, and in the ongoing practices of the signature practitioner herself or himself, is a matter of considerable interest, but under-represented in performance-writing. At this point I want to identify performance survival simply in terms of *performance continuities* – a term I have borrowed from Brian Massumi[3] – noting, as I do so, that performance-continuity, in the university, tends to be assured first by *writing*, in certain specific registers, and second (but less frequently) by the professional documentation of performance by or through co-operation with expert performance practitioners.

Writing 'practice'/practicing 'writing'

Writing is far from being a neutral communicative tool. Gregory Ulmer once suggested[4] that the writing promoted in the university adopts a number of registers and a number of functions, including:

1 The role of 'explanatory myth' – here we might find a feminist approach to the work of Ariane Mnouchkine.
2 Expert or technical registers – dealing, for example, with the scenographic production processes entailed.
3 Popular registers – often used in theatre reviews with a wide general readership in the popular press, and tending to be characterised by an unreflexive use of evaluative language.
4 Personal/anecdotal registers, made popular in the later twentieth century in both action-theoretical approaches and in first-person accounts,[5] to explore some of the lived implications of the more conventionally theoretical.

I have included this rough paraphrase of Ulmer here in order to draw your attention to what continues to be the major mode of production in performance studies or performing arts in the university; to what writing is variously 'up to', in such a context; and to ask you to ponder, as I do so, what becomes of professional performance practices when these sorts of interpretative apparatuses are brought, by spectators, to their processing. In order to explore the pertinency of Ulmer's topographic account and its topological implications, you might consider David Williams' *Collaborative Theatre: Le Théâtre du Soleil Sourcebook*.[6] This published text provides an exemplary late twentieth-century account which ranges across the written registers identified. It signals an instance of *theatre-historical discourse and metadiscourse*, innovative at the time of publication in its recourse to fragments of writing in the full range of registers identified by Ulmer, and its attempts to include practitioner-accounts (often first-person/practitioner-anecdotal and/or popular) of performance making and reflection.

Despite this *performance* of a multi-vocal account of performance production and processing, however, Williams' expertly edited (and *signed*) text is largely restricted to writing across those registers. 'Restricted', when it comes to the work of this notorious and inspirational company of practitioners, for the simple reason that 'the (performance) work itself', by way of contrast, is *mixed-mode at source*: to a significant extent it operates through processes too fine, fragile and subtle to give way to the particular fixings that writing tends to impose. In what follows, I shall make the curious suggestion that a professionally produced video account of the making of the Théâtre du Soleil's *Tartuffe*,[7] produced from a privileged 'insider' perspective, better '*theorises*' Ariane Mnouchkine's work with the company than does any published written account, whether 'academic' or journalistic in register.

What might be the implications of my suggestion that mixed-mode practices 'themselves' better *theorise*, in this sort of case, than do expert or explanatory registers of writing? I shall return to this question, but would invite you, at this point, to entertain two notions: the first is that 'theory' is itself a complex 'knowledge-*practice*', always *performed* somewhere (this includes published texts destined for the university resource centre), by and for someone, to certain explicit and implicit criteria; second, that in ancient accounts 'theoria' was also used to refer to a mode of public performance by a trusted, ambassadorial performer. The theoretical, in this case, is 'processional' and by implication mixed-mode performance-based. In the images which follow, I am arguing that we can see aspects of the video production company's *processional theorisation* of professional performance-making practices. I am also arguing that these signal professional processes are generally unavailable as such to expert spectating, and – perhaps more importantly – unable to be inferred in a spectator's engagement with performance product.

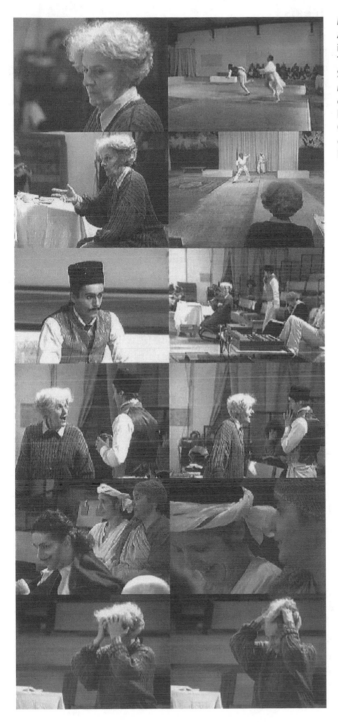

Figure 8.1
Ariane Mnouchkine
in rehearsal at the
Théâtre du Soleil.
Stills from *Au soleil
même la nuit, Scènes
d'accouchements*,
É. Darmon and
C. Vilpoux, Théâtre
du Soleil/Agat Films/
La Sept Arte, 1997.

Signature practices?

What is it that is particular to performance practices which have excited the ongoing production of writing in the university? I want to return here to the problematic notion of *signature* – necessarily a metaphor of writerly implication (and imposition) when it comes to complex mixed-mode performance-making practices – and to what 'signature' might seem to mean in performance studies *writing*. Plainly writing – its *techne* or craft, or art – involves identification and naming of a *subject*. I have already produced a key instance of identification through naming above – by implication, I have reproduced and reinforced the notion that in writing, at least, certain performance practices are not just named, but signature-bearing, and a matter of intellectual property ownership; yet at the same time, these uses reproduce a widely-evidenced *misrecognition* of collaborative professional practice. I know, from experience, that what I have called 'Ariane Mnouchkine's work' is actually the outcome of a series of professional collaborations, without which that name would not have achieved public prominence. My point of principle, then, is in part counter-intuitive: I both know (intuitively) that this '*is*' 'Mnouchkine's work' (my use of the possessive plus the verb 'to be' is ontologising, or asserts being); and I know, at one and the same time, that 'it *is* the work' of a number of relatively speaking unnamed/unwritten professional practitioners, who have effectively *contracted for* that erasure of their own names where 'the show itself' is concerned. Certainly I have no easy recall of the name of the lighting designer who works with (indeed, 'illuminates') Mnouchkine, and I am assuming that my amnesia here is in large part at least effected by the reproduction of dominant discursive forms.

Multi-participant relationality

In theoretical/expert-technical terms, relating to the production of the work itself, the show is both collaborative *and* it is 'owned' and 'signed' by Mnouchkine herself – to whom, writing rapidly, we might even be prepared to attribute the work of the actors and the vital contribution of, for example, Jean-Jacques Lemêtre's music composition and performance. Yet that work is, in *metatheoretical terms*, entirely relational and multi-participant. In addition, the performance-making work for *Tartuffe* at the Théâtre du Soleil has been acknowledged, by Mnouchkine herself in the video account to which I refer above, to be far from unusual in its capacity, in the making, to have exceeded her own knowledge processes; to have exceeded her professional ability, in the short term at least, to conjure it forth, suggesting that her professional work *does more than she knows*, and differently.

Signature survives, nonetheless, and accrues authority; it outlives the largely forgotten realities of professional collaborative practices, and to this extent it turns out, curiously enough, to be non-identical with 'the show' (its 'eventness') which drew our attention to it. It would also seem to be the case that 'the show', in the processes of its making, is similarly non-identical with the event, bearing the same name, of spectators' experience. To utter the words 'the work itself' is, thus, a nonsense, if we have any concern for the professional undertaking it entails, as distinct from the spectators' experience and engagement with 'it'.

From this point of view what is at stake, from the perspectives of professional performance making, is what writing in certain genres and registers, in particular sites, performs upon the body (so to speak) of complex, mixed-mode, multi-participant professional practices. It is licensed to perform this in the university, with a confidence and an authority which *ontologise* in terms of spectator experience – as though the writing were naming 'the show itself'. In my argument here, this authorised wording has little to do with the relatively fragile and forward-looking, *inventive* economies of performance-professional practices themselves.

These economies are action-based, concerned with movement (and, in metaphoric terms, with moving any number of participants); and they are concerned with what Massumi[8] has called 'continuities' under 'qualitative transformation'. Work driven by the need to move (hence with *affect*, from which we obtain 'teleoaffective' choices[9]), and by the need to effect qualitative transformation of the given, is work characterised by a continual becoming. Work already made, once submitted to spectating and to the ongoing production and reproduction of spectator-centred writing, is by way of contrast *ontologised* according to the orders of spectating and (writerly) semantics.

Move me

In my own experience, the work I have identified with 'Ariane Mnouchkine' at the Théâtre du Soleil is 'affectively invested', a number of times over, but this is far from claiming that its 'knowledge status' is thereby 'subjectively' compromised. On the contrary: first, no professional performance work fails to be regulated by the logics of performance production – and what is regulated includes affective and teleoaffective choices; second, in the 'practice theory' of Karin Knorr Cetina, we find the suggestion that *all* 'creative and constructive', 'non-routine' research practices are systematically driven by affective investment[10]. What moves, plainly, in live performance, both literally and figuratively, has something to do with present and material bodies, some named-performance-expert, some spectatorial and anonymous. Massumi points out with regard to movement and affect, however, that cultural theory over two decades has been revealed to include no widely available discourse about affects. Cultural theory, over recent decades, has thus lost 'the very notion of movement as qualitative transformation'. 'There is "displacement",' Massumi adds, in cultural-theoretical approaches drawing on the tradition of psychoanalytic theoretical writing, 'but [there is] no transformation; it is as if the [expert, performing] body simply leaps from one definition to the next'.

In addition, because 'the positional model's definitional framework [that is, in critical-interpretative registers] is punctual', giving us a sense of historical change in tranches of activity, 'it simply can't attribute a reality to the interval, whose crossing is a continuity'.[11] It is to this continuity, plus the drive to effect qualitative transformation, that I am attributing 'signature'. In these terms, the quest for *qualitatively transformed continuities – which move, in/as the event* – patently involves recourse to disciplinary tradition and its mastery, to aesthetic judgement and to institutionally approved value systems. In this sense, professional performance making requires that we bring the notion of normative practices into play. It also involves a particular challenge to the writers amongst us: to attempt to deal with professionals' *looking forward with curiosity*, at the constitutively not-yet-imaginable.

It is the emergence of the not-yet-imaginable that surprises performance professionals themselves, at work. That work, from this perspective, is affectively driven, necessarily orientated to a future event: acutely fragile as such, systematically speculative in mode. I cannot over-stress the importance of this complex observation, in the context of the backward-looking ontologisation which writing performs (and into which my own choice of medium here binds my enquiry): renowned practitioners whose work has been pursued over a considerable period of time are effectively professional-creative researchers. Their professional activities, which calculate a future, qualitatively transformed event, constitute one field of what have been called affectively invested 'epistemic practice' in a knowledge economy.[12] Epistemic practices are driven, as far as I have been able to tell, by *curiosity* – which Ulmer, at least, has identified as central to the practice of the theoretical.[13] In other words, qualitative transformation requires not so much a quest for a crudely figured 'newness', but rather, the means to enable the emergence of something not yet seen but recognised, something both continuous with, and judged to be *better* than, the already-seen. It involves the intermix of *continuity* with *futurity*.

2 Professional-affective continuities, 'radical' thematisations

The notion of signature seems to me to be applied, *in the university*, to practitioners whose work has achieved a certain notoriety over a period of time. It is used as short-hand to exemplify professional performance practice at a given moment. Curiously enough, however, that named work tends then to be abstracted from its situation and context of emergence – to be approached, in the university, as though it were historically transcendent. Its university-guaranteed transcendency seems to be linked to the 'academic' identification of challenges, 'in the work', to, and/or subversion of, dominant and established forms of performance.

Looking at challenging performance practices from the perspective of their mastery, their professional production values, and the place they have won for themselves within the dynamic institutions of performance, I have been inclined to assert, instead, that it is only through that mastery of the discipline or disciplines that *ongoing, signed* creative practices – which together come to constitute an oeuvre or body of work – can effectively *thematise* challenges to dominant forms. The claim, from performance studies, that the work of a particular practitioner is 'cutting edge', 'radical', interrogative or subversive of dominant forms, seems to me to misrecognise the *fact* of disciplinary mastery, upon which the success of 'radical' thematisations singularly depends.

Mnouchkine's work at the Théâtre du Soleil in the late 1960s and 1970s at least has been widely described as 'politically engaged', as 'radical' in its thematics and its uses, for example, of theatre spaces and performance stylistics and scripted or scriptable material. Yet, in my own argument here, it was always also *professional*, in its modes of operation and consistent production values, and has grown more so. The company's increasing professional, disciplinary expertise and mastery suggest to me at least that it is on the basis of their conservation *and development from within*, of professional production values, as well as their aspiration to the qualitative transformation of performance continuities, that certain practitioners are able to produce performance material which serves as medium to the performance articulation of a 'radical' thematics, *and not vice versa*. It seems to me to follow that in applauding 'radical', or 'liminal', or 'subversive', or 'culturally interrogative' performance practices,[14] certain performance studies writers have tended to overlook issues relating to the necessary mastery of performance disciplines, performance professions, performance institutions and institutional set-ups, performance expertise (and how to get it) as well as performance production values.

Theatre 'contexts' and historicity

Further contradictions are revealed when some of us in the university claim, with regard to expert practices or practitioners, that performance work has been produced upon the basis of, and hence reveals, the impact of historical contexts. The attempt at matching performance thematisations, after the event, to putatively determinant elements of cultural context seems to me to be wrong-headed, regardless of the appeal of such a formulation. Historical impact tends to be better grasped with the benefit of hindsight, as a number of recent reappraisals of cultural studies in the post-Second World War decades have pointed out, apparently ruefully.[15]

Žižek,[16] for instance, argues that certain cultural practices actualise and illuminate aspects of contemporary and other contexts and situations, *for their own spectators*, rather than vice versa: 'their own spectators', for the simple reason that decisions made in performance production are always calculated (even where this is denied) in terms of a relationship to and a triggering of certain sorts of engagements and actions in contemporary audiences. Just as *1789* – at the Roundhouse in London in the 1970s – actualised and illuminated for British audiences certain perceptions of the late 1960s in Paris, *Richard II* in the early 1980s functioned, for this spectator at least, to actualise and illuminate the compromise of the French Left under the presidency of Mitterrand – and not vice versa.

The affective signature

By what compositional means does Mnouchkine's work manage to function both as complex theatrical metaphor illuminating the everyday-political and the historical, and as what Banu once called a theatre of the Imaginary,[17] while inventing itself anew with each new production? I want to suggest that the 'art' in performing arts practices tends to involve and to emerge through the arts-professional *working* of 'resistant materialities'.[18]

Such *workings of resistant materialities* (in Mnouchkine's work, the video document suggests, this includes the apparently exasperating contribution in rehearsals, with a deadline looming, of a performer trained in older and intellectualising or psychologising traditions of directing and acting[19]) involve, in live performance practices, the director's engagement with a human actional and interactional plasticity which has already excited her professional curiosity; mixing and moulding the human aspirational with the human affective, through the application of one or another complex abstraction. Others have called the application of the abstract to the material – where expert performance is concerned – *mise-en-scène*. *Mise-en-scène* remains virtual, even when it is actualised in performance, to the extent that it is not identical with the fullness of the performance-materiality itself – which nonetheless it seems to regulate, and which serves, in addition, as its vehicle. Perhaps this complexity is involved, once again, in the mysteries of the signature.

The *working of the material by the (disciplinary or expert) immaterial* is pursued in significant part, in my experience, to the end of effecting those particular qualitative transformations of performance 'continuities' – within a disciplinary tradition and involving its further elaboration – which are likely (but not guaranteed) to *bind* a significant percentage of members of an expert audience *in* to the perceptual experience, to what it seems to conjure, its magic. It is this curious and fragile working of the resistant material by the immaterial, informed (as it is in my experience of

Mnouchkine's stagings) by what remains a startling sense of generosity, which seems to me to signal the gift that this work represents.

Mixed-mode theoretical practices

I have suggested above that the processes and the expert performance practices which bear a practitioner signature *are non-identical with* the practices – *bearing the same name* – which provide spectators (and spectator studies) with their preferred objects of analysis. I have suggested that spectator perspectives and practitioner perspectives are non-identical from a number of points of view, including those concerned with the differences between processes and outcomes; multi-participant production processes contrasted with single-spectator positioning; signed practitioner work and anonymous spectating. Théâtre du Soleil's *Tartuffe* is now, however, fixed and objectified; it is a matter of theatre history, not least because its production processes have been the subject of (and subjected to) video documentation by a professional video production company, and marketed through the theatre company itself in these terms. The resulting video document provides an insider account of a complex and lengthy production process, carried out in circumstances quite peculiar to the theatre company's work. I can replay it at will.

The account is an excellent 'multi-participant-relational' and 'multi-dimensional schematisation' of the sorts of work practices which the company regularly engages (and has done over some thirty years). Patently, it bears witness from a number of favoured positions, and has benefited from an ongoing access to (selected) performance-making processes. These processes seized 'on the (performance-making) ground' are contextualised here by scenes relating to budgetary difficulties, set design and construction, wardrobe and general management matters, as well as everyday scenes from life at the Cartoucherie on the literal margins of Parisian life.[20]

The video account actualises perceptions of theatre-making processes over a considerable period of time, in a way that no published written account has been able to. Its authorised 'bearing witness' recalls that earlier understanding of the term 'theoria' to which I alluded early in this chapter. Setting aside the dangers of the 'etymological fallacy' (where ancient definitions of terms are spuriously replayed in the current context), I want to bring the 'processional' account of 'theoria' into play in the case of this visual and actional 'theorisation' of the Théâtre du Soleil's working processes.

Theoria, in ancient Greek,[21] referred both to the action of observing and contemplating, and to the solemn procession, to a public audience, of the ambassadors who performed those actions. The 'first recorded "theorist" in Western history' was Solon, a 'Greek sage' who lived around 550 BC in the city of Athens. His reporting back was oral/embodied and performative in terms of maintaining its own authority over its audience, rather than written. The *theor*'s performance was embedded within a ritualised event, performed, it is noted, 'with ostentatious pomp', and he thereby gave his listeners the benefit of his acts of observation, contemplation, speculation and reflection, actions linked etymologically to the term 'theoria'.

'Others,' adds Ulmer, 'could see and make claims, but their reports would merely have the status of "perceptions" rather than public witness'. The term implied 'a complex but organic mode of active observation . . . that included asking questions, listening to stories and local myths, and feeling as well as seeing'. It encouraged 'an open reception to every kind of emotional, cognitive, symbolic, imaginative and sensory experience'. The best word for '*theoria*' in English, Ulmer adds, is 'curiosity'.

Curiosuty/ies

The video document seems to me to attempt to operate, with regard to these performance-making processes, in a particular professional context, in terms of what has been called *parallax*, which 'involves the apparent displacement of an object caused by the actual movement of its observer'.[22] In terms of the video-making processes, the video maker effects 'the apparent displacement of the [performance-making processes] by the actual movement of the [camera person]', but at one and the same time, the whole account – almost ambassadorial – is biographical, relating to the persona, in all of its various complex facets, of a wholly singular theatre-practitioner. The video document, through identification, selection, filming and editing processes (wholly banal, in this case), '*theorises*' her professional identity, and in so doing it also provides an exemplary account of the contemporary theatre director.

The account is both exemplary in the singularity of its subject – it is monstrous, in the scarcely-concealed self-affectation it also articulates – and it is banal, in its homage to her professional activity, with its endless, apparently pedestrian (but in fact expert) renegotiations. It shows how work proceeds when professional-creative expertise in collaborative mode provides its starting point, its moments of 'equipmental breakdown',[23] its attempts at coping, its necessary compromises, its intuitive flashes and the recentring consequent upon these; the operations of contingency, its retrieval, as well as its outcomes.

If you return to the first set of back-and-white images, included in Figure 8.1, you will see plainly that 'Mnouchkine's work' is not simply collaboratively produced, a matter of passion, and relational in its making processes, but also that, in the making, its detail occasionally escaped Mnouchkine's expert-practitioner will. It resisted in the short term at least her attempts at its development; it resisted her *wanting*, as well as – if I might put it this way – her 'knowledge-project', while also seeming to

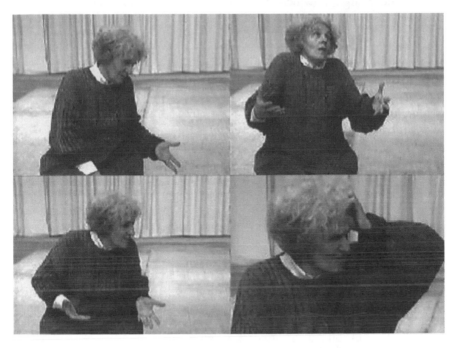

Figure 8.2　Ariane Mnouchkine in rehearsal at the Théâtre du Soleil. Stills from *Au soleil même la nuit, Scènes d'accouchements*, É. Darmon and C. Vilpoux, Théâtre du Soleil/Agat Films/La Sept Arte, 1997.

threaten her company's professional contracts. The nature of the work is such that, despite her experience and particular expertise, its quality as multi-participant and relational means that she is unable, in one notable case, to call forth the performer contribution which she seeks, from the actor cast in a central role.

Mnouchkine indicates elsewhere in this video account[24] that she will recognise what she wants from this performer's interaction with the others concerned, but cannot identify it in advance of their producing it in rehearsal, because it is interrelational, multi-participant and a matter of catalysis.[25] It will emerge (if indeed it does, within the time available in terms both of rehearsal budget and opening night) as something new conjured in the space between the two performers concerned and the onlooker(s), where that space-between is overlaid a number of times: a second set of 'transparencies', 'grids' and schematisations is specific to *mise-en-scène*; other abstractions (such as desire, such as performance aesthetic, such as an ethics of practice, such as signature) overlay these, and need to be juggled. Within each the Mnouchkine positioning is key, but so too is the positioning of the rest of the company, which you can see in Figure 8.1. These company members take up, in the rehearsal process, the positions and a ferocious version of the modes of expert spectating. Together this participation produces *in the event* that 'parallax' effect identified by Hal Foster, and to which I refer above. But they do so with this very clear difference, which is that 'the artist', in Foster, tends to be a solitary figure, and 'the work' an art 'object'.

The interconnected and shifting positionings, in 'epistemic'[26] terms, are affectively invested in the performance making a number of times over, and their working is teleoaffectively regulated – that is, such as to participate in the quest for a particular objective: not just 'the show', but its binding-in of a maximum of spectators to perceptions of a shared cultural history. Not only do the various professional participants share this objective, but it motivates their growing contribution, intervening, and not necessarily unproblematically, in all decisions taken. The work will be expected, by those involved in its production, to demonstrate a 'qualitative transformation' experienced in large part in individual terms, by each of the individual practitioners concerned – including Mnouchkine, and in relation to her own grasp of her preceding work. The full implications of that professional experience may emerge gradually, over a matter of years. Once again, its 'knowledge status', and how this is experienced, is variously lived, and difficult to generalise upon.

Mnouchkine herself, as far as I have been able to discern, articulates her grasp of these complexities twice over and differently: in words, she prefers humanist and popular registers, mixed with some performance technical/expert elements, but refuses what Ulmer calls 'explanatory myths'. Her discourse tends, despite the complexities of the practice, toward widely accessible registers. By way of contrast, in her complex heterogeneous professional performance-making practices, she exercises the various schematisations, their overlayering; the affective investments, the juggling of 'knowledge-engagements' and expertise; the trust in the contribution of other professional artists; the irritations, the delays, the developing expectations, the 'emergent premises'; the intuitive flash and recentring enabled by the Aha! moment; the drive, the revisions, the 'equipmental breakdowns' and the compromise, but also the 'knowledge-withholding mastery'.

Mnouchkine's expertise is such that she can count on her already-proven ability to conjure and/or to summon forth what will, in her own experience, *work* in public performance, with this particular cluster of performance professionals, even at the most extreme moments of creative crisis and 'equipmental breakdown', yet it is as clear, from the video account of performance-making processes, that her considerable expertise cannot predetermine what might spring forth from the particular intersections which she establishes, and which she overlays with the specificity of Molière's dramatic writing of *Tartuffe*.

Her own excitement, which seems to me to be palpable in the video document, and her own professional-artistic challenge, lies then in her *not knowing what will emerge* when she seeks to actualise that dramatic writing in a performance arena whose own architectural and design specifics relate, twice over, to the traditions of the Cartoucherie itself, and to the Franco/Algerian colonialist thematics which this production will also enable her to work with.[27] She does not know what will emerge, yet patently, when 'it' emerges in the space between the individual performers, she will recognise its aesthetic force and its contribution to the growing production. This sort of observation about knowing and not-yet-knowing, plus the phenomenon of recognition, tends to challenge the supposition, in many parts of the university, that *we know (in expert practice) what we know*.

Affective conclusions

The production of *Tartuffe*, by the Théâtre du Soleil, could only *work* professionally if the production company had made decisions relating to the interface of affective investments, disciplinary mastery and production logics, and was able, in professional terms, to carry these through to each event of spectating. Affect was once defined by Deleuze and Guattari[28] in terms of something mediated by 'the moving body in itself' – which I should want to further qualify here, with performance expertise in mind, in terms of 'performance-expert moving bodies'. Affects, then, involve 'speeds and compositions of speed among elements', and they 'are projectiles just like weapons' in the competent hands of the master *metteur en scène*. Mnouchkine's work emits projectiles, however much it is also the case that these are passionate and tender, at one and the same time. 'Feelings', on the other hand, 'are introceptive like tools', and thereby become available *to me*, when I am attempting to deal with questions relating to the interface, between stage narrativity, the operation of performance systems, and questions relating to thematics and spectating. It has always appeared to me to be the case, *after* my experience of each of Mnouchkine's productions, that I have sought to qualify my own affective engagement in terms like 'reconciliation', 'loss', 'generosity' and 'joyfulness', which emerge when I have been able to map aspects relating to context, situation – even 'history' – over the surviving traces of my own affective engagement. Emotions, according to Brian Massumi, are affects requalified, in the sorts of terms which are conventionally available to us.

Now, the production will have *worked* its professional engagement if and when a majority of individual spectators are bound-in, experiencing and participating in any number of little affective 'events'. I have been struck, over the decades, by the quantity and quality of the applause which has met each production from the company – at a sense of something like a gift offered and a gift received; at a sense of generosity, on the part of performers and production team, and our acknowledgement of that generosity. As spectator I have experienced my own little affective events, which seemed to be political in the late 1960s, but emerged as openly 'metatheoretical/theatrical' in the early 1980s. For the rest, I can only, as writer-educator, fall back on my sense of what the applause, at the end of the show, seemed to signal with regard to others' experience.

Notes

1 See reference to the constitutive operations of hypotyposis in my 'Textual Turn . . .', at http://www.sfmelrose.u-net.com.
2 'Ephemerality' figures in Eugenio Barba's writing published in the 1980s and 1990s (see, for example, his 'Four Spectators', in *The Drama Review*, 1, 1990), as well as in Peggy Phelan's *Unmarked: The Politics of Performance*, London and New York: Routledge, 1993.
3 B. Massumi, *Parables for the Virtual*, Durham and London: Duke University Press, 2002.
4 G. Ulmer, *Teletheory: Grammatology in the Age of Video*, London and New York: Routledge, 1989.
5 P. Phelan, *Unmarked*. On p. 11, Phelan considers 'the political dimensions of the encounter between self and other', noting that theoretical writing is always also autobiographical, and should proceed to identify itself as such.
6 D. Williams, ed., *Collaborative Theatre: Le Théâtre du Soleil Sourcebook*, London and New York: Routledge, 1999.
7 *Au soleil même la nuit, Scènes d'accouchements*, É. Darmon et C. Vilpoux, Théâtre du Soleil/Agat Films/La Sept Arte, Paris 1997.
8 Massumi, *Parables for the Virtual*.
9 T. Schatzki, 'Practice Mind-ed Orders', in T. Schatzki *et al.*, eds., *The Practice Turn in Contemporary Theory*, London and New York: Routledge, 2001. The prefix 'teleo-' signals a concern with objectives; hence these are performance choices calculated, in part at least, in terms of their contribution to the Mnouchkine 'little world' and their likely contribution to the production of spectator affects. Even choices in casting may well be teleoaffective in part: Georges Bigot, who played Richard in Mnouchkine's *Richard II* (1982), offers – as one detail of the Mnouchkine signature – a stark, dark-featured facial clarity across which spectator projections readily play.
10 K. Knorr-Cetina considers the epistemic (or 'knowledge-practice') status of research strategies and processes in her 'Objectual Practice', in Schatzki, *The Practice Turn in Contemporary Theory*, pp. 175–88.
11 Massumi, *Parables for the Virtual*, p. 4.
12 Massumi, *Parables for the Virtual*, p. 4.
13 G. Ulmer, *Heuretics: The Logic of Invention*, Baltimore and London: Johns Hopkins University Press, 1994.
14 See, for example, J. McKenzie's *Perform . . . Or Else: From Discipline to Performance* (New York and London: Routledge, 2001) on this question of the 'mainstreamisation', in the university, of interrogation, through performance, of dominant forms (except those represented by the university itself as institution).
15 Hal Foster's introduction to *The Return of The Real: The Avant-Garde at the End of the Century* (Cambridge, MA and London: MIT Press, 1996) provides one example of this rather rueful return to (his own writerly past in) the 1970s and 1980s art-critical and art-theoretical scenes.

16 S. Žižek, *Organs Without Bodies: On Deleuze and Consequences*, New York and London: Routledge, 2004.

17 G. Banu, *L'Acteur qui ne revient pas*, Paris: Aubier, 1986.

18 The notion of resistant materialities comes from a number of sources, including N. K. Hayles, *How We Became Posthuman: Virtual Bodies in Cybernetics, Literature and Informatics* (Chicago and London: University of Chicago Press, 1999). Most, if not all, bear the impact of the psychoanalytic theory of Jacques Lacan, for whom 'the Real' is one of three linked terms: the Imaginary, the Symbolic and the Real. The Real, in Lacan, is neither symbolic (like language) nor imaginary (like image-stuff), both liable to a certain extent to be accessed and exchanged; the Real resists, as an 'ineliminable residue of all articulation', an impossibility which is resistant to human attempts at capturing it (J. Lacan, *The Four Fundamental Concepts of Psycho-Analysis*, ed. J.-A. Miller, trans. A. Sheridan, London: Vintage, 1998).

19 You can see a detail of this difficult process in Figure 8.1.

20 The Cartoucherie, former munitions factory, is on the eastern edge of Paris, just outside the *Périphérique*.

21 G. Ulmer, *Heuretics*, p. 120.

22 H. Foster, *Return of the Real*, p. xii.

23 I owe this term to the Heideggerian tradition, reread by a number of 'practice theoreticians', including Knorr Cetina, in her 'Objectual Practice', and Herbert Dreyfus, 'How Heidegger Defends the Possibility of a Correspondence Theory of Truth . . .', both in Schatzki, *The Practice Turn in Contemporary Theory*.

24 You can see some shots of her speaking on this subject in Figure 8.2.

25 Catalysis has occurred when the outcome is greater than the sum of its parts; that is, when those individual elements catalyse each other, in a process of mutual (and qualitative) transformation.

26 Or 'knowledge object' and 'knowledge practice', in Knorr Cetina, 'Objective Practice'.

27 The Molière text permits her to show the entry of the stranger into the heart of the 'North African' domestic scene, and in the mid-1990s that stranger is both fundamentalism and it is an older French colonial 'invasion' of Algeria.

28 G. Deleuze and F. Guattari, *A Thousand Plateaus: Capitalism and Schizophrenia*, trans. B. Massumi, Minneapolis: University of Minnesota Press, 1987, p. 400.

Chapter 9

Marshfield Mummers
The Old Time Paper Boys

Mike Pearson

It's 11am on Boxing Day in the village of Marshfield in Gloucestershire, England. In the Market Place, the carol singing has just ended and the silver band has put away its instruments. Amongst villagers and visitors alike, there is growing expectancy. Faintly, in the distance, a hand bell rings, begins its approach. To one side of the square the crowd parts and the Town Crier appears, wearing black coat and top hat trimmed with a yellow band. Behind him, in single file, there emerges a file of extraordinary figures, fantastically dressed, covered from crown to knee in strips of paper, with faces hidden, shimmering as they move. First comes Father Christmas in red and white streamers; next the braggart Little Man John (*'If anyone defy me, let them come on'*) in tea-stained, brown paper and carrying his wooden sword; then heroic, multicoloured King William (*'A man of courage and bold, With my sword and spear all in my hand, I gained three crowns of gold'*). Doctor Phoenix (*'I'm a noble doctor, I can do more than any man can. I can cure the itch, the stitch, the palsy and the gout, All pains within and none without'*) wears a costume covered in yellowing newsprint. Saucy Jack, Tenpenny Nit and Old Father Beelzebub all follow, accompanied by several money collectors in similar attire, and the Sheetman, who – at the centre of the space that the performers have begun to clear – lays a square of canvas bearing the words 'Marshfield Mummers'.[1] The main figures halt and stand equally spaced around the circle that their entry has described.

So, it begins. The Town Crier introduces *'The celebrated Marshfield Mummers, The Old Time Paper Boys'*, removes his hat and bows: *'God save the Queen.'* One after another the figures enter, identifying themselves and their purpose in a short text. Father Christmas, the main presenter, steps in with the words *'In comes I, Old Father Christmas.'* He speaks a few lines whilst turning and occasionally flourishing his incongruous sword: *'Christmas comes but once a year, Then we generally get good cheer. Roast beef, plum pudding and mince pies. Who likes that better than King William and I?'* He exits with the words *'Room, room, a gallant room I say, If Little Man John is in the room, Let him step this way.'* In comes Little Man John who, after a short boast whilst slashing with *his* sword, challenges his adversary: *'If King William is in the room, Let him step this way.'* King William enters, also extolling his own prowess whilst brandishing his two weapons: *'I fought the fiery dragon, And brought him to the slaughter, And by the means of that, I gained the hand of the Queen of Europe's daughter.'* They fight – in a perfunctory clash of wooden props – and with few histrionics Little Man John falls dead upon the tarpaulin. The crowd boos. King William calls upon Doctor Phoenix, who proclaims his own powers and with a small bottle of 'old English turpentide [sic]' – *'I place a drop on his lips, And a drop on his thigh'* – revives and helps to his feet the fallen warrior: *'Rise, arise Little Man John, I long to see thee stand. Open thine eyes and look around. I'll take thee by the hand.'* The crowd cheers. There then follows the so-called *quête* of subsidiary characters: Saucy Jack – *'Wife and family at me back'* – who bears a haversack filled with small dolls, including a single black one; local hard man Tenpenny Nit – *'With my big head and my little wit'* – who strikes himself on the head with his sword as if to prove *'My head is hard as iron, My body's tough as steel'*; and Old Father Beelzebub – *'On my shoulder I carry my club. And in my hand my money pan'* – who concludes with an appeal: *'A little of your Christmas ale, Would make us boys dance and sing. A little of your money in our pockets, Would be a jolly fine thing.'* All finally sing an enigmatic song in three verses – *'It's of a noble Welshman I heard the*

Figure 9.1   The Marshfield Mummers. The fight. Photograph: Mike Pearson.

people say, As I rode up to London all on St David's Day' – to accompany a shuffling, circular dance. The bell rings, the canvas is lifted and they are gone. Their performance has not lasted more than six minutes.

The Town Crier leads them away. Proceeding along the High Street, they repeat their play at the junctions of Sheep Fair Lane/Touching End Lane and St Martin's Lane – where further crowds await them – and then at the western edge of the village in front of the almshouses, founded in the early seventeenth century. On their return they perform outside one of the village public houses, the landlord offering them sherry or whisky. In recent years their last performance has taken place in front of the house of the late Edgar Lewis – builder, stonemason and one of the original troupe of 1930. After this, they are invited inside by his daughter for more drink and mince pies. The whole event – six performances – has taken just over an hour. Shortly each man will put his costume back into a suitcase in the attic, until next year.

This form of traditional drama or mummers' play – a short dramatic performance with an orally transmitted spoken text, mostly in rhyme and seasonally performed by young men and boys mainly in the midwinter period around Christmas and New Year – was once found widely in agricultural communities of lowland England (and the industrial north).[2] The Marshfield play is of a type known as the *hero-combat* in which there is usually an introduction, a boast, a fight – often between St George and the Turkish Knight – a death, a lament, a cure and a resurrection at the hands of a quack Doctor, followed by the *quête* and collection.[3] Throughout the nineteenth century these plays were presented annually by groups of labourers who visited the large houses and farms, often over a wide area of their district. Their object – in a season of little work and material hardship – was to gain admission and to extract food, drink and money as reward for their performance. The activity also served to nurture camaraderie amongst its participants, particularly in their collusive acts of domestic intrusion. In return, the exhibition of hospitality by the hosts was socially cohesive. In the Marshfield text there are constant reminders of this, of the 'indoors' now become 'outdoors'. Father Christmas demands, *'If Little Man John is in the room, let him step this way.'* Old Father Beelzebub incites us to *'sit down at your ease'* and adds *'And give us what you please'*. By the 1880s the mummers' plays had begun to disappear – with rural depopulation resulting from agricultural depression, increasing mechanisation and the breaking of large estates; through the dispersal of labourers and the drift to the cities. Few survived the traumatic effects of the first world war and the killing and demoralisation of so many carriers of tradition. But their passing also proceeded from a change of tone in the nature of rural culture, not solely through the influence of educational advancement offered by the 1870 Education Act but wrought by working people themselves in their embrace of Primitive Methodism, Temperance and Friendly Societies – with shifting attitudes to prudence and mutual- and self-reliance – and the nascent collectivism of Joseph Arch's National Agricultural Labourers' Union of 1872. All these movements espoused degrees of independence and individuality and offered new varieties of popular entertainment and 'rational recreation': parades, dinners, outings, galas, sporting events. The begging implicit in mumming and the increasingly attendant consumption of alcohol were viewed as undesirable. From as early as 1840 the *Stamford Mercury* regularly criticised the activity in Lincolnshire – my home area – as 'a subsidiary of getting money for drink', leading to 'riot and excess', and as heathen and pagan. '[The] frequent adjournment to the public-houses is a material drawback', it noted in 1884.[4] In 1898 the Barrow-on-Humber troupe were fined for assault, and when one of the West Halton team froze to death after a drunken fall, the constable of Alkborough 'set his face against the practice'.[5]

Yet such customs were venerated by an emerging generation of folklorists as relics of a threatened and vanishing Arcady. Organisations such as the Folklore Society, founded in 1878, were dedicated to collecting and preserving lore and ceremony. But Cecil Sharp's English Folk Dance Society of 1911 had the added aspiration of promoting English folk dances; Sharpe was both an advocate of traditional practices and participant in the first revival movement, publishing dances for new middle-class participants. Similar enthusiasms fired Violet Alford, author of *Introduction to English Folklore*;[6] the play at Marshfield is itself a revival under her influence. In an apocryphal story, her brother C. S. L. Alford, the rector of Marshfield, still at that time a largely self-sufficient community, was greeted by his aged gardener Edwin Harding with the words *'In comes I Old Father Christmas.'* He informed Alford, and in 1930 she encouraged three older men of the village to remember all they could of mumming from the 1880s and to teach the text to a group of younger inhabitants – nothing was written down; all words and actions were committed directly to memory. Whilst apparently careful not to school them, her attention was demanding and Edgar Lewis was himself coerced into participating as Old Father Beelzebub. The current play is thus a *reconstitution* of the remains of what its initial participants knew and recalled: there is a break in its history. Indeed we should suspect any claims of unbroken continuity in such practices. They were always susceptible to changes, additions, losses, to alterations during oral transmission, through the inheritance of actions by one body from another. And this was compounded by the lack of a permanent cast: untenured labourers annually moved from farm to farm, bringing, and taking, performative and dramaturgical knowledge and abilities with them. The plays were always in flux; there was never a moment when they were 'how they were supposed to be'. They were ephemeral, existing only in moments of performance. And this perception might cause us to doubt any claims of authenticity – of 'this is just how it was' – in the exposition of contemporary heritage culture.

Folklore scholarship has long concentrated upon the origins of mummers' plays and upon analysis of their textual components. Mid-twentieth-century commentators such as Alex Helm imagined ritual origins for the plays, seeing the action – the recurrent motif of combat, death and resurrection – as a survival, with the text as an accretion, a later rationalisation of a pattern of activity that had lost its ritual function.[7] The term 'mumming' possibly derives from the Old Danish root *mumme* – to mask or hide – and Helm was much concerned with the significance of disguise: 'The anonymity made the performers entirely different beings, remote from their everyday lives'.[8] Recent academic analysis has focused upon the scripts themselves, pointing to theatrical precursors and to the wide dissemination of the plays through chapbook versions in the nineteenth century, although no one single source-text has been identified. However, concerted efforts by the Traditional Drama Research Group have done much to demonstrate and illuminate performative aspects of mumming.[9]

The plays might best be viewed as sanctioned forms of alms gathering that incorporated novelty and theatrical elaboration – from a variety of sources – as a means to an end. Transmuted from this original purpose, they have now become *ludic* pursuits, although the collection of money still gives an ostensible sense of purpose to the activity: it has charitable (and altruistic) objectives. Beyond personal reasons for involvement – of social responsibility (keeping tradition alive) and desire (the enjoyment of performing) – it enables the Marshfield performers to rationalise what they do. The collectors regard the opportunity to meet the crowd as an active stimulus to sociability. The money will go eventually to local charities, though specifically which ones will not be decided for several weeks. So, the crowd gives – gives to the Mummers – who respond with performance, with all that they have. All present are linked in giving, in gift exchange: it is this that nurtures the provisional, and pleasurable, communality.

I first saw photographs of the Marshfield troupe in the late 1960s in Alan Brody's *The English Mummers and their Plays*: King William with his sword and sceptre, figures in the Market Place captioned 'The Stage as Circle' and the sword fight outside the Almshouses entitled 'The Play as an Action'. Whilst Brody's work is now regarded as largely derivative[10] – he probably never witnessed a live performance – he sees the questions central to an understanding of the mummers' plays (the relationship between actor and spectator, the nature of the playing area, the purpose of performance) reflected in the then contemporary work of The Living Theater, Jerzy Grotowski, Barba's Odin Teatret and Bread and Puppet Theater. 'The occasion, the stage, the performers, the costume, the style of acting, the attitude of the performers to the text, and the audience are all subject to conventions far removed from those of the realistic proscenium theater,'[11] he surmises, and proposes that his study might help in the understanding of these experimental initiatives with their emphasis upon ritualistic qualities and elements

– significantly he begins by quoting Artaud. For him the mummers' plays represent conflict at an elemental level, stripped to the basics of opposing forces, and his structural analysis lays emphasis upon the performing of the action – identifying the visit, the circle and the acting style as constitutive features. And all this was suggestive for a young imagination seeking an effective genealogy for, and conceptual and analytical approaches to, the burgeoning alternative theatre of the late 1960s.

But it was in the scratchy drawings in Richard Southern's *The Seven Ages of the Theatre* – themselves impressions of the photographs Brody would later publish – that I first encountered the Marshfield Mummers.[12] For Southern, theatre – 'an address through "doing"' – 'depends on a concentrated effort on one particular occasion',[13] involving the employment of the personal resources of the player – voice, gesture, appearance, instruments/properties – and the secondary resources of place, stage and scenery. His *seven ages* model is based upon an ahistorical evolution of theatrical space in phases rather than dated periods: each of his phases may exist contemporaneously, although he, too, constantly appeals to primitive origins. He places the Marshfield Mummers in his first phase, that of the Costumed Player: 'The whole man is transformed into a walking, rustling, white anonymity of fluttering.'[14] In this earliest moment of theatrical encounter, there is *visitation* by men in disguise, at a particular season. For him as well the action is at the core of the mummers' play: he focuses his critical attention upon the procession, the circle and the killing. And again this was instructive for a nascent physical theatre, identifying potential predecessors and a genus of unlikely fellow practitioners.

I first saw the Marshfield Mummers perform on a frosty day in 2001. They were revelatory: their performance – in its simplicity and clarity of exposition   utilises, demonstrates and displays for scrutiny a series of foundational mechanisms and organising principles enacted elsewhere – albeit schematically or momentarily – in contemporary forms of alternative theatre. Cass has pointed to the inappropriate use of conventional notions of drama and theatre in the critique of the plot, text and performance of mummers' plays:[15] early commentators frequently lamented the expressionless, declamatory style with little attempt to represent character. They are more effectively apprehended, I suggest, through the interdisciplinary approaches of performance studies, and – in the use of space, modes of engagement and dramaturgical structure – may further inform analytical approaches to the nature of performance. And in the disavowal of realist conventions for the staging of dramatic literature – favouring figure over character, manifestation over psychological depth, sequence over plot, site over stage – the work is itself, I contend, resolutely contemporary.

The genesis, delineation and formalisation of performance space is precisely enacted and – springing from the action itself – almost instantaneous here: there are no ropes or tapes or bollards to orientate either performers or spectators. The Mummers are drawn into a circle by the Town Crier, who may walk round once, twice, before stopping at his point of entry. 'I get them settled, then get them on their way,' he told me. Processing and entering in the same order, they always take up the same position on an unmarked street corner: their knowledge of this landscape is intimate. They know where they stand, ready to cue each other, although by the performance at the Almshouses they are confident enough to change places, to confound King William and to add moments of humour as he seeks his old enemy. They adopt a circle as the most basic of performative configurations.[16] The circle affects the type, nature and quality of the activity and its reception. They have an empirical understanding of the requirements of performing here: they walk and turn whilst speaking; they stand at the centre to declaim. With their backs to the crowd, they hold the circle intact. And the fall of Little Man John is mediated by the road surface; there is the restraint of enactment here.

The Mummers inscribe a performative map upon that of the everyday: a group of men – now rendered 'other' – visit their fellow inhabitants and spread the effect of their work through the village. For one hour traffic stops and streets fill with people as they move through a series of precise *locales* that – although these have changed within memory – are currently perceived to be the best places *for* performance. Local public houses formerly had a unique dispensation to open on Boxing Day, leading to a sense of reverie and contravention. There is still a suspension of the social order, and it is political. As Marshfield becomes a commuter village for local towns and cities, the cottages of farm labourers change hands for inflated prices. For a short time the Mummers repossess their community, a community within which increasingly few of them will be able to afford to live. Significantly, new voices have begun to voice opposition to the disruption they bring. With the advent of laws demanding that each locale shall have a separate licence to ensure public safety and crowd control, their activity may yet become transgressive once more, as the traditional confronts the bureaucratic: performance as social action.

The pattern here is that of a *punctuated procession*: a traversing of the village, a precise choreography within an extant architectural configuration with irregular nodes or densities of activity. Encounters, events and physical intercourse are prescribed, choreographed and staged in relation to a particular space. The costumed bodies of the Mummers – strategically deployed in extra-daily practices – are framed and observed in relation to particular facades, backdrops and screens; their movement is channelled through crowded streets that regulate patterns of visibility and hidden-ness – an articulation of watchers and watched. Performative analysis here might better focus upon the *ergonomic* relationships between body and environment and upon the shifting nature of viewpoint. For the Mummers there are two basic modes of engagement – procession and performance

– with very different degrees of formality, though no periods of rest, and signalled spatially rather than by major changes in rhetorical expression. It resembles an interrupted practice, with varying degrees of intensity of engagement. On procession, they may talk to visitors and greet villagers, though this is difficult in single file, especially when windy.

Strips of paper must have been a rare commodity in rural communities in the mid-nineteenth century and the Mummers value the uniqueness of their costume: this is not 'fancy dress' but a symbol of identity, and of links to the past. Several of the costumes – such as those of Father Christmas, Saucy Jack and Old Man Beelzebub – are original, dating to 1930, with paper that is sewn on and that must be regularly renewed; it is possible to find on them dated fragments of newspaper of different ages, literally to read their past. One costume was made by the village carpenter, the paper affixed with wood glue: even today it is impossible to pierce it with a needle. They are extremely durable   surviving adverse weather – though they do require recurrent renovation. Each costume is maintained by the individual performer and there is a concern that some performers are not taking enough care to cover their faces. The performers are in disguise, although their community knows each individual by voice and demeanour. But perhaps their covered faces do help release inhibitions: Father Christmas appreciates the fact that he can't see much, though few like wind as the blowing paper strips affect vision and cut the face.

The Mummers never rehearse the play together, apart from a cursory recitation of lines shortly before 11am. Preparation is an individual responsibility and this is done over different trajectories of time: one individual never rehearsed with the others for fifty years and regarded it as 'a damn waste of time'. But all acknowledge that this is what they do on Boxing Day – this gathering of a particular group of men, who may not meet from one year to the next. It is what Boxing Day consists of, for them and their ancestors. There are too the imperatives, the disciplinary requirements, of tradition and continuity, ways of doing things, that – given the longevity of performers – ensures a direct connection with the aesthetics of the performers of the revival. There is a strong sense of how texts should be spoken; what actions are appropriate. And since the tradition is carried by certain families there are direct links to former Mummers, to their ways of doing things: several older Mummers still admit to hearing former colleagues in the roles. As John Barrett suggests, they write into existence the presence of ancestors.[17] One admits to thickening his local accent during the play, as an homage to the past, to this place. There is 'the possibility of a meaning which seems to originate beyond their own world of everyday experience'.[18] Succession is through a number of related family lines though there is an agreed process of apprenticeship. The novice begins as a collector and advances to Sheetman who, as first reserve, must know all the parts lest someone falls ill, though most learn the complete text as children. The present Father Christmas knew his part when he took it, though he is conscious that he uses different hand movements and reactions and emphasises different words, without changing the text. But he can hear his own father's voice as he does it; his father avers that he could step back in if required.

The performance of the Marshfield play involves the modification of the vocal and physical resources of the performer, including elements of *mimesis*: 'hard man' Tenpenny Nit is portrayed in his posture *as* a hard man, King William swaggers after the fight. There is, however, little attempt at characterisation (King William: 'When I've got the costume on, I am King William. That's it, end of story'). There is need of different tones of voice and extra-daily physical behaviour. And it's in the detail that innovation occurs, sometimes through accidents of speech or loss of memory, more often through conscious additions: changes are both momentary and glacial. Tenpenny Nit wears a helmet so that he can strike himself on the head to show that it is indeed made of iron; it is locally agreed that his build and demeanour fit the part. He himself comments,

> In drama you try to assess how good your performance was and whether the audience appreciate it but I don't think we're quite the same when we perform our play in the streets. We're not really that worried. You know, we want the audience to be able to hear it and enjoy it but it's more important to us to get it right rather than get it right for the audience. It's a difficult feeling to explain but we're doing it for ourselves as much as we're doing it for anyone else whereas if you're in a play or something you want to try and perhaps get into the character more and portray it whereas I feel that I know my character is supposed to be hard man or whatever and I try to portray that a little bit but whether Father Beelzebub is trying to get himself psyched up to be the devil or King William is psyching himself up to be royalty is another matter isn't it.

The Mummers admit that their performance has become more theatrical: formerly there were few movements to accompany the words. The performance of late nineteenth-century mummers was characterised by a seriousness of demeanour, upright stances and minimal and stylised gestures. But the Mummers retain a strong sense of their own stylistic conventions, without resorting to pantomimic gestures. They do not seek audience approbation through their performance and opportunities to monitor response and to alter the dramatic engagement accordingly are few, given the duration of the play and the limited visual and auditory capacity of the costumed performers. They are engaged rather in declamation, addressed neither directly to their colleagues nor to specific sections of the crowd. The need for strength of voice is stressed (even if this involves shouting and hoarseness), and increasing quietness is deemed a potential reason for retirement, though longevity is a feature of Marshfield. There are only seven speaking roles and some individuals spend fifty years in the part – several current performers are in their seventies. Wind is again regarded as problematic as it 'takes' the voice and makes hearing and cueing difficult; cold, clear mornings, when the voice 'travels', are generally favoured. And in the short rehearsal there are constant exhortations to slow down, to keep the articulation of text clear against the street noise.

Some of the Mummers admit to nervousness. 'But once you're actually there doing it, it's totally different, once you're all dressed up and you see everybody else dressed up' says Saucy Jack. Some stress the potential distractions of performing in the circle – the danger of looking at the crowd, of recognising friends and relations – as the mind might wander and they might miss the cue, forget to come in; memories of mistakes linger in the collective memory. Several deny that they are a person 'to stand up and perform', insisting it is just what they do on Boxing Day. 'The thing is it's nothing major really, is it? You just go in the circle, say your lines and get out again and that's it. But to actually do it, that's something else.' Several have particular strategies of survival: walking round the circle once will get them to the end of their text; watching for dance steps may be more effective than listening for the song. If one forgets his lines, he can rest assured that they will emerge from another of the shrouded figures. The performance in the Market Place enables them to remember their performance in front of the largest crowd: 'But as soon as I open my mouth it just comes out . . . apart from once last year.' And they have superstitions. Father Christmas always wears the same pair of gloves and King William carries a sprig of mistletoe in his top pocket. As the morning progresses the performers become tired, but they also relax   they've remembered how to do it! So they catch each other with moments of tactical improvisation and humour: Little Man John changes places in the circle to confuse King William.

The narrative structure of the play derives from the single incident of conflict: the fight is preceded by boast, challenge, counter-challenge; it is followed by death, revival and celebration. But the performance exists rather as a sequence of directives and obligations not predicated upon dramatic notions of motive, character and timing: *'If Tenpenny Nit is in the room, Let him step this way.'* The dynamic is one of inevitability: figures must enter when they are announced and must in turn announce their fellow. First, they stand and wait. Each performer must ensure a continuum of presence, which, whilst it may be informal, must not jeopardise the overall tenor of the occasion; this requires decorum. They watch each other; they do not commit irrelevant acts. They exercise self-restraint – in words and actions – for the communal good of the performance. Then, they enter and perform: the resources of the performer are assembled and committed in a single impulsive moment, with the words '*In comes I*'. And each figure enters with an explicitly performative utterance, denoting his intentionality. '*In comes I*' is at once an annunciation, a declaration of intent, an existential affirmation, a transitive action, an identification, an entrée . . . He is solely responsible for the delivery of his text and in his few lines, with extreme brevity, he must establish his identity, his history, his prowess and his purpose and then introduce and cue his colleague before exiting. Yet he performs with only a limited range of gestures to emphasise moments in the text, without the audience empathy that might result from facial expression and the intricacies of character and narrative development that dramatic interplay might presume. Early entries constitute *inciting incidents*, changes of consequence and their trajectories; they advance the story such as it is. But the figures of the *quête* – freed from any function within the narrative – have an autonomous and ambiguous performative existence: their presence, their function and the effect they create are effectively conflated.

There are complexities to positioning the Marshfield Mummers genealogically. This is certainly not some kind of *ur*-drama from which all theatre has evolved, though commentators have pointed to features shared with the surviving Romanian *kalusari* play,[19] 'Les Rouges' and 'Les Noirs' in the French Pyrenees[20] and examples from Thessaly and Macedonia.[21] The Mummers themselves distinguish their activity *from* drama – several deny that they are actors – although their play may have theatrical antecedents and constitute a very degraded form. In relocating it within a spectrum of alternative performance practices, it must first be acknowledged that the Mummers themselves – and similar exponents – have informed and influenced the development of these very forms: there is a debt to their visual aesthetics in the celebratory events of Welfare State;[22] in his film *Being and Doing*[23] Stuart Brisley juxtaposes representations of English customary practices with performance art. But the Mummers are themselves present and effective in the public domain: they know 'how to go on' there. In their work, we see enacted familiar features of contemporary performance: the creation of transitory space as in the street performances of Odin Teatret[24] and the uncompromising actions of La Fura dels Baus; interrupted or discontinuous practice as employed by the performers of Forced Entertainment;[25] the use of costume-as-disguise as in the projects of André Stitt;[26] the creation of task-based performances as in the work of many contemporary performance artists.[27] At Marshfield we see them clearly, without ironic intent or in the hope of adulation. They are present in ways that might assist clearer understandings of their existence elsewhere.

In March 2003, I interviewed all the current Marshfield Mummers and several retired members. I asked no questions about origins or meanings, concentrating instead upon the play in performance and their own practices, hoping to reveal – performer to performer – mutualities of interest and inclination. Most were surprised to be asked about nervousness and superstitions and feelings, and then forthcoming, delighted to reveal their empirical knowledge: in personal anecdote, candid opinion and vague recollection. Some of this was familiar – the common experience of performing in front of others, some surprising – a certain ambivalence about the need for preparation. But all reinforced an increasing personal urge to reorientate the enquiry of performance studies from spectatorship – both aesthetic and academic – and towards a more acute concern with – a closer listening to – what practitioners themselves perceive that they are doing. This may always have been the intention of Eugenio Barba's theatre anthropology project.[28] But I am concerned to reposition the *articulate practitioner* at the heart of the discipline. Unique experiences such as those of the Marshfield Mummers – appearing on one occasion per year with little rehearsal in often difficult environmental conditions – begins to provide ways of discussing modes of contemporary performance within which the familiar terminology of character, motive, plot no longer seems useful. 'The thing is it's nothing major really, is it? You just go in the circle, say your lines and get out again and that's it. But to actually do it, that's something else.'

The activity of the Marshfield Mummers, The Old Time Paper Boys, is a calendar custom: it takes place at a particular time on a certain day in a specific place. It will, with luck, be there next year and in ten years' time, too.

Acknowledgements

My sincerest thanks go to the Marshfield Mummers and particularly to Bernard Fishlock, tireless secretary and advocate of the Mummers . . . and Tenpenny Nit.

Notes

1 B. Fishlock, *The History of the Mummers*, Marshfield: Marshfield Mummers, 1999.
2 See E. C. Cawte, A. Helm and N. Peacock, *English Ritual Drama: A Geographical Index*, London: The Folklore Society, 1967, pp. 31–66.
3 E. Cass and S. Roud, *Room, Room, Ladies and Gentlemen . . .: An Introduction to the English Mummers' Play*, London: English Folk Dance and Song Society, 2002, pp. 35–9.
4 R. C. Russell, *From Cock-fighting to Chapel Building*, Heckington, Lincolnshire: Heritage Trust of Lincolnshire, 2002, pp. 18–20.
5 M. W. Barley, 'Plough Plays in the East Midlands', *Journal of the English Folk Dance and Song Society*, 7, 2, 1953, pp. 68–105 (p. 76).
6 V. Alford, *Introduction to English Folklore*, London: G. Bell & Son Ltd, 1952.
7 Cawte *et al.*, *English Ritual Drama*, pp. 29–30; Cass and Roud, *Room, Room*, pp. 17–18.

8 A. Helm, *The English Mummers' Play*, Woodbridge, Suffolk: D. S. Brewer/The Folklore Society, 1980, pp. 37–45.
9 http://www.shef.ac.uk/uni/projects/tdrg.
10 E. Cass, M. J. Preston and P. Smith, *The English Mumming Play: An Introductory Bibliography*, London: FLS Books, 2000, p. 7.
11 A. Brody, n.d., *The English Mummers and their Plays: Traces of Ancient Mystery*, London: Routledge and Kegan Paul, 1969, p. 14.
12 R. Southern, *The Seven Ages of the Theatre*, London: Faber and Faber, 1962, pp. 45–61.
13 Southern, *Seven Ages*, p. 23.
14 Southern, *Seven Ages*, p. 47.
15 Cass and Roud, *Room, Room*, pp. 41–44.
16 M. Pearson and M. Shanks, *Theatre/Archaeology*, London: Routledge, 2001, pp. 20–2.
17 J. C. Barrett, 'Towards an Archaeology of Ritual', in P. Garwood, A. Fitzpatrick and L. McInnes, eds., *Sacred and Profane*, Oxford: Oxford University Committee for Archaeology, 1991, p. 5.
18 Barrett, 'Towards an Archaeology of Ritual', p. 5.
19 Brody, *The English Mummers*, pp. 163–6; Helm, *The English Mummers' Play*, pp. 46–8.
20 Helm, *The English Mummers' Play*, p. 46.
21 Cawte *et al.*, *English Ritual Drama*, p. 30.
22 T. Coult and B. Kershaw, *Engineers of the Imagination*, London: Methuen, 1983.
23 K. McMullen and S. Brisley, *Being and Doing*, film, London: Through Match Films (London)/ACGB, 1984.
24 T. D'Urso and F. Taviani, *L'Étranger qui danse*, Holstebro, Denmark: Maison de la Culture de Rennes, 1977.
25 T. Etchells, *Certain Fragments*, London: Routledge, 1999.
26 A. Stitt, *The Bedford Project*, Bedford, England: BCA, TRACE and Fort Sztuki, 2003.
27 See A. Howell, *The Analysis of Performance Art*, Amsterdam: Harwood Academic Publishers, 1999; C. R. Garoian, *Performing Pedagogy*, Albany: State University of New York Press, 1999.
28 E. Barba and N. Savarese, *A Dictionary of Theatre Anthropology: The Secret Art of the Performer*, London: Routledge, 1991.

Chapter 10

The gift of play
Übung and the secret signal of gesture

Andrew Quick

A man's maturity – consists in having found again the seriousness one had as a child, at play.[1]

Quivering life is never symbolic, because it lacks form.[2]

Revolutionary play

Writing in 1929, four years before Hitler is made Reich Chancellor of Germany, Walter Benjamin puts forward a 'Program for a Proletarian Children's Theatre', although it remains unpublished in his lifetime. Reading this six-page essay in 2005, I am struck by how much the times have changed. In an era in which global capitalism seems to have reached into every nook and cranny of our daily lives it is hard, if not impossible, to conjure up a theatre that might be Proletarian, that might explore the possibilities of a society that is founded on the principles of Marxist doctrine and ideology. Even harder is the thought that such a form of theatre could exist *for* children. Just imagine the headlines in our tabloid newspapers. They would surely rage against the alleged misuse of taxpayers' money pursued in the name of indoctrination (remembering, of course, that the hypocrisy of this accusation is always lost to the leader writer and news-paper editor). Even taking this into account, such a programme sounds dour and somewhat irrelevant. It is an invention emanating from a world that is so completely different to the one that we live in today; one in which the political dividing lines were clearly marked out and particular ideological formations were seen to provide the answer to all the ills of society.

However, as with so much of Benjamin's writing, there is something extraordinarily astute and pertinent in his thinking on childhood, some-thing that not only tests the limit of any form of doctrinal thought, but one that also offers hope in that the concept and condition of orthodoxy itself is put to the test. Benjamin's Marxism, if it can be called that, is evinced in his programme through his emphasis on a form of revolution that provokes an endless transformation, a revolution that works to prevent

orthodoxies from stagnating and fixing society, one that always looks
forward to a future that is forever in the process of being built.[3] What is
more, it is around the figure of the child that Benjamin invokes this concept
of a future that is based on revolutionary principles, where the limits and
constraints of any form of political orthodoxy are always exceeded by the
child's action and imagination: action and imagination that would put to
the test all the pre-established rules and assumptions upon which societies
are constructed.

Consider the closing lines of his 'Program for a Proletarian Children's
Theatre':

> what is truly revolutionary is not the propaganda of ideas, which leads
> here and there to impracticable actions and vanishes in a puff of smoke
> upon the first sober reflection at the theatre exit. What is truly revo-
> lutionary is the *secret signal* of what is to come that speaks from the
> gesture of the child.[4]

A little earlier in the essay Benjamin elaborates on his concept of the
child's gesture, the secret gestic impulse that for him resonates with revolutionary potential. According to Benjamin, 'every childhood action and
gesture becomes a signal'. These gestures are not signals of unconscious
desire or repressions, they are signals, he writes, that arrive 'from another
world, in which the child lives and commands'.[5] For Benjamin, such
gestures literally point towards notions of truth. They are actions that
surface as a consequence of judgements that take place in pragmatic conditions, which, in certain circumstances, are clear of the absolutism of
intention, prediction and authoritarian rule: the regime that arranges and
directs adult experience. Or, at least, these gestures emerge as the transitory outcomes of decisions that are made when particular sets of rules are
unable to determine forms of action and thinking. This is the basis of their
secrecy, since what gives life to these gestures (and directs what they might
signify) always remains beyond the comprehension of the adult.

Significantly, it is the theatre that provides the revolutionary environment for Benjamin, one which would set in motion what he calls a 'radical
unleashing of play – something which the adult can only wonder at'.[6]
Benjamin does not really define or expand upon what he means by 'play'
in his programme, but he does indicate that the concept of improvisation
is central to an understanding of what might be at stake in this emphasis
on the child's gesture as the instance of revolutionary potential.[7] For
Benjamin, improvisation provides the framework for the production of
gestures. He claims that gestures (or signals) emerge from the creative
activities that the practices of improvisation promote. Improvisation domi-
nates the world of play; 'it is the framework from which the signals, the
signifying gestures emerge'. It is via the synthesis of these gestures that

performance/theatre is created because, Benjamin explains, performance or theatre 'alone have the unexpected uniqueness that enables the child's gesture to stand in its own authentic space'.[8] According to Benjamin, theatre's uniqueness is founded on the fact that everything that is produced on its various stages is ephemeral. While the walls of the theatre, the auditorium and the stage are permanently fixed, the events that take place on the stage are always transitory and ultimately lost (except to memory) when the performance is over.[9]

Performance's ephemeral nature is highly significant for Benjamin because it provides what he calls a 'creative pause' in the presumed (by adults) continuity of everyday social life. Performance, Benjamin maintains, is constructed through the constellation of gestures and each gesture institutes a kind of pause or rupture in any attempt to construct a synchronic organisation of experience. As such, gesture can be seen as an occasion that disfigures linear temporal flow. Gesture, according to Benjamin, as a product of play, retains an essential playful and disruptive quality. Gesture stills, but refuses being stilled as meaning. As Benjamin observes in an essay on Kafka published in 1934, theatre functions to dissolve events into gestures. However, the 'codes of gestures' that constitute Kafka's entire work, Benjamin asserts, are not grounded in symbolic meaning. Rather, he maintains, Kafka, like the child in the Proletarian Children's Theater, attempts 'to derive such a meaning from them in ever-changing contexts and experimental groupings'. Hence gesture, he writes, is 'an event – one might say a drama – in itself'. Gesture, Benjamin concludes, is 'the decisive thing, the centre of the event'. Gesture, in the world of the child, in the worlds created by Kafka, cannot be contained by what he calls 'its traditional supports', supports that would give an untroubled account of what a gesture would signify. In the improvisatory hands and body of the child, in the unsettling words presented by Kafka, gesture provokes an endless reflection, one in which 'you look up in fright and realise that you are already far away from the continent of man'.[10]

This 'continent of man' is knowledge and our removal from those realms with which we are familiar produces a profound disturbance. According to Benjamin, gesture shocks us out of what we presume to know. It disfigures any notion of symbolic unity that we might cling on to, to orientate ourselves in the world. This is not to say that gesture solely participates in the collapse of the symbolic. As interruption, gesture initiates and brings something forward from the 'quivering life' that is the ground of all being, the chaos from which all life and art emanates. Consequently, gesture does not wholly participate in the act of repetition that signification always relies upon to establish its network of symbolic meaning. As an interruptive and arresting moment, gesture becomes astonishing, not through the reproduction of reality, but rather, as a revelation, an opening on to, 'a discovery' of a situation *as a situation is occurring*.[11] In this sense, gesture marks the present time of happening itself, the 'now' that is an occurrence. This is the centre of the event that Benjamin alludes to, a centre that in its revealing can never be fully known because, like play and gesture, it occurs as an interruption in any attempt to configure temporal continuity. In the act of revelation (revealing), gesture does not reveal (point towards the revealed) anything except its potential to signify: the capacity to be meaningful in the future. This is the basis of 'the secret signal of *what is to come* that speaks from the gesture of the child' (my emphasis).[12] Although a gesture carries with(in) it the possibility of communication, the *act* of gesturing clouds communication and the stilling required to create meaning is always deferred as the gesture disappears or is transformed into another gesture. The gestural act necessarily takes place in the 'differentiated' time of the present, a time Benjamin describes as a time of showing ('I need not say anything. Merely show').[13] This is the time of enactment itself. Yet, what this enactment signifies cannot be grasped until that differentiated time has been subsumed by historical time and transformed into knowledge. In this sense, as an occurrence, gesture presents a radical rupture in the continuity of experience (of History) upon which the adult world of order and law is established. Gesture signals the future that has yet to be conceived as knowledge. Thus, according to Benjamin, this rupture, far from being a negative dynamic, is rooted in the very idea of progress, in how we might comprehend and imagine the future. He writes: 'progress has its seat not in the continuity of elapsing time but in its interferences – where the truly new makes itself felt for the first time, with the sobriety of dawn'.[14]

When placed in the hands of the child, Benjamin constructs performance as a liberating activity. He rejects the psychologically rounded characterisation that makes up certain genres of theatre practice. He pours scorn on realism's claims for authentic representation, configuring it as a mode of practice that attempts to diminish improvisatory practice in the performance event itself. Nothing, he writes, can compete with the authenticity that is the child's improvisational activity. This is the 'moment of the gesture' and such instances are always ephemeral, exorcised by the activity of time and the transitory nature of performance itself, where the condition of improvisation is inevitably founded upon impermanence. This is why, Benjamin intimates, theatre is *the* space in which the child can be at play. Of course, anybody observing children at play can see how they create 'theatres' for their games and role playing, how improvisation and rule testing are utilised and pushed to various limits within particular spatial and temporal configurations. This is why children often make rooms within rooms, utilising cushions, blankets, creating their own 'child(ish)' space within the adult space that always attempts to organise them. The worlds they create are temporary and fragile, built out of found materials that stand in for the permanence and ordered materiality of the 'real' world.[15]

As an adult I might be allowed into this childish space, but, more often than not, I am forced to stand on the edge, both excluded and included, dependent on the child's whim – on the never fully comprehended signals that she gives me.

We're playing 'Three Little Pigs' and I, of course am the big bad wolf. I blow the house down and another is quickly and hysterically rebuilt, resurrected in an atmosphere infused with a mixture of glee and fear. The game goes on too long, I've lost count how many times the house has been blown down and I am becoming bored with the story's repetitive structure. I wish to bring it to an end. Admitting failure as the wolf, I become an earthquake and then a storm, hoping to destroy the house for good, hoping that this manoeuvre will finish off this space that seems impervious to all the disasters that I attempt to throw at it. But I'm ordered to stop. 'It's hot now, it's summer – let's have a picnic'. The game has morphed, a different space is quickly established and I'm sucked into a new narrative and a new set of inventions, my attempt at establishing any sense of ending is artfully thwarted.

The space that makes up Benjamin's concept of theatre is also bound by rules. He is not advocating an authenticity that is established solely on spatial grounds – the creation of a place in which the child can be absolutely or completely 'free'. The 'authenticity' that Benjamin rather cryptically alludes to occurs as a result of the improvisational moment that takes place in rule-bound space. This is because a space without rule and order cannot exist, since laws and limits are involved in any spatial formation.[16] Even utopian spaces are built upon rules, rules that are based on an exclusion of authoritarianism and the desire to establish a way of life governed by the principles of absolute freedom and equality. It is important to remember that the enactment of 'Three Little Pigs' described above takes place in a space that is marked by history, by narrative conventions and by specific sets of rules that order and control particular patterns of behaviour (the child's and my own): teatime, bathtime, and *bedtime* – the activity that would signal the end of the day, the activity that the child always seems ready to resist most intensely, or at least endeavours to negotiate under her own terms. Similarly, according to Benjamin, the authentic moment occurs in the improvisational instant that takes place in a space that is, inevitably, circumscribed and ordered by rules. Gesture, as improvisation, however, does not necessarily bend to the will of rules. It plays within the very co-ordinates of what governs and orders, what ordains what is permissible and inadmissible. Consequently, rules are not banished or permanently excluded, but rather they are suspended and pushed aside, as the rule of what is being 'done' is worked through in the improvisational moment. This 'being done' is, I would like to assert, an ontological constituent of play.

Practising play

Since Benjamin makes no attempt to contextualise his somewhat cryptic theorisations of gesture and play through any specific analysis of performance, let me attempt to ground what I think he is alluding to by making reference to Josse De Pauw and Victoria theatre's extraordinary production of *Übung*, which I saw in London and in Glasgow in 2003.[17] In many respects the structure around which *Übung* operates is relatively straightforward. A black and white film of events that make up an evening and following morning are played on a large screen, which is placed at the back of the playing space. In the film, a couple, Robert and Rolanda, invite a group of friends to their house in the country. This group includes another couple, Ivo and Ria, Olivier (a poet) and György (a Russian violinist). They drink aperitifs and all have a meal together. During the evening they get progressively drunk, tell and listen to awful jokes, witness Olivier's recitation of Dylan Thomas's poem 'And Death Shall Have No Dominion', and make bungled attempts at seductions. A fight breaks out, furniture is smashed and everybody re-emerges, with much embarrassment, at breakfast the next morning. The film closes with everyone taking a morning walk in the woods in their winter clothes.

Something in the cinematography reminds me of the work of Lars von Trier and other Dogme filmmakers. The film has an expressionist quality: the camera work is often hand-held and the action jump-cuts from shot to shot, rather than being seamlessly edited together. Shots linger on faces and objects: an immaculately arranged bowl of fruit, state-of-the-art telephones, televisions and music systems, a modernist chair, paintings, sculptures, a BMW sports car – all the trappings of bourgeois life. An abstract rhythmic pulse on the soundtrack underpins all the ensuing action. The characterisation of the hosts and their guests draws on particular social stereotypes in order to expose the unhappiness and violence that exists under the surface of bourgeois living, although the acting itself appears rooted in psychological observation/motivation. In front of this film, six children of varying ages (I guess they range from around eight to fifteen) 'play' the adults on the screen. This 'play' entails the wearing of clothes that are identical to those that are worn by the adults and speaking the adult voices throughout the events that make up the film.

In contrast to the film, these live elements of the performance are not founded on the basis of psychological investment; the ability to seamlessly identify with and embody the character portrayed. The processes demanded by the performance set-up are indicated by the title: *Übung*. *Übung* can be translated as 'practice' or 'exercise' and I would argue that the term (and the performance) *Übung* approximates what Benjamin is attempting to describe, all too briefly, in his 'Program for a Proletarian Children's Theater'. The children in *Übung* move within a space bound by specific rules: they have to lip-synch in time with adults and speak the adults' words, they change clothes before us to approximate the transformations that take place on the screen, they watch television monitors to guide their actions and the timing of their speaking. Yet, within this tightly organised and controlling structure, the children appear to have room to improvise, to roam and move between the different sets of activities that the performance demands of them. Glances are exchanged and particular physical actions – a circling move across the playing space – evoke the 'gesture of the moment' that Benjamin eulogises. Of course, in one sense, the very nature of filmic reproduction denies such moments of gesture to the adults on the screen. Their action is condemned to eternal repetition, which will make their gestures and words exactly the same in every performance. On the other hand, the film also incorporates qualities that are gestural. The use of jump-cuts and the lingering shots of single objects and faces interrupt the continuous flow of time (and disrupt the spatial order) in the film. The cinematography introduces ruptures within the filmic frame of the performance, creating temporal breaks that the children make use of in their live interactions with the screen action. These ruptures give the children time to exchange glances, change clothes and move around the stage, as they process the information that the film presents to them.

One of the youngest children (Basiel Roberts) plays Ivo (Dirk Roothooft), a boorish bear of a man who tells jokes that are often in bad taste. This child does have an uncanny resemblance to the man on the screen and I can imagine that he could be a younger version of the character in the film. Sometimes the child looks directly at the screen to co-ordinate his movements and words with the adult figure. Sometimes he looks at the downstage television monitors positioned at the far corners of the playing space. Occasionally, he glances at the other children and sometimes directly at the audience. His movement in and across the space intrigues me, as I focus on the ways in which he relates to the other performers, the screen and the audience. His body is constantly on the move, his hands barely still, as he endlessly shifts positions between the screen, the other children on the stage and the audience. I realise that I am searching for patterns, for structure, attempting to work out what is being 'done' before me. I fail. And thinking this over, as I watch the performance, I conclude that the performer is working and walking through numerous possibilities, making particular sets of performance choices *before* me. He is 'practising' and 'exercising' throughout the performance. This is *Übung* in practice. His, I would surmise, is a performance of *moves*, of *gestures*, that signal a state of troubling and unsettling impermanence often lost to those of us who dwell in the world of adults. It is a practice built on ruse and guile, on the ability to be permanently on the move as if avoiding being fixed by adult modes of behaviour.

I distinctly remember one particular move across the playing space made by the child version of Ivo. He begins by looking and speaking in direct relation to the screen. He then ambles downstage, still speaking, but now addresses the child that 'plays' the character that is being harangued by the adult version of him in the film. My eye flickers between the figures on the stage and the larger-than-life adult glowering on the screen. Then suddenly, the child turns his back on the screen and seemingly speaks directly to us in the audience. It is as if he has broken any connection with the figure that he is portraying, signalling both the proximity and distance between himself and his adult version that he is supposedly portraying in the film. Possibilities press into my mind, possibilities that I cannot definitively find an answer to:

> *The child becoming adult? The adult becoming child? The child performer turning his back on a version of adulthood becoming a child once more? Am I like the adult on the screen? Am I like the child on the stage?*

The exchange of looks implies some form of complicity, but I cannot work out the rule of this exchange, and what my relationship is to it. Once again, as in 'Three Little Pigs', I am on edge – included and yet excluded; identifying and immediately excluded from identification. I am caught up in the swirl of movement and gesture, where the signals, I am sure, are not entirely planned and fixed. There is something undirected in the arc of this child's movement, in the playfulness of his use of gesture, in the jauntiness of his walk – or rather, not necessarily determined by the adult framework within which he is placed. As such, I am unable to fasten down what the signals, the gestures, might represent, although I am able, in turn, to play with their possibilities. Watching in utter admiration, I am caught in the improvisational moment, implicated in the 'exercise', the 'practice' that is unfolding before me. And Benjamin is right: as an adult I can only wonder at it, even though it disturbs me, as it brutally reminds me of the rule-bound and materialistic existence that I am so happy to inhabit.

Of course, the demands made by imitation regulate all the children's actions that take place during the performance of *Übung*. Consequently, as a direct result of the requirements exacted by the command to repeat, one might expect to witness a certain dampening in the child's improvisational activity. However, the repetitive acts pursued by these children appear to be driven by processes that are always improvisational. These improvisational moments, I would like to surmise, arise as a direct result of the technical demands that the repetition of words and gestures, taken from the film, make on the live performer. These words and gestures are negotiated in the act of listening and watching *as* the film unfolds before both the performer and the audience. Importantly, the child's negotiation

of the adult world takes place in a space that makes no attempt to reproduce the spatial realities of the film (and, by implication, adult reality).
Indeed, there is little attempt, beyond repeating the rhythm of speech and
selectively appropriating gestures, to recreate the interactions that occur
in the film. For example, when two figures are shown dancing together
on the film, the children playing these adults move separately as they both
look up to the screen from different parts of the playing space to time
their repetitions. What I witness, then, is a stop–start relationship to imitation, one that refuses to participate in the temporal, spatial and
psychological continuity that is always implied in the film's order of representation. Imitation takes place in a moment-by-moment response to the
screen, where the reproduction of the film's fictional reality is rendered
impossible and where the words and gestures of the adults can never be
fully embodied. In the temporal and spatial ruptures that ensue, what I
witness is the differentiated time of showing that occurs in the child's *practice* of imitation, an imitation of a world from which he or she always
appears alienated.

Importantly, the performance of *Übung* reveals that the practice of imitation is not limited to the activities of the child. On the screen, as the
evening descends into drunkenness, one of the women dances outside in
the garden. The camera pans back to the house to reveal Ivo parodying
her movements as he observes her through the window. Suddenly, I am
presented with three sets of dancing figures: the woman, the adult Ivo
impersonating her movements, and (live on the stage) the child imitating
the adult version of himself on the screen. However, when articulated by
the child, the parodic element of the adult's imitation of the woman's
movements disappears, seemingly as a direct consequence of the child's
struggle with the task of imitation itself. Whereas the woman's movements
evoke the modernist dance language that presumes to articulate a direct
spiritual relationship to nature, and Ivo's movements are a comic under-
mining of such presumptions, the child's gestures, unburdened by
signification, appear to have a reality in and of themselves – a reality to
which I am unable to attach any particular meaning. My eye oscillates
between the three different sets of movements that find themselves caught
up in the same nexus of imitation, although I am confused as to the origin
of this imitation. In this extraordinary moment, I fleetingly think that both
adults on the film are struggling to imitate the child, each failing to embody
the child's gestural playing. It is as if the child's abstract gesturing, a
struggle in and of articulation itself, is the reality (the origin) to which their
movements are referring. It is a reality that they are unable to capture.
In this instance of re-presentational failure I am aware that something is
occurring. This occurrence is the gestural moment itself, a happening now,
an event, during which signification is forced to wait a while. Caught in
this pause, this rupture, the adult world appears to break apart, its order

and rule incapable of accounting for what is occurring. Here, I glimpse gesture as practice and practice as gesture. Here, nothing is said. There is merely showing.

During the after-show discussion that followed the performance of *Übung* in London, I listened to criticisms that implied that the children had been compelled to work within what were identified as adult constraints in the performance. Were the children informed of the director's intention? Why were the children not permitted to be whatever they wanted to be, to change characters, to ignore the strict 'adult' rules that they were forced to obey? I found the questions difficult to fathom, as if the questioners had been watching a different performance. Perhaps these adults believed in the existence of a rule-free space that would enable the children to operate outside adult constraints. Perhaps the directorial hand was perceived as being too dictatorial, too directional. What I witnessed in *Übung* was a practice, an exercise, which put into play, as 'play', the crucial question of how the child fulfils the promise of his or her childhood in becoming adult. It was an exercise that reminded me of the ways in which I have undoubtedly made compromises in fulfilling the promise of my own childhood, compromises that are deeply personal and always perturbing.

In those repeated instances in *Übung*, where the adult looks down on his or her version of themselves as a child on the stage, where the child looks up to an adult future that can only be imagined, I am reminded that the promise of childhood works both ways. We look forwards and backwards: towards a future, but owing a great debt to the past. Yet, it would appear that there is a definite limit to what might be retrievable from the past. It is striking that the state of infancy, that vital condition of childhood, is absent from this and many other representations. Perhaps we should not be too surprised by this absence, since, if Benjamin is correct, it is the instance of gesture that causes our wonder. Indeed, people's descriptions of their children would appear to bear this out. What is remembered, and what is looked forward to, is communication with the child: its coming into language, its attempts at working physically with objects, its capacity to learn from us as adults, to surprise us and to teach us through the ways in which it learns.

With its limited ability to communicate, the infant is usually banished from the stage. If it does appear, as it often does in children's nativity plays, the infant is reduced to a doll or a tightly wrapped bundle of cloth, where the face and limbs are deliberately obscured. Not that I experience this usurping of the infant by its stand-in as a loss. In the playful hands of children, the inert doll somehow retains a certain infancy. Anyway, I cannot think how I might become engaged in watching a 'real' infant in a performance, just as I cannot muster the same interest that my friends have for their own very young children. Yet, I am still fascinated by the infant's absence, since the word 'infant' implies the very origin of being itself: the being from which the child and then the adult emerges. Does not the presence of and in improvisation, the practice, the exercise, inevitably haunt this state of infancy, where all rules are seemingly suspended, waiting to be learned in the process of growing up? If improvisation implies a being there in the moment, as signalled by the gesture that points towards the contingent materiality of things, an ephemeral testing out that speaks of judgement and possibility, then similar processes are existent in the infant state. The crucial question then becomes whether we can we ever go back to or rediscover such a state. Such a return is, perhaps, impossible. But does not play return us to that moment of infancy where improvisation reigns until the 'I' of the individual is borne into the world of language, a world based absolutely upon rules and laws? This is play's gift.

Coda: interrupting play

In his short essay 'The Gift of Organs', Lyotard urges us to be open to an object's plasticity, a plasticity that resists all attempts to distil it into information, to render it meaningful. The plastic object gives, he argues, because it offers something up that cannot be read, because it produces something that exceeds (or resists being stilled by) any signifying system. Lyotard writes:

> The plastic object is not a message, it is not a vehicle of communication chartered for the best possible transport of information. The more plastic it is, the fewer informative elements it contains. The painter, the sketcher, do not talk to us through their lines and colours. The thing they make is meant to be given. The child also gives his shit to what he loves.[18]

In words that echo Benjamin, Lyotard asserts that nothing is given in acts that signify. These acts simply reveal what is already comprehended. For signification is always the outcome of our being able to attach signs to objects and this requires a prior knowledge of both the object itself and the sign that would stand in for it. This is how all signifying systems operate. The gift, like Benjamin's gesture, on the other hand, being unrecognisable (it being made anew), takes us by surprise and interrupts communication. 'One gives when speech is lacking', Lyotard observes; 'one gives things, not messages, even if these things are made of words'.[19] Lyotard playfully reminds us that the child without language will often present its own excrement as a gift to its parents. As a by-product of its own corporeality, excrement becomes an object of play for the pre-linguistic child. This gift, at least for the child, has no association with the sense of revulsion that it generates in the adult to whom it is given.

In *Powers of Horror*, Julia Kristeva asserts that excrement presents an external threat to identity, to the borders and limits from which the self is constructed. 'Excrement and its equivalents (decay, infection, disease, corpse, etc.)', she writes, 'stand for the danger to identity that comes from without: the ego threatened by the non-ego, society threatened by its outside, life by death'.[20] However, as Kristeva points out, it is not excrement per se that causes subjectivity to buckle and break apart, which results in the I being expelled, as she words it. Subjectivity is displaced by that which jeopardises those symbolic systems that are constructed to enable the subject to exist as a subject in the first place. These systems are founded on the ability to differentiate between and thus define objects, to locate the points of difference that identity relies upon for its very existence. It is the encounter with the 'jettisoned object', what she describes as the abject, that draws the individual towards 'the place where meaning collapses',[21] to the site where the self might disintegrate. If subjectivity is created through a process of ordering, then it is disorder that poses the most direct threat to its continuation. In the encounter with disorder (dirt, filth, waste, the cadaver), in the confrontation with that which has to be expelled to instil order, the world, Kristeva insists, falls away. In words that echo Lyotard's thinking on plasticity and Benjamin's on gesture, Kristeva observes that, 'in that thing that no longer matches and therefore no longer signifies anything, I behold the breaking down of a world that has erased its borders: fainting away'.[22] This, she maintains, is the effect of abjection.

Play, it would seem, also keeps the I at bay. This is another of its gifts. Like the encounter with the jettisoned object, play produces a profound rupture in those organising systems that presume to order the world and make it sensible. Of course, both toys and gestures are, in their different ways, 'jettisoned objects'. One only has to think of the countless occasions in which children make play with those everyday items that are the waste products or the redundant materials that are recovered from adult life. If play always exceeds signification, then it too is wasted, as it is unable to be accommodated and consumed within any representational economy. It would seem, then, following Kristeva, that play provokes the self's dispersal and ultimate disintegration. This is what causes our wonder and astonishment. Does not this assertion mark out play as a deadly pursuit, one that always leads to the final fainting away that is death? This would explain children's apparent obsession with death and account for the multiple expirations that constitute so much of their playful activities.

However, the plasticity implicit in the gestural activity of play, as Lyotard reminds us, brings us back to the act of giving, an act that feels far removed from the final act of dying. Lyotard implies that the gift brings something new into the world, something that, in being brought forth, being born(e), always exceeds our knowledge of it. According to Lyotard, birth is not merely tied to biological reproduction. Rather, it is a profound displacement of similitude. He writes:

> Birth is not merely the biological fact of parturition, but under cover and on discovery of this fact, the event of a possible radical alteration in the course compelling things to repeat the same. Childhood is the name of this faculty, in that it brings to the world of being the astonishment of what, for a moment, is nothing yet – of what *is already* without yet being *something*.[23]

This disruption of repetition, this being born, which is always a product of play, of improvisation, of gesture, carries an ethical obligation. This disruption, which Lyotard and Benjamin both call an event, does not leave us merely swinging in the wind (an activity most children take much delight in) or permanently fainting away. The event, as *Übung*, points to the future, the making of a new rule – perhaps one that might be more just; one that will, of course, be broken in a further exercise. This is its secret signal.

Notes

1 F. Nietzsche, *Beyond Good and Evil*, trans. W. Kaufmann, New York: Vintage, 1966, p. 83.
2 W. Benjamin, *Selected Writings, vol. 1, 1913–1926*, eds. M. Bullock and M. W. Jennings, Cambridge, MA: Harvard University Press, 1996, p. 224.
3 For an analysis of Benjamin's thinking on Marx, see Allegra De Laurentiis's 'A Prophet Turned Backwards: Materialism and Mysticism in Walter Benjamin's Notion of History', *Rethinking Marxism*, 7, 4, winter 1994. In this article De Laurentiis maintains that Benjamin combines both Marxist and Jewish-mystical traditions in his analysis of that which history occludes in its accounting for past events. The task Benjamin sets himself, De Laurentiis argues, is to explore how a materialist understanding of history might be juxtaposed with the glimpsed or experiential comprehension of the past event (as a singular occurrence) in order to reveal history's redemptive potential. Art, De Laurentiis explains, provides an opening for Benjamin to gain an access to the singular event(s) that history seeks to reorder and conflate within its narration of the past.
4 W. Benjamin, *Selected Writings, vol. 2, 1927–1934*, eds. M. W. Jennings, H. Eiland and G. Smith, Cambridge, MA: Harvard University Press, 1999, p. 206.
5 Benjamin, *Selected Writings, vol. 2*, p. 204.
6 Benjamin, *Selected Writings, vol. 2*, p. 205.
7 Benjamin gives a more explicit definition of play in his essay 'Toys and Play', published in the same year as the 'Program for a Proletarian's Children's Theater'. Play is described as an activity that the child engages in to 'create the entire event anew' and also as 'Not a "doing as if" but a "doing the same thing over and over again," the transformation of a shattering experience into habit – that is the essence of play'. Benjamin, *Selected Writings, vol. 2*, p. 120.
8 Benjamin, *Selected Writings, vol. 2*, p. 204.
9 Benjamin's observation that ephemerality is a defining feature of theatricality corresponds to Peggy Phelan's conceptualisation of disappearance as the ontological constituent of performance. See P. Phelan, *Unmarked: The Politics of Performance*, London and New York: Routledge, 1993, pp. 146–66.

10 Benjamin, *Selected Writings, vol. 2*, pp. 801–2.
11 Benjamin, *Selected Writings, vol. 2*, p. 778. For an excellent analysis of Benjamin's thinking on the caesura, see Werner Hamacher's 'The Gesture in the Name: On Benjamin and Kafka'. Hamacher gives the following definition of gesture: 'Gesture is what remains of language after meaning is withdrawn from it, and it is gesture that withdraws from meaning. The rest of language – and so language itself, language irreducible to meaning – is gesture'; W. Hamacher, *Premises: Essays on Philosophy and Literature from Kant to Celan*, trans. P. Fenves, Stanford: Stanford University Press, 1996, p. 330.
12 See G. Agamben, *Potentialities*, ed. and trans. D. Heller-Roazen, Stanford: Stanford University Press, 1999, especially 'Kommerell, or On Gesture', pp. 77–89. See also D. Heller-Roazen's introduction in the same publication, pp. 22–3.
13 W. Benjamin, *The Arcades Project*, trans. H. Eiland and K. McLaughlin, Cambridge, MA: Harvard University Press, 2002, p. 460. See Andrew Benjamin's essay 'Time and Task' for an excellent analysis of Benjamin's thinking on the temporality of the present (A. Benjamin and P. Osborne, *Walter Benjamin's Philosophy: Destruction and Experience*, London: Routledge, 1994, pp. 216–50).
14 Benjamin, *Arcades Project*, p. 474.
15 In his essay 'In Playland: Reflections on History and Play', Giorgio Agamben makes a clear distinction between ritual and play. Following Lévi-Strauss, who argues that ritual fixes time in order to preserve 'the continuity of lived experience', Agamben insists that play both distorts and destroys temporality. He observes that 'the function of rites is to adjust the contradiction between mythic past and present, annulling the interval separating them, and reabsorbing all events into the synchronic structure'. Play, in contrast, severs 'the connection between past and present, and to break down and crumble the whole structure into events'; G. Agamben, *Infancy and History: Essays on the Destruction of Experience*, trans. L. Heron, London: Verso, 1993, p. 74.
16 I engage in a more detailed analysis of how rules operate to organise space and place in 'Taking Place: Encountering the Live', *Live: Art and Performance*, ed. A. Heathfield, London, Tate Publications, 2004, pp. 92–9.
17 For a brief description of the production and the work of Josse de Pauw, see http://www.kunstenfestivaldesarts.be/archief/en/2001/stl/stl18.html.
18 J.-F. Lyotard, *Driftworks*, New York: Semiotext(e), 1984, p. 85.
19 Lyotard, *Driftworks*, p. 86. It is important to note that Lyotard observes that all acts of signification retain a certain plasticity, a plasticity that disrupts their power to describe. Lyotard is not privileging the signifier's materiality above what it represents; he is not making a claim for a beyond to representation. The plasticity of an object indicates that there is something in/of the object that escapes signification (comprehension) in the signifying act itself. Lyotard describes this plasticity as 'the other side of words, the order of silence, of the scream . . . It imposes the other to discourse, it is movement in its simplicity erecting sense.'
20 J. Kristeva, *Powers of Horror*, trans. L. S. Roudiez, New York: Columbia University Press, 1982, p. 71.
21 Kristeva, *Powers of Horror*, p. 2.
22 Kristeva, *Powers of Horror*, p. 4.
23 J.-F. Lyotard, *Towards the Postmodern*, eds. R. Harvey and M. S. Roberts, New York: Humanity Books, 1999, p. 151.

Chapter 11

Authority, empowerment and fairy tales

Theatre for young people

Bridget Escolme

I walk into a performance space underneath a theatre. I take off my shoes and get into bed. It is a very pleasurable act, reminiscent of childhood on two counts. It reminds me of being told stories, and of games of make-believe. I am pretending to be a child getting into bed to be told a story, as are the other adults and children around me. The space is full of these narrow beds; some are in rows, some above one another in bunks. As I shiver beneath a crisp white sheet and a rough brown blanket, a giant stomps about above us, making the ceiling shake. The bulb swings ominously when the giant passes.

The woman telling the story has long dark plaits and a medieval-looking smock. She could be the giant's wife, trying to keep us safe as he storms around. She appears at first to be mistress of the whole event as she sits on a stool beneath the bare bulb with her storybook and reads us the story of *Buchettino* – Tom Thumb, Thumbkin or Hop O'My Thumb. But as the piece progresses, neither her telling of the tale nor our own safety seem to be perfectly under her control. Her voice is amplified, so that it can be possessed by other voices – the giant's is a particularly startling throaty roar. The beds seem idyllically safe as each audience member chooses one, neatly leaves his or her shoes by its side and gets in. But the bedroom in the story is the place where Buchettino tricks the giant into slitting the throats of his own daughters.

The performance of *Buchettino* produced, in me at least, a delicious nostalgia for a time when fears and sorrows could be experienced and survived at the one-remove of fairytale fiction. I imagine that the five or six year old me would have experienced moments of absolute terror during the show – but would still have enjoyed it. What am I assuming about children and their potential relationship to this story when I remember myself thus? Much has been written on the nature of the 'folk tale' and the 'fairy tale' in terms of their essential, and by implication universal, moral, ethical and psychological purpose. In contrast, politicised critiques of these narratives and their production have traced their development from oral, community-owned narratives to bourgeois morality tale. The questions raised in this essay are around what happens to these tales when we make theatre out of them, and the kinds of children we imagine and produce when we do so.

Children in Europe are a sensitive issue. Child abuse and pornography are both a genuine problem and a tabloid mainstay: we must protect our children from the real-life monsters that lurk round every corner. Delinquency and disruption hold equal pride of place in popular mythology: we must control and punish our children more effectively, they are the twenty-first century's real-life monsters, though German psycho-analyst Alice Miller's work on 'child-rearing and the roots of violence'[1] suggests that fear of children underpinned European childrearing phil-osophy and practice as early as the eighteenth century. The work analysed here is all remarkable in having found ways of confronting the fears and discomforts of both children and adults, riding roughshod over 'sensitivi-ties' whilst remaining acutely sensitive.

The origins of fairy tales have little to do with children or, at least, such tales in their early forms were told to them only as they might have been part of a wider community. Jack Zipes traces the history of the form from oral folklore to literary tale, observing, for example, how the Brothers Grimm edited the tales they had collected to suit bourgeois sensibilities of the early nineteenth century,[2] and how it was only 'from 1830 to 1900, during the rise of the middle classes, that the fairy tale came into its own for children'.[3] The French fairy tale emerges in the literary form in which we now have *Beauty and the Beast* from an explicitly adult tradition of salon storytelling and collection,[4] stories from which tradition were adapted for children during the mid-eighteenth century. Bruno Bettelheim in his *Uses of Enchantment* suggests there is something essentially pedagogical in the themes and motifs of the well-known tales to which he applied his psycho-analytical critique. However, as Zipes argues, Bettelheim tends to ignore the cultural conditions of the tales' production and revision, and regards them – and some basic and somewhat simplified tenets of psychoanalysis – as timeless and universal.[5] Moreover, where Zipes reads power struggle and dialectic tension both in the tales themselves and their reproduction, Bettelheim sees a benevolent pedagogical practice that enables children who are read to to reach an idealised state of social adjustment and hetero-sexual love. Zipes' historicist accounts of the essentially conservative changes made to folk tales in the process of literarisation pose some important questions for this essay. How has making theatre from this material foregrounded, challenged or changed its sexual and cultural poli-tics? What much of the work explored here suggests is that reality for a child is both social *and* psychosexual and that theatre for children is strug-gling to be at once therapeutic and politically challenging, to enable its audiences both to cope with the world as it is and to interrogate it. In what follows, I focus particularly on the relationship – and on the power relationship – between performer and audience. Bettelheim figures the parent reader of the fairy tale as simply and transparently bringing tale to child – he insists that the reader must let the tales do their therapeutic work and that they must not be overtly interpreted.[6] In reading to their children, however, Bettelheim's parents have a clear pedagogical role: they should know that these stories will be good for their children, and Bettelheim's book explains how. The theatre pieces explored here, I am going to argue, productively shift the power relationship between teller and told.

König Lindwurm

The Danish story of the dragon prince and his queen is told by Ania Michaelis of Berlin's Theater o. N. (Zinnober), in the black box studio of Freiburg's Theater im Marienbad, a conversion from an old baths which is dedicated to work for young people. She begins as a queen who longs for a child but who gives birth to a Lindwurm, or wingless dragon. Michaelis both embodies the characters in the tale, putting on and removing simple costumes, and uses children's toy figures – a mix of differently sized, modern plastic ones – to enact scenes as a child might. Like the young wife in *Bluebeard* who cannot resist opening the forbidden door, the queen of this tale eats two flowers, against the advice of an old woman she has met in her garden, who has told her that eating a white rose will give her a girl, and a red one a boy. Eating both, it turns out, gives her a dragon. The Lindwurm grows up, is reluctantly accepted by his father, and is keen to marry – but has the unfortunate habit of consuming all the princesses who are presented to him. Eventually a shepherd's daughter outwits the dragon prince, also on the advice of an old woman, by demanding that, as she takes off her clothes on their wedding night, the prince takes off his skins. She flays the last skin from him with birch twigs, and the monster groom (as is the wont of monster grooms in this cycle of stories) becomes a man.[7]

Ania Michaelis' performance, directed by Gottfried Röszler, is startling on two counts – in the violence and viscerality of its narrative and in the compelling mix of controlled wit and vulnerability exhibited by Michaelis. She begins surrounded by a semicircle of costumes and objects. Some of these have a certain archaic, storytelling authenticity about them: the twigs that in the tale are used to flay the Lindwurm's last skin from him are real twigs, bare and beautiful, like driftwood; the military coat used to denote the king is red and gold, with epaulettes, like a soldier's coat from a children's illustration; indeed, the one piece of substantial set is a box, whose sides are hinged so that it can be made by Michaelis into a variety of structures. When the king first returns home from the wars to discover his Lindwurm son, however, and during the sequence of princess-eating, figures in the story are embodied by the modern plastic toy figures. *König Lindwurm* thus gives equal status to what a middle-class parent might idealise as imaginative play (Michaelis can make a battered set of hinged planks into anything) and to a child's enjoyment of commercially produced collectible figures.

What is produced by the deliberate lack of aesthetic consistency in the choice of objects, and her rapid switches of focus from object to embodiment, is vulnerability in the moment of performance that seems particularly appropriate and unpatronising in a storytelling theatre piece for children. It is not that Michaelis does not perform with confidence. *König Lindwurm* contains wonderfully observed comic set pieces, such as the moment when the plastic figure king comes face to face with his plastic dragon son and splutters pompously that there is little he can do, he has been at the wars after all. This provokes much laughter of recognition – not, of course, at the situation of being presented with a dragon as a son, but at the comic portrayal of a pompous man out of his habitual position of control. Michaelis' evident ability to control her audience, however, is set against an improvised metatheatricality that she establishes from the opening moments of the piece, when she repeatedly insists 'I am the queen' in a way that reminds us that she is not a queen at all. There are times when she hesitates as if unsure as to the turn the narrative is about to take, and makes clear that the piece is improvised. Throughout *König Lindwurm*, her use of the third person and her distance from the figures in the narrative – she has to tell us when she is 'being' the king or queen, she clearly does not ask us to believe that she 'is' any of the plastic figures – produces an effect of presence in the performer herself that always leaves her exposed, like the Lindwurm without his skin. One is left with the impression of a narrative that Michaelis is compelled to tell, that she hopes we will like and that she tells us as equals.

This mode of address to the audience and its simultaneous suggestion of relaxation and exposure recalls the Puppen-Theater der Stadt Halle's version of *Beauty and the Beast*. This piece is performed by two actor/storytellers using masks, both conventionally – on the faces of the actors as they embody the figures – and as puppets, held away from the actors' faces. Primarily a puppet theatre, the Halle company come from a tradition of puppetry that Michaelis, a West German actress who received a Grotowski-influenced training in Switzerland, describes as specifically East German in origin. In interview, she is unsurprised to hear me recall Halle's work, as she views her own as inflected by similar traditions. She spent time in Berlin just after the fall of the wall, and speaks both of puppetry and Brecht's Epic theatre as producing the kinds of relaxed alienation effects evident in her work. Her engaging propensity to undermine herself with casual, throw-away asides – at which I find myself laughing even when my lack of German means I don't actually understand the joke –

has even led to her being mistaken for East German in birth and training. The distance between performer and figure theorised by Brecht lends itself to a form of theatre in which only one or two performers and some plastic figures/masks/objects play all the characters.

What this alienation effect produces, however, is, *pace* Brecht, a demand for empathy from the audience. The object of empathy shifts back and forth from performer to fictional figure as the predicament of the former – exposed in the presence of the audience with whom she shares her story – is presented simultaneously with the exposure of the latter to the trials of the fairy-tale narrative. The Halle company maximise this sense of dual exposure by spending much of *Beauty and the Beast* with their masks held in front of but a little away from their faces, revealing the storyteller behind the mask, so that in remembering the performance one remembers the 'Beast' as both the grotesque monster the beast mask represents, and as the man he not only eventually becomes in the narrative, but who portrays him throughout the piece.

Lars Frank, who begins *Beauty* and plays the Beast, seems relaxed but a little severe; he is not a storyteller who appears particularly to like children. He demonstrates a quiet, stern authority that at first has the audience, comprising mainly children around seven and eight years old, their teachers and some practitioners, giggling a little nervously.[8] At first, then, he is more of an authority figure than Michaelis, entirely in charge, as indeed the Beast is when he catches Beauty's father stealing from his garden. However, his status as storyteller shifts compellingly as the Beast's story unfolds. In similar style to *König Lindwurm*, the Halle performers play a black box studio, with objects and structures placed casually around the playing space. The most striking of these is a hive-shaped metal cage on wheels, which Ines Heinrich as Beauty both stands inside, spreading her blue skirt over it so that the skirt stands out, crinoline-like, around her, and crouches within, refusing to answer 'Yes' to the Beast's daily question, 'Do you love me?' The cage suggests both a trap and a refuge. From standing inside the cage, Heinrich crouches and slips out of her blue skirt, leaving the fabric to make a tent around her. Beauty clearly colludes in the trap of female self-sacrifice that is expected of her by going to live with the Beast to save her father's life. She is also clearly not going to open up this skirt-like structure to the beast against her will. In the face of her refusal to emerge, Frank's Beast/storyteller appears more and more exposed and ridiculous, both fictionally and theatrically, as he presents ever bigger bunches of flowers to Beauty and, once she has disappeared inside her skirt, takes to posting gifts for her into the hole in the top of the cage. The controlling status of the theatrical storyteller is undermined as we both laugh at and pity the Beast.

Both pieces refuse to engage in overt acts of interpretation, in the sense of informing the audience of the possible social or psychosexual meanings for the narrative. However, they are always and inevitably overt acts of interpretation as the performers shift from one embodied persona to another and from one means of embodiment to another, permitting empathy with figures exposed to the trials of the tale and with the figures exposed in the moment of performance. Notions of authority are in a constant state of play as the audience laugh with or at the performer/fictional figures, approve or disapprove their actions. As Bettelheim repeatedly suggests, the figures in the stories are childlike in that they continually face seemingly insurmountable material and existential problems and are obliged to surmount or submit to them. Here, the performers are child-like too, not because they are 'acting' child characters or embodying any kind of supposedly childlike energy, but because they are audaciously pretending things are other things, and appear to be asking for our attention and empathy in the full knowledge that the audience is free to give it or not. The child spectator is empowered in a way that the child listener in Bettelheim's pedagogical narrative, wherein the child is read psychologically healthful narratives by a parent, is not.

Hansel and Gretel

The Grimms' *Hansel and Gretel* is a tale around which psychoanalytic and historicist/materialist readings of the fairy tale such as Bettelheim's and Zipes' respectively, become particularly polarised. Bettelheim reads fairy tale as psychoanalytic cure, figuring gingerbread-house-eating as a childish 'fixation . . . to primitive levels of development',[9] a symbolic gorging at the mother's breast, which the brother and sister must abandon to attain well-adjusted adulthood. Zipes, on the other hand, points to the material roots of the Grimms' version of the tale, adapted by Wilhelm during a time when famines in Central Europe were causing the kinds of hardship that might truly lead to the abandonment of children.[10] By moving next to Leeds-based Theatre Company Blah Blah Blah's work on *Hansel and Gretel*, I want to contrast a storytelling approach with an adaptation of the tale rooted in dramatic realism. I have suggested so far that the figure of the actor-storyteller potentially acknowledges a child's identification with the vulnerable heroes and heroines of the tales, whilst putting the adult figure that controls the tale by telling it in a vulnerable and ambivalent position, too. Blah Blah Blah have made a range of pieces based on *Hansel and Gretel*. One uses a storytelling figure; the other is a Theatre in Education project, still in progress, that involves its ten-year-old audiences in the action of a narrative transformed to an unspecified European country in the twenty-first century. The latter piece uses a range of participatory techniques to blur the boundaries between actor and audience, so that on one level the tellers of the tale share the power of its interpretation with its recipients. However, I want to interrogate the dramatic realism of this piece, as, in the early version I witnessed, it gave rise to some interesting tensions between the progressive and conservative potential of adapting the Grimms.

The Theatre Company Blah Blah Blah's first version of *Hansel and Gretel* is one of three works in progress stimulated by artistic director Anthony Haddon's fascination with the Anthony Browne illustrations of the Grimms' version in Eleanor Quarrie's 1949 translation.[11] The illustrations are an engaging and eerie mix of fairy-tale forestry and soap opera realism, in which it is suggested that the stepmother is not simply the nastier pragmatist of the parents when it comes to abandoning the children in time of famine, but a self-indulgent, tackily glamorous figure complete with dyed black hair, an animal-print coat, a cigarette and a sluttish collection of make-up and potions on her dressing table.

The Blahs' first telling of *Hansel and Gretel* comprises storyteller Brian Higgins, who wrote this version of the story, actors Abi Horsfield, Barnaby King and Anthony Haddon himself, dancer Carolyn Baker, cellist Kate Rose, and installation artist Amy Todman, who has created a set from plastic, paper, wood string and masking tape and continues to do so throughout the performance. This debris demarcates a number of seating and performance spaces and is manipulated, tied and balanced by Todman to make different structures during the performance. The precarious-looking spaces and artefacts sometimes appear to represent places and figures in the story and sometimes appear to be made for their own sake. The making of them can be functional to the narrative of *Hansel and Gretel* but is at times juxtaposed to it, so that the spectator is left to make connections between narrative and action. Similarly, performance itself is sometimes clearly representational, or is simply placed alongside the story. As 'families lay awake at night with the hunger gnawing at their bellies',[12] a family of performers writhe and grimace with hunger; but when Baker leaps and ducks her way over and under the carefully balanced debris, it is the effort of dancing we connect with Hansel's precarious plan to save himself and his sister by leaving a trail of pebbles, rather than any attempt at representation on the part of the dancer of this part of the story.

The work in progress performance takes the notion of representing children's play present in Ania Michaelis' work and pushes it to an aesthetic extreme. Todman and the performers can make anything represent anything – a puppet witch is made from a gnarled hand of twigs and a head of wood, cotton wool and masking tape; the house of sweets and gingerbread has no bright book-illustration colours but is assembled from the rubbish like everything else. It gives the piece the sense of an urban rather than a rural setting and, though it is the forest of the story to which Brian Higgins refers in his narrative, the image is of Hansel and Gretel abandoned on a landfill sight or in a refugee camp, although there is no overt attempt to give the tale a 'modern' setting. The audience watch foregrounded acts of making and interpretation, and are invited to make links between artefact and narrative. They are asked to enjoy being told a story, and to critique, it seemed to me, aspects of their enjoyment – particularly when they are offered the chance to gorge themselves on a rather lurid-looking Battenberg cake to celebrate the children's return from their first period of abandonment in the forest. The performance foregrounds famine and indulgence, emphasising the presence of both in the tale and delicately reminding the audience of their presence in our own society.

Blah Blah Blah's second *Hansel and Gretel* piece – despite the use of participation, which of course takes it far from the passive spectatorship of some modes of dramatic realism – is fundamentally dependent on the conventions of realism. Hansel and Gretel are transferred to current social life, and the piece is peopled by actors playing individual characters, as opposed to actor-storytellers narrating and embodying the tale. In fact, a social realist *Hansel and Gretel* makes a fleeting appearance in the first work-in-progress performance. There is a point in Higgins' text in which one of the performers breaks from the narrative and speaks as Gretel to the puppet witch; Gretel is forced to work for the witch – as Hansel is fattened for the pot:

> GRETEL: What do you want me to do?
> Am I doing it right?
> Do you want me to do that over there?
> I did all that yesterday.
>
> How old are you? You look really old . . .
> Have you always lived here by yourself?
> Have you ever seen a wolf?
> Did you used to have a husband?
> It's not right to live by yourself, you'll get lonely . . .
> I feel safe here.
> I like it here.
> When we go home, will you come with us?

Here, Gretel begins to relate to the witch rather as hostages are reported to do, becoming attached to her captor. Her speech hints at the possibilities of realist motivation for the witch, who for a moment becomes an old woman deprived of social interaction. The moment is brief, and there is no sense of a moral dilemma for Gretel when it comes to saving her brother by tricking the witch to her death. However, it is an important moment in this version of the story for director Anthony Haddon, who is interested in the witch as a potentially attractive figure, rather than the one of pure evil that an analyst such as Bettelheim needs such figures to be.[13]

The pilot phase of the participatory *Hansel and Gretel* piece breaks from the fairy-tale narrative almost entirely. In preparing it, The Blahs have worked with Theatre in Education practitioner Jane Holden on Dorothy Heathcote's participatory drama tool, 'the mantle of the expert'.[14] This is a technique whereby the drama teacher or Theatre in Education practitioner endows a group of participants with a role of expertise in the narrative. 'Mantle of the expert' may involve the facilitators taking on roles of lesser status than the children with whom they work, asking the advice of the experts, giving them responsibility in the fictional moment, and a degree of responsibility for the way in which the narrative itself develops. For me the technique epitomises British Drama and Theatre in Education practice in its underlying motivation – student empowerment.

The ten-year-olds with whom the Blahs work on the pilot project are asked to consider a realist parallel to Hansel and Gretel, the story of two children put on a train by their mother, who thinks they have a better chance of survival in the city at the end of the line than they will in the war zone where the family lives. The children are introduced to the Hansel and Gretel figures, Adlan and Aida, who won't speak except in their sleep; they are clearly troubled by terrible dreams. The children's expert role is a psychotherapeutic one. They are specialists in dream interpretation, and their first encounters with the company are based around building these roles – deciding what kinds of problems or incidents lead to distressing dreams and how one might speak to, treat, gain the trust of a traumatised person. The theatrical act of play whereby objects can be made to represent objects and figures in a narrative is transferred to a realist setting, which not only lends itself to interpretation but demands it. The children watch and listen to the sleeping Adlan and Aida, played by Russell Dean and Ruth Cooper, turning and murmuring in their sleep; they see the boy character play with a structure he has made out of wood, string and paper. Their role at this point in the drama is, essentially, to get the boy to speak of whatever trauma has brought about his silence and dreams.

The class I witness working on the pilot is fascinated by watching the adult actor play a child playing; the children maintain a concentration as intense as Adlan's as he plays with his paper figures. When the class look into Adlan's box they find what they take to be a warscape, the site of an explosion, or a dump on which the child and his friends have been secretly playing. They also have the opportunity to look at pictures that the girl of the pair has drawn and screwed up. When asked for suggestions for how to find out more, the children seem remarkably well versed in therapeutic techniques. They suggest playing alongside the boy at first, getting the child to talk about his play rather than asking him outright if there are links to his own experience.

The semiotic workings of this participatory drama appear to be more strictly delimited than they are in the performance piece. The relationship between dream and reality at this stage in the project is literal: the lines Aida and Adlan mutter in their sleep as the dream experts watch them are directly related to the narrative of abandonment, abduction and escape that emerges as their 'true story' as the drama unfolds. It is eventually revealed through fragments of Aida's burnt diary that, when they reach the city, the children have been befriended by a woman called Angela, who eventually betrays them. Aida's sleep-talking and the diary show that Aida has been excited by the adult status this befriending stranger has given her, allowing her to try on her clothes and make-up, while her brother remains locked away, purportedly because he does not have 'the right papers'. The suggestion that Aida is being groomed by her captor for sexual abuse, and that she eventually kills her captor, makes one teacher uncomfortable about the explicit nature of the violence in the narrative. What disturbed me about this stage of the development of the project, on the other hand, is the archetype of the witch as it emerges from a series of realist modes: the Grimms' adaptation of the tale suits mid-nineteenth-century bourgeois sensibilities, while Antony Browne's sexualised illustration of the mother and witch evokes a twenty-first century child-trafficker who tempts Gretel with the trappings of womanhood. Treachery comes in the form of a glamorous, sexualised woman. It seems in foregrounding the reality of a mother who abandons her children – and in the pilot project she is played delicately and empathetically by Abi Horsfield – her demonic other, the child abuser, must always lurk in the background,[15] and we are in danger of reinforcing rather than challenging media-hyped fears around children.

What is exciting about both Blah Blah Blah explorations of Hansel and Gretel is their envisioning of the child as both interpreter and maker of meaning, and it is this that is emerging further as the company move away from the parallel *Hansel and Gretel* narrative they devised in the pilot. The intention is to return more explicitly to the fairy tale, to have motifs from it emerge in the two 'modern' children's dreams and paintings. This would seem to be an approach closer to Bettelheim's psychoanalytic one – which insists on the power of the 'original' tale – but there is a crucial difference. Bettelheim insists that there are particular and universal meanings to be found in fairy tales, albeit ones which vary according to the age of the listener. He also insists that these meanings are not to be made explicit to the child: interpretation of the child's enjoyment of the narratives would be an intrusive and disempowering probing into what, at any given moment in her life, might need to remain unconscious.[16] What the Blahs might offer through a combination of the 'mantle of the expert' technique and a return to the broad metaphors of fairy-tale is an opportunity to interpret and to make meaning themselves.

I began by getting into bed for the Socìetas Raffaello Sanzio's *Buchettino*, and I will end with that tale. Visually it is the simplest of the works described here. As narrator Monica Demuru explains to her audience, a large book on her lap, 'there is nothing to do here, and nothing to see;

you just have to listen. So, put your head on your pillow, close your eyes and open your ears because, you know, I want to tell you a story'.[17]

Perrault's tale, from which the piece is adapted, privileges hearing as the sense of the wise and sensitive. In Società Raffaello Sanzio's version, as in Perrault's, Thumbkin says little, but 'to make up for keeping his mouth closed, he kept his ears wide open, and his silence was a sign of cleverness and intelligence'. Thumbkin is the smallest brother of seven; like Hansel, he devises pebble and bread trails to return to his parents but eventually has to face the world – in this tale a child-eating ogre. Though Società Raffaello Sanzio cut Perrault's lightly misogynistic asides about women's propensity to nag and faint, they maintain Perrault's lightness of tone through some of the sound effects, little aural jokes on Thumbkin's tiny footsteps or the giant's unwholesome snoring and scratching. At the same time, the piece pulls no punches with regard to the violence and viscerality of the tale, and it places a similar emphasis on the materiality of food and eating as the Blahs' first *Hansel and Gretel* performance. Though *Buchettino* is the closest of all the pieces described here to the literary experience of being read to, what it shares with the other pieces is a relationship with its audience that shifts from authority – of the teller and the tale – to a relinquishing and interrogation of authority, not through the fiction alone but through the shifting status and meaning of the adult performers. Ania Michaelis' *König Lindwurm* in Freiburg and the Halle company's *Beauty and the Beast* present control and vulnerability in their performance personas, just as the tales deal with control and vulnerability. The Theatre Company Blah Blah Blah is experimenting with the degrees of control of meaning their audiences might be offered in both their performance and participatory work. Lying in our beds listening to the Società Raffaello Sanzio's sounds and narrations, we are being told a story – and we are enacting being told a story – which appears to be, excitingly and terrifyingly, somewhat out of the storyteller's control.

The strength of all this work is the role it gives its audience in the production of meaning. It assumes that a child is an interpreter and a maker of the meanings of tales whose motifs and first conditions of production are partly analogous, partly other to their own experience. The theatrical embodiment of the tales brings the child face to face with vulnerability and loss in manageable form, as Bettelheim suggests it should; these pieces also suggest a child capable of interrogating his or her own vulnerability and the authorities that protect them or render them so.

Notes

1 A. Miller, *For Your Own Good: Hidden Cruelty in Child-rearing and the Roots of Violence*, trans. H. and H. Hannum, London: Virago, 1987.
2 J. Zipes, *When Dreams Came True: Classic Fairy Tales and their Tradition*, London: Routledge, 1999, Chapter 4, 'There were Two Brothers called Grimm', pp. 61–79 (p. 72).

3 Zipes, *When Dreams Came True*, p. 20.
4 See M. Warner, *From the Beast to the Blonde: On Fairy Tales and their Tellers*, London: Chatto and Windus, 1994; see also Zipes, *When Dreams Came True*, pp. 38–43.
5 See Zipes, *Breaking the Magic Spell: Radical Theories of Folk and Fairy Tales*, London: Heinemann, 1979. Chapter 6, 'On the Use and Abuse of Folk and Fairy Tales with Children: Bruno Bettelheim's Moralistic Magic Wand', pp. 160–82.
6 B. Bettelheim, *The Uses of Enchantment: The Meaning and Importance of Fairy Tales*, London: Penguin, 1991.
7 When Michaelis enacts the story for a group of predominantly very young children (the piece is advertised as suitable for children aged six and above), this is where the story ends. For an older group, or mixed group of adults and children, the story continues as in the Danish version. Sven Grundtvig's version in *Gamle danske Minder i Folkemunde* (Copenhagen, 1854–1861), vol. 1, no. 216 can be found in 'Folklore and Mythology: Electronic Texts', trans. 1998 D. L. Ashliman at http://www.pitt.edu/~dash/snake.html#lindorm.
8 The performance referred to took place at the Traverse Theatre, Edinburgh, as part of the 2004 Bank of Scotland Children's International Theatre Festival organised by Imaginate.
9 Bettelheim, *Uses of Enchantment*, p. 160.
10 J. Zipes, *Happily Ever After: Fairy Tales, Children, and the Culture Industry*, London: Routledge, 1997, pp. 48–9.
11 *Hansel and Gretel*, illustrated by Anthony Browne, London: Julia McRae Books, 1981. It is interesting to note that Quarrie's name appears in this edition with the publication data, and the name 'Grimm' not at all. The same assumption appears to have been made here as Bettelheim's – that Victorian literary versions of these tales are the 'originals', their authors and their period immaterial to interpretation.
12 All quotations from the first Theatre Company Blah Blah Blah work-in-progress performance are from Brian Higgins' text.
13 Bettelheim objects to realist revisioning of fairy tales and insists that children need figures of pure good and evil.
14 For a full account of this technique see D. Heathcote and G. Bolton, *Drama for Learning: Dorothy Heathcote's Mantle of the Expert Approach to Education*, Portsmouth, NH: Heinemann, 1995.
15 There are obvious stepmother/witch parallels in the Grimms' tale, which Anthony Browne's illustrations highlight by giving the stepmother and witch the same thin, rouged lips and beauty spot; at the end of the Grimms' tale, the children return to their father's house to find that their mother (like the witch) is dead. Zipes explores the parallel in *Happily Ever After*, pp. 49–55.
16 See Bettelheim, *Uses of Enchantment*, p.18.
17 Sociètas Raffaello Sanzio, *Buchettino*, trans. Gillian Hanna, from the version of the tale by Charles Perrault, *Histoires ou contes du temps passé, avec des moralités: Contes de ma mère l' Oye*, Paris, 1697. For Andrew Lang's English version, see Lang, *The Blue Fairy Book*, London: Longmans, Green, and Co, c. 1889, pp. 231–41.

Chapter 12

Make-believe

Società Raffaello Sanzio do theatre

Nicholas Ridout

I

The curtains are white. As the house lights go down the crack of a whip is heard through the auditorium. A spotlight shines brightly, getting brighter and fiercer, on the white curtains, at the point at which they meet, as though someone were about to slip out between them on to the forestage and speak to us, to make some kind of announcement. Perhaps an actor is indisposed and an understudy will appear in his or her place tonight. Instead of someone stepping into this light, a small sign, bearing a word or a message of some kind, is pushed out into the light. The hand of whoever is holding it is briefly visible. The sign says '. . . vskij'. This sign, perhaps, will stand in for someone, for Stanislavski[j] perhaps,[1] the actor, director and teacher of theatre who has done so much to shape our modern understanding of what it means to stand in for, to represent, another human being.

The sign disappears, but the spotlight remains. The curtains billow outwards and flutter. Someone or something is moving or pushing against them from on stage. The curtains billow outwards again, and again, in what starts to feel like a predictable rhythm, and eventually they open to reveal, swinging in the grey cold light of the stage, a huge battering ram with a carved face: a monstrous, simple mechanical thing that seems to be the only thing alive here. Like the sign '. . . vskij', this wooden ram is dead, but it is the image of something living. It is animated, given soul and breath, just as an actor might be said to give life and soul and breath to the dead. The great actors, it is said, bring their characters to life before our very eyes.

When the curtains open again there is a pile of shoes centre stage right and a man in a white robe, long brown hair and a beard, sitting centre stage left. This makes him look like Jesus Christ.[2] Not, of course, like a real historical figure, of whom we have no images, but like the countless images produced by Christian iconography, by Raphael, Leonardo and the rest. He looks like he is a copy of an image of a man who was, they say, the Word of God made flesh (given life and soul and breath, and ultimately, the weakness of mortality). The God who became man – incarnated, embodied – and then died was then represented in paint and is now re-embodied, reincarnated or perhaps, we might say, resurrected, in the form of this actor with long hair, a beard and a white robe. Brought to life before our very eyes.

Beside him there is a machine with little glowing lights. This turns out to be an endoscope, which the actor inserts through his nostrils so that it transmits a live image of his vocal cords to a circular screen above his head. As he speaks the first lines of the play, we see how his voice is produced: we see, that is to say, the word made flesh. Or rather, we see an image that represents the word made flesh. The medium of the endoscope represents the man's vocal cords. It puts them somewhere else. In reproducing them it *makes* them somewhere else. The most striking thing about this particular reproduction is how real it feels. It feels so real that many people in the audience can barely look at it. No one, it seems, experiences this as an image. It is experienced as reality: 'I actually, literally saw his vocal cords!' But it was an image, all the same.

This describes the opening of Societas Raffaello Sanzio's *Giulio Cesare*, a production premiered in 1997, and which toured extensively in Europe until it finally played for the last time in Le Mans, France, in 2003. The production is Shakespeare's *Julius Caesar*, with additional material from the Roman historian, politician and orator, Cicero.[3] This production, like the company's *Oresteia* (1996), was often remarked upon for the extraordinary way in which human and non-human bodies appeared on stage,[4] and the company has, more generally, been acclaimed for the intensity of the 'reality' of the action presented on stage. Such accounts of the company's work tend to identify it as a further (and belated) contribution to the traditional European avant-garde, for which, in theatre, Artaud tends to stand as the emblematic figure. Typically, the avant-garde is understood to be interested in collapsing the distinction between art and life, and therefore part of its programme was to do away with an art that tries to copy life. Painting will rid itself of slavish dependency upon the real world by suspending its figurative activity (painting things) and will instead just paint. Theatre finds it hard to make such a radical break, of course, since people appearing on stage find it very hard to avoid looking as though they are supposed to represent other people. Theatre seemed irredeemably contaminated by its historic entanglement with representation, and it was difficult to conceive of a way of breaking with this past. Artaud sought a solution, by insisting that the theatre should reverse the usual theatrical relationship, in which the actors and objects on stage represent a life off stage, and that it should offer instead an encounter with 'life'[5] of which human individuals are merely representations: through a theatre of sound and gesture, human actors would offer a revelation of an inhuman 'life' in which we are all cruelly caught up.

What I would like to suggest in this essay is that this tendency to see the 'real' in the work of Societas Raffaello Sanzio is in fact an effect of the success of their theatrical pretending. Far from making theatre that follows Artaud into a denunciation or transcendence of theatrical representation,[6] or that aligns itself with artists such as Marina Abramovic, for whom 'theatre was an absolute enemy',[7] they are actually doing good old-fashioned theatre, in which representation is absolutely the central concern. My own first encounter with the work, which was with *Giulio Cesare*, felt like an encounter with something absolutely alien, unlike any theatre I had ever witnessed before. The obvious explanation for this might be offered in terms of the real, live horse, the emaciated bodies of the two women playing Brutus and Cassius, the visceral impact of an actor playing Mark Antony without a larynx, the sheer volume of the wrestler in the role of Cicero, not to mention the extraordinary experience of being shown another person's vocal cords. The overwhelming sense of an encounter with something strange and powerful would be attributed to the impact of all this 'real' stuff. But, as I've already suggested, it wasn't real at all. An image of vocal cords was displayed, not the cords themselves. The horse was caught up in a complex system of representations (involving the skeleton of a horse and a model of a seahorse), so that its value as real, live horse was subsumed by its position as one of several signs for the idea of 'horse'. The actor without a larynx spoke 'viscerally', but as part of a rhetorical strategy in which the character Antony claims not to be speaking rhetorically, a subterfuge clearly articulated and amplified by the way the actor pointed out to the audience the Latin word '*Ars*' (art), inscribed upon the pedestal from which he stepped down to speak. The strange and alien thing that I had encountered here was theatre. The tendency in critical responses to the work to emphasise the 'real' as opposed to the pretend is testimony to the success of the pretending. The theatre is working; it is making us take its make-believe for real. The intensity of the encounter was produced by the fact that I had never seen anyone else taking the imitation game so seriously. It was as though no other theatre had considered that it might be possible to make representations that might be taken for the real thing; as though no one else believed that the theatre might be a kind of magic.

Perhaps even the most naturalistic drama of the twentieth century ultimately knew (or thought it knew) that it was only pretending, and that nothing real could be made by pretending. Indeed, the rational scientific basis for theatrical naturalism would surely compel a denial that anything as supernatural as magic might be possible. That the contemporary theatre company most commonly associated with the fervently anti-naturalist European avant-garde should turn out to be devoting itself so thoroughly to the old theatrical 'magic' of mimetic representation is perhaps both paradoxical and inevitable:

> Iconoclasm was a maternal and important word for us. A powerful word for those of us who were experiencing the same horror as regards art as had Plato. For him optical reality was deceitful in relation to the incorruptible truth of ideas. Instead of eliminating the deceits of optical reality, art reproduced them, seeking in vain to transcend them. But how could it be possible to transcend reality while making abstractions from its phenomena? How could it be possible to re-make the world without holding in your hands all the elements of the world itself, including your own hands? It is this paradox that entangles in contradiction that art which is in every respect most similar to existence itself: the theatre.[8]

From the very beginning, then, the company made a commitment to 'iconoclasm':[9] a critical practice that deploys images or representations in order to explore how their work of deceit is achieved. As Nick Kaye and Gabriella Giannachi suggest, the company 'address the limits of their own rhetorical means from within'.[10] Like all genuinely critical practices, the work becomes an investigation of the conditions under which something might be possible: in this case, how it might be possible to make theatre. Theatre's own representational tools will be turned on themselves, just as, in order to make a copy of the world, you would need to make first a copy of your own hands. Everything about the project is contaminated by doubleness or irony. So even the clearest statement, in the classic avant-garde rhetorical form of the manifesto, turns out to be turned against itself. The reader must believe Claudia Castellucci to be speaking both truth and deceit when she writes in the manifesto that accompanied the production of *Santa Sofia, Teatro Khmer*:

> This is a theatre that refuses representation. . . . We know the real and we've been disappointed with it from the age of four. Perhaps it's not like that for you? . . . This is the khmer theatre, we declare it loud and clear: which is about making a clean slate of the whole world. This is an iconoclastic theatre: it's about throwing down every image by adhering to the only fundamental reality: the anti-cosmic Irreal, everything which is not thought.[11]

A theatre may 'refuse representation', but it can only do so by means of representation – in a play, in this case, in which two iconoclasts (Leo III and Pol Pot) are represented on stage. Rather than a decisive statement, this ironic rhetoric opens up the space for the questions posed by critique, questions about the nature and purposes of theatre itself. How do you make things come alive? How do you make people die? How do you make the dead come back to life? How do you conjure ghosts? What are the powers and the terrors of representation?

2

Announcing a 'Year Zero' of theatre in which everything that had gone before must be swept away, the company, naturally, set about a rigorous education in theatre practice and history. In an interview with Federico Tiezzi, Chiara Guidi (one of the four founder members of the company in 1981) explains their process:

> In the first years of work, we did tremendous exercises for the voice and for the body. The first texts of theatrical theory we familiarised ourselves with were Aristotle's *Poetica* and Grotowski's *The Poor Theater*; these were followed by Stanislawski's and Diderot's texts.[12]

Tiezzi also records that 'It was Chiara who introduced the group to Artaud's *The Theater and its Double*, while Romeo tried out the theater of the Weimar Republic, and then introduced Appia, Craig and Schlemmer'.[13]

One might therefore conceive of the company's work as a series of acts of resurrection or reanimation, constantly bringing back to the theatre the basic problems that have always haunted it: how best to make actors appear as though they were real people, and how best to make the stage appear as though it were a real world. Perhaps the core problem might be simply posed: How do we create truth in a place which is not the 'real' world? Unlike a modernist avant-garde practice, that might want to eliminate the past (perhaps using the rhetoric of Year Zero iconoclasm), Sociètas Raffaello Sanzio pursue this question along their own 'iconoclastic' path by means of acts of restoration rather than destruction, or rather, by means of a destruction that both creates and preserves.

The history of theatre and theories about how to make it are only one aspect of the company's commitment to historical research. Their creative practice is a continuous research activity, and one particularly fruitful source of inspiration, and methodological example, has been the work of Aby Warburg. Aby Warburg was an art historian who devoted much of his life to the exploration of the reappearance of images of pagan antiquity in the art of the European Renaissance.[14] There is an immediate parallel that might be drawn between Warburg's lifelong project and Sociètas Raffaello Sanzio's polemical engagement with Attic tragedy, in which, like Warburg exploring images of pagan antiquity in renaissance art, Sociètas Raffaello Sanzio seek out the pre-tragic within the tragic, and also attempt the impossible act of restoring tragedy itself to the contemporary stage.[15] In both practices there is a clear determination to identify the persistence through historical time of images and symbolic forms. There is also, perhaps most importantly for this particular line of thinking about the work, a shared interest in the nature of mimesis, its relationship with magic and magic's strange affinity with scientific rationality.

In 1895, as part of this exploration of magic, mimesis and rationality, Warburg undertook an anthropological study of various ritual practices of the Pueblo people of the southwestern United States, eventually published as the text of a lecture given in 1923.[16] Of particular interest to Warburg was the Serpent Ritual, in which dancers summoned up thunder and thus rain by means of a dance in which they held live rattlesnakes in their mouths. Warburg saw in this not only a survival into technical-rational modernity of a form of magical thinking, but also an act of mimesis – the dancers imitating the snakes who, in turn, stand for the lightning, which, with thunder, will accompany rain. The idea that mimesis might have a magical impact upon the real world is what Warburg wanted to insist upon, and in so doing suggest that there has been a shift from one kind of mimesis (magical) towards another, in which symbols and images are no longer believed to possess magical powers in the real world, but merely represent aspects of the real world. Mimesis is not in the world, so much as supplementary to it. Like Walter Benjamin,[17] Warburg developed a notion of mimesis in which there is still supposed to be an intrinsic or natural connection between sign and thing, rather than the merely arbitrary connection suggested by the rational linguistics of Saussure, in which there is no intrinsic connection between, say, the word 'cat' and the furry feline sitting on the mat, but only a conventional one, in which all the speakers of the language tacitly agree that the word 'cat' refers to the furry feline in question.

Warburg's interest in the possibility that mimesis might do more than just produce conventionally recognisable copies of the 'phenomena' of 'reality', if only we might allow ourselves to see things that way, continued right through to *Mnemosyne*. This was his final project, an unfinished collection of diverse images mounted in groups on boards, designed to uncover or assert profound associations between superficially unrelated instances of the human will to make images. As Matthew Rampley suggests in his account of *Mnemosyne*,

> In his last work, the incomplete pictorial atlas *Mnemosyne*, mimesis again plays a crucial part, in that the atlas maps out the visual signs of a transformation in human experience, from magical-mimetic identification to the logical-dissociative objectivism of the modern scientific world view.[18]

Mnemosyne[19] thus presents in images a narrative not unlike the implicit narrative of the Serpent Ritual lecture: scientific rationality gradually strips creatures and objects of their magical-mimetic powers, but these powers leave traces in the persistence of these images, and the beliefs that they inspire. Belief in the truth and power of images is the currency of mimetic theatre. Theatre seems thus to stand opposed to scientific rationality or, rather, exists (at least as conceived through the work of Societas Raffaello Sanzio) as a trace of the pre-rational magic that still has the power to offer a critique of post-magical rationality.

This transformation from magical identification to technological objectivity involves, for Walter Benjamin, for example, a loss of experience, and theatre might, one supposes, be in the business of restoring to its audience an experience of that lost experience, but doing so, cruelly, through illusion, through a restoration that is also destructive, because in seeking proximity it inscribes distance. The moment, that is, you try to get close to something, you become acutely aware of how far away it is. The restoration of the lost experience only accentuates the extent of the loss. The better the theatre gets at restoring an experience of the world, the more we experience it (the theatre) as the place where the world is not and cannot therefore be experienced.

For Warburg, this loss of experience – this theatricalisation of the world by means of mimesis   was the precondition for human progress. The opening sentence of his introduction to *Mnemosyne* reads: 'One may consider the conscious creation of distance between oneself and the external world as the basic act of human civilisation'.[20] Theatre is a conscious creation of a distance between oneself and another (possibly external) world. It becomes a space for the exploration of our own magical-mimetic powers and thought, the place where we start to look at our own mimetic behaviour and ask questions about it, a kind of constant mid point between magic and rationality. Matthew Rampley suggests that this is precisely what Warburg saw in the survival of the Serpent Ritual: an activity that combined aspects of both.

> The Indians themselves no longer exist in the state of absolute savagery, but stand in a hybrid condition between magic and logic; while certain primitive impulses have been sublimated into symbolic representation, others, particularly the urge to imitate, continue unabated.[21]

In the theatre, perhaps, there is a wavering between the pleasures of imitation and the responsibilities of representation, between magic and scientific knowledge, between truth and illusion, in which neither term will ever be quite what it seems. Diderot's famous paradox (in which it is claimed that it is the actor without feeling who can best express emotion on stage[22]) seems to be another way of looking at just this problem: the theatre can only approach its aim of complete identification between itself and the world — between actor and character, that is, by completely detaching itself from the world. Rather than feeling the feeling of the character, the actor must consciously stand to one side of the character. Perhaps Warburg himself, had it not been for a trick of nature, might have tested out this proposition for himself, for, as Kenneth Clark reveals:

> He should not have been an art historian, but a poet like Hölderlin. He himself said that if he had been five inches taller . . . he would have become an actor, and I can believe it, for he had, to an uncanny degree, the gift of mimesis. He could get 'inside' a character, so that when he quoted from Savonarola, one seemed to hear the Frate's high compelling voice; and when he read from Poliziano there was all the daintiness and the slight artificiality of the Medicean circle. Symbols are a dangerous branch of study as they easily lead to magic; and magic leads to the loss of reason.[23]

3

In January 2002, Societas Raffaello Sanzio opened the first episode of *Tragedia Endogonidia* at the Teatro Comandini (their permanent workspace) in the northern Italian town of Cesena. As with all subsequent episodes – there have been eleven in all – it took its title from the initial letter of the town and from its number in the sequence. This first episode was therefore called *C.#01*, and the final episode, which was presented (again in Cesena) at the end of a cycle that had produced episodes in Avignon, Berlin, Brussels, Bergen, Paris, Rome, London, Strasbourg and Marseille, was therefore *C.#11*. In the context of the discussion of theatrical representation and reproduction it should be recalled here that the title of the whole project – *Tragedia Endogonidia* – refers to an organism, in this case Tragedy, that is capable of reproducing itself. One might say that it is therefore an organism in which the gap between the thing and its re-presentation has closed to nothing, in which a kind of magical identification rather than a symbolic representation is taking place.

In *C.#01* an adolescent boy is lying on stage, as if dead, in a golden room which has contained most of the action of the episode. He wears a white shirt, black trousers and a black ski-mask. Lying beside him on the stage is a red fire extinguisher. This image is a theatrical reproduction of a photograph, widely reproduced in the Italian media, of the anti-globalisation protestor Carlo Giuliani, killed by the Italian police at the demonstrations in Genoa on the occasion of the G8 summit meeting in July 2001. Its efficacy as a reproduction of these reproductions depends upon our distance from the boy on stage, and upon his abstraction from anything else that might have been in the photograph, in that this allows us to read him as being the same size as the murdered Giuliani, whereas he is in fact a lot smaller. He is closer and smaller, reversing the usual rules of perspective, in which the further away you go, the smaller you get. Now, in front of the box a young man enters, wearing black trousers and black boots, but with his torso naked. He stands in profile and sings. He sings a song of lament, mourning, it would seem, the dead boy upstage. The song is in a language I do not understand. But that's not what really captures my attention. The voice seems to come from somewhere else. This is partly the effect of some very peculiar and almost undetectable amplification – all sounds here are manipulated live by the composer Scott Gibbons – but mainly because it is a soprano voice. This voice does not belong to this body; except that it seems to. The man's naked torso allows me to watch his breathing, to register the movement of his muscles and his ribcage. And, in fact, it turns out that the voice does belong to this body. The singer is Radu Marian, an endocrinological castrato.[24] Not only biologically incapable of reproduction, but also biologically capable of a peculiar gap between body and voice, a gap presented in this theatrical event as both obvious and indeterminable. The fact of his voice enables him to appear to be pretending to copy; that is to say, it looks very much as though he is miming, although he is not. This difficulty in making out the difference between the real thing and its copy grows progressively more intense through the episodes that follow.

In Brussels there is an almost intolerably extended sequence, which begins when an actor dressed in Belgian police uniform pours stage blood into a pool on the marble floor of the stage. He then places cards bearing numbers around the pool of blood, as though marking in advance for a press photographer the key pieces of evidence of the 'crime' that is about to be committed on the 'scene'. Another actor, also wearing a police uniform, undresses to his underpants and is then 'beaten' repeatedly by the first 'policeman' and an accomplice, until his body is covered in 'blood'. With each 'blow' of the baton comes a shattering noise from Scott Gibbons's live sound performance. It is almost as though the 'staging' of this event is so obviously signalled, and yet so meticulously 'mimed', that it is experienced as something intolerable, intolerably real. In Rome I enjoy the absolutely bizarre experience of watching a chimpanzee on stage for about ten minutes, wondering all the while whether it isn't perhaps just a man in a chimpanzee suit. In Strasbourg the evening ends when a real tank drives on to the stage through the back wall of the theatre, and for some weird theatrical reason it looks and feels like a make-believe tank. But both the chimpanzee and the tank are real – until, it seems, they get on stage. Like Claudia Castellucci's rhetoric in the manifesto that accompanied *Santa Sofia* in the theatre, the sheer fact of entry into the space of theatre condemns all reality to duplication, inversion and deceit. In the theatre, it's all make-believe.

Finally, back in Cesena, in December 2004, for *C.#11*, the stage is another room, not gold this time, but brown and beige. A perfect traditional naturalistic box set. Carpet, ceiling, ceiling light, table lamp, bed,

Figure 12.1   Socìetas Raffaello Sanzio, *Tragedia Endogonidia* (C.#11). Photograph: Luca del Pia.

telephone, door with a frosted glass panel. Everything you might want for a good game of naturalist make-believe. On the bed there's a cat. Yes, it's real. A small boy enters. He puts out the cat and settles into bed, reading from a picture book that looks like it's one of those graphic novels, still very popular in Italy, which we might think of as little hand-held domestic cinemas. His mother (we suppose that's who she is) enters, prises the book away from him, replacing it with a teddy bear and encouraging him to lie down to sleep. As the lights go down on this scene, a white curtain is pulled across the front of the stage, and the mother backs away from the bed towards centre stage. It is completely dark. Here in the Teatro Comandini, Raffaello Sanzio can play it their own way with no need to obey health and safety regulations. There are no exit lights. I can't see anything. I can't even tell whether my eyes are open or not. A sound starts to rise. It sounds at first like a little motor, rather tinny, regular, mechanical. Soon it increases in both volume and depth. Its sonority thickens into a vast motor roar. The air is moving in the auditorium, blowing a breeze across my face. This is both terrifying and exhilarating. I remember a terrifying dream from my childhood in 1970s America, a dream in which I was hiding with my brother and sister and mother and father underneath the kitchen table as a sinister aeroplane came high overhead, clearly about to release its atomic bomb. The following evening, however, I experience it differently. This time it is a thrill, a ride, as though I were suddenly in the plane myself, full of power, hurtling above the world on an unimaginably vast and thrilling journey. As the theatre vibrated around me, I felt that I had never flown so far or so fast. Gradually the sound started to subside, returning towards its initial tinny grating. On both occasions the whole experience must have lasted at least a couple of minutes. Surely this sound must have some utilitarian function: covering up an elaborate and noisy scene change, of course. As the lights came up, the white curtain was drawn to reveal the amazing new location to which the theatrical machine had transported me. The same room. Exactly the same. Except that the boy is gone from the bed, and a woman is now vacuuming the carpet. In the intensity of the restored experience I have been deceived into believing that I must be somewhere else.

Such deceit can be deadly, as the little boy (whoever he is, but with whom I find I have identified myself) will soon find out. It is not me, but the boy, my double, who has been transported. Seduced it seems by the mimetic lure of the graphic novel, he has been drawn, it seems, by fairy magic into a place that really is (and yet is not) somewhere else, for in the second half of the episode, the audience is conducted from one theatre space to another. In the second space there is eventually revealed a dark and sinister forest, with rain dripping through bare branches, car headlights on a nearby highway flashing through the gloom and, finally, the probing torch beams of the men who are hunting the boy down. Caught in the forest of his imagination the boy meets his death at the hands of a merciless child-killer, make-believe victim of a make-believe murderer to whom he was led by his own belief in make-believe.

The pain of this theatre is that every effort made to make make-believe work is made to unmake itself. We who believe in magic, in this brief traffic with the ghosts of the stage, will always be cruelly deceived by the truth that there is no life here, only death (life's copy, its double). At least the death performed in this theatre is make-believe, too. That may be a consolation: no one is dead, yet; but it is also, perhaps, true that it is death that we really came here to experience, and that we might perhaps have got away with it, just.

Notes

1 The programme booklet for the production includes, on its back cover, a photograph of Stanislavski in the role of Brutus in his own production of Shakespeare's *Julius Caesar*.
2 The image reproduced on the front cover of the programme booklet is of a fifteenth-century icon, *Christ's Face*, by Beato Angelico.

3   A full dramaturgy of the production is published, in Italian, with production photographs, in C. Castellucci, R. Castellucci and C. Guidi, *Epopea delle Polvere*, Milan: Ubulibri, 2002.

4   See, for example, P. Conrad, 'Shakespeare Made Sick', *Guardian*, 6 June 1999, in which the production of *Giulio Cesare* is discussed very largely in terms of the exposure of the actors' bodies, as 'scavenged exhibits' and 'specimens of privation'. As Bridget Escolme notes in her account of the production in *Talking to the Audience: Shakespeare, Performance, Self* (London and New York: Routledge, 2005, p. 172, fn. 15), Conrad also assumes that there is some kind of real-life endurance and torment being imposed upon the actors, a practice that he, mistakenly, associates with Artaud's Theatre of Cruelty.

5   By 'life', here I am trying to suggest the existence of a force that endures beyond the life of any individual. Today's most obvious way of thinking about such a 'life' would be to think of DNA: a code of life which makes use of individual human beings as a medium for its own self-perpetuation. The realisation that this is what is 'really' going on, and that our own little lives are simply means to an impersonal end, is one way of describing what Artaud meant by 'cruelty'.

6   See, for example, A. Artaud, *The Theatre and Its Double*, London: Calder Publications, 1993 and, for an influential essay on this aspiration to replace representation with 'life' or 'cruelty' in Artaud's writing, see J. Derrida, 'The Theatre of Cruelty and the Closure of Representation' (*Writing and Difference*, trans. A. Bass, London and Henley: Routledge and Kegan Paul, 1978, pp. 232–50).

7   Marina Abramovic in N. Kaye, ed., *Art Into Theatre: Performance Interviews and Documents*, Amsterdam: Harwood Academic Press, 1996, p. 181.

8   Claudia Castellucci, cited in Romeo Castellucci, 'L'iconoclastie de la scène et le retour du corps, la puissance charnelle du théâtre', in Castellucci and R. Castellucci, *Les Pèlerins de la Matière: Théorie et praxis du théatre, Écrits de la Socìetas Raffaello Sanzio*, pp. 99–100 (author's translation).

9   Iconoclasm normally refers to the destruction of images, such as, for example, Emperor Leo III, who ordered the destruction of all the icons in the Christian Church. It was taken up by the company as the theme of one of their early productions, *Santa Sofia, Teatro Khmer* (1985), in which the central characters are Leo III and the Cambodian revolutionary leader Pol Pot.

10 N. Kaye and G. Giannachi, *Staging the Post-Avant-Garde: Italian Experimental Performance after 1970*, Bern: Peter Lang, 2002, p. 144.

11 Claudia Castellucci, in C. Castellucci and R. Castellucci, *Il teatro della Socìetas Raffaello Sanzio, dal teatro iconoclasta alla super-icona*, Milan: Ubulibri, 1992, p. 9 (author's translation).

12 F. Tiezzi, 'Socìetàs Raffaello Sanzio: L'anima mentale e l'anima passionale, La memoria di un incontro di Federico Tiezzi', in *Westuff: Quarterly Magazine of Art, Fashion and Music*, 5, November–December 1986, p. 69.

13 Tiezzi in *Westuff*, p. 69.

14 See A. Warburg, *The Renewal of Pagan Antiquity: Contributions to the Cultural History of the European Renaissance*, introduction Kurt W. Forster, trans. David Britt, Los Angeles: Getty Research Institute, 1999.

15 'Our intention with this production is to rethink tragedy, bring it into the here and now', Romeo Castellucci, in 'The Universal: The Simplest Place Possible', interview V. Valentini and B. Marranca, trans. J. House, *Performing Arts Journal* 77, 2004, pp. 16–25.

16 Aby Warburg, *Images from the Region of the Pueblo Indians of North America*, trans. M. P. Steinberg, Ithaca: Cornell University Press, 1995.

17 See W. Benjamin, 'On the Mimetic Faculty', in *One Way Street and Other Writings*, introduction Susan Sontag, trans. E. Jephcott and K. Shorter, London: Verso, 1985, pp. 160–3.

18 M. Rampley, *The Remembrance of Things Past: On Aby M. Warburg and Walter Benjamin*, Wiesbaden: Harrassowitz Verlag, 2000, p. 19.

19 In May 2004, as part of the presentation of episode IX, L.#09 of *Tragedia Endogonidia*, Romeo Castellucci presented an 'Atlas Room' of images that had played a part in the creation of the episode, in a form and with a title that directly responded to Warburg's uncompleted project (which is now archived at London's Warburg Institute).

20 A. Warburg, 'Mnemosyne – Einführung', in Warburg Archive, Warburg Institute, 102.1.1, p. 2.

21 Rampley, *The Remembrance of Things Past*, p. 37.

22 Denis de Diderot, 'The Paradox of the Actor', in *Selected Writings on Literature and Culture*, introduction and trans. G. Bremer, London: Penguin, 1994, pp. 98–158.

23 K. Clark, 'A Lecture that Changed my Life', in *Mnemosyne: Beiträge zum 50. Todestag von Aby M. Warburg*, Göttingen: Gratia-Verlag, 1979.

24 Radu Marian, born in Moldova of Romanian parents in 1977, is a natural male soprano whose voice resembles those of the so-called castrati (boys castrated before their voices broke mainly in order that they could sing soprano roles in opera).

Chapter 13

After the fall

Dance-theatre and dance-performance

Adrian Heathfield

What is the cultural significance of the artistic innovations of European dance-theatre, the interdisciplinary movement that transformed the aesthetic contours of Western dance and experimental theatre in the 1980s and 90s? How did this movement reflect and reconfigure understandings of the body, social relation and movement itself? How might this body of choreographic practice be related to the current European scene of prolific experimentation at the interfaces of dance and performance art? Given performance art's status in contemporary cultural and critical discourse as an art form that epitomises transience and thus perturbs the cultural mechanisms and economies that seek to name, place and capitalise it, how is time re-figured across these shifts in choreographic practice? What might dance-theatre and dance-performance have to tell us about the manifestation and perception of time in the contemporary?

Pina Bausch's response to the empty formalism of the dance against which she turned was to assert through dance the drive to move. The inaugural question of this work was not, How does the body move, but Why? In the wake of this question, dance-theatre went in search of the psychological and emotional drives of physical expression, and against the context of the personal and sexual politics of the 1980s and 90s, found its *métier* as an embodied language of desire. Its aesthetics asserted the performer's personal history and identity as an indispensable *content*, overturned hierarchies of power in role and relation, exploded the repressive postures of grace and poise, stretched the performer's body and the audience's nerves through highly energised risk-taking, resisted narrative structures, opened the status of the musical score and generously liberated meaning through a sensual poetry. Dance-theatre had a powerful influence on Western choreographic practice, but it also spawned forms of physical theatre conducted by directors and dramaturges outside of dance-trained contexts. Physical expression was placed in a new relation to the verbal in these moves, but the body *in extremis* became dance and physical theatre's primary instrument and site of relational and cultural critique. The work pressed hard against psychic and physical limits, finding insights and new means of articulating the dynamics of gender, sex and sexuality in human relations. Ecstasy and agony were often intertwined in this work as a way to relay the personal and cultural resonances of the interdependence of presence and absence, masculinity and femininity, sex and death, attainment and loss. As such, dance-theatre and physical theatre articulated a certain wounding in the nature of sexual (and social) relation. Positioning the performing body as the vital means through which to access and articulate this wound, they also offered it up as a promising means of cure, or at least resistance, through the exertion of movement itself. Perhaps this is why the repetition of falling became such a dominant figuration in the choreography of dance-theatre: trusting in relation, in the will and flesh of others, dance-theatre's emblematic, sacrificial body fell again and again, subject to the violent disregard of the other. The other couldn't catch that fall. But the fall contained an imperative, like all sacrifices, for the social body (the audience): the imperative to recognise, remember and repair.

I want to linger for a little while in one specific work of Bausch's that I cannot help thinking of as a kind of exemplary origin of many of the formal and discursive co-ordinates of 1980s and 1990s dance- and phys-ical-theatre. Bausch's late 1970s work *Café Müller* inaugurates a terrain of questioning around the relations between gender, desire, memory, love and loss. As such it is a groundbreaking, intense and complex work. Whilst this short analysis will inevitably betray the philosophical weight and cultural resonance of this piece, it may at least enable insight into some of the ideas at stake in a particular interdisciplinary move between dance and theatre. This crossing of forms facilitates a questioning of relations of body, identity and place and hence a realignment of their cultural reso-nance. Here in *Café Müller*, and perhaps even more extensively in Bausch's later work, the wounded body, and the wound at the heart of sexual and social relation, attests to a profound instability in the structures of belonging that anchor bodies and identities to place. Bausch's later works will see this question of belonging articulated in relation to notions of nation, of the new Europe and the global subject, but here in *Café Müller* belonging is manifested more as a psychosexual and interpersonal question.

What is this place, *Café Müller*, where Bausch's dancers enact their fleeting encounters and broken relations? Beyond its simple function as an urban resting place in which to eat and drink, a café is a gathering place, a place of social exchange, pleasure and consumption; it is a place from which the social itself is observed and discussed. The café holds a particular place within European cultural imagination as a scene of modern innovation, of prolific artistic and social mixing. But Rolf Borzik's scenography creates a blank, indeterminate and cavernous space through which this history must only echo. In Borzik's design, the café's main and determining facets are its entrances and exits, its walls and glass partition walls, and its chairs and tables, which act as 'obstacles' to the dance. Whilst these facets are themselves nondescript, the scale of the doors and walls, and the high number of tables and chairs, suggest that this is a kind of post-social, evacuated space; a residue of a once bustling, intense and productive social scene. It is tempting to read this evacuation, this night-of-the-social, as a reflection of the cultural and historical wounds of Europe, or as a kind of post-modern limbo, but its scenic resonance is hard to resolve. What is clear is that this is an after-space: a space of remembrance and re-enactment within the present. In the wake of the party or catastrophe, Bausch's performers seem somewhat like revenants or ghosts, re-staging the forces and dynamics of a life that has already been left behind.

If the scenography of *Café Müller* gives little clue towards the location and nature of this social catastrophe, Bausch's dance furnishes us with multiple possibilities of definition. Here, the discursive terrain is the nature of relation itself – amorous and sexual relation, in particular – within the broader context of the constitution of the social. Movement is formulated as the locus of both the conservation of social and cultural orders of power, and their disassembly through subversive reiteration. As most dancers will tell you, the body is a house of habituation: one holds oneself, acts and moves, according to learned customs laden with often unknown and undisclosed values. Power relations are thus inhered in habitual practice. But a body is also an agency for unlearning, and the subversive reiteration of the habitual practice within an aesthetic may come to question the inherent values upon which that practice is founded. Bausch's deployment of simple physical action alongside choreographic fragments, the reiteration of driven gestural phrases, her use of inequalities of agency, power and tension in partnering, her attention to the materiality of scenic elements, enables her to conjure a set of relations where the psychological, emotional and phenomenological qualities of relationship are privileged as content. She replaces the cultural logics of relation with experiential soundings of subjection; an alterior, emotive and sensual logic is asserted. One might then see Bausch's reiterations of the violence of the inter-subjective, as a means to unlearn the political, emotional and psychological blueprint of gendered identity upon which relation is founded. Each reiteration produces a difference and, in its spectator, recognition both of a particular knowledge at a limit and the force by which it may be exceeded.

Bausch asks: How does the self know itself, and how does it know the other? What place do love and desire occupy in this quest? What role does memory play, in the experience of amorous exchange? Reflecting a social and cultural milieu that increasingly values transient connection over long-term bonding, Bausch's figures are desperate to relate but wary of being related. Their fleeting encounters, missed affinities, locked inequities, misrecognitions and divergent trysts, draw on, re-enact and proliferate in their spectators emotional and sense memories whose realm is the insufficiencies and failures of erotic relation. The stage is strewn with material objects that block reciprocity: the flows of movement crash through the café setting, chairs are strewn and walls are hit in Bausch's choreographic cycles of capture and escape. If the material fabric of the social sphere might seem to represent an obstacle to connection, obstruction is predominantly asserted as both a psychological and phenomenological dynamic. The female performers moving 'blind' through this potentially treacherous terrain are sporadically guarded by a male figure who hurriedly casts aside the obstacles in their flight paths. This figure acts as a kind of desperate and always belated protector, a witness, or surrogate audience figure. Pina Bausch dances through these scenes, somewhat cut off from her fellow performers, simultaneously floating and shuffling. She moves gripped by an interior reverie and repeatedly holds a gesture of open giving that seems already withdrawn. The inability of these figures to be in the present space of enactment suggests that each is re-enacting the pattern of dynamics that precede the present and hamper and restrict relation. The dancer's intense swings between capture and release, synergy and disarray suggest the impossibility of reciprocity is resident within the matter of bodies themselves. In *Café Müller*, the figures function as mutable personae ('characters' is perhaps too strong a word); they are ciphers for fleeting embodiments of sense-relation fragments. The anonymity and indeterminacy of these figures creates in the spectator an unanswerable need to name and know the figure, to stabilise their identity and return the work to the solid ground of clearly delineated identification. Sociality is thus manifested as an incomplete play, a relay, conducted by absenting agents, in the space between self-knowledge and self-loss, remembrance and forgetting, desire and its realisation.

Café Müller is an interrogation of the nature of the social bond, and in particular the relation between love and desire as forms of affinity creation. This relation is seen as an antagonistic interplay where love seeks the sustenance and protection of the other, and desire comes to consume that other, and by consumption, to discard it, destroying the cohesion of affinity. Bausch's question then, seems to be, how to hold another? How to sustain personal and social bonds given the antagonism of the forces that found our attraction to others? This question is asked relentlessly across gender division, within co-ordinates of power inequality. The answers are in fragments, and they are insistently phrased, not as meaning or as rational knowledge, but as sensory, emotional and embodied knowledges. Bausch stages experiential reports from love's battlefield, the performance of somatic testimony, whose purpose is survival, and perhaps, an ethics through which this survival may be sustained. The frame of relationship is insistently that of amorous or desirous relation. Relationship does not extend beyond the triangulated set of self, other and another who comes to break apart the pair, and, while this set at least speaks of the psychic presence and wreckage of hetero-normative familial relation within love relations, it barely comes to constitute a more extensive notion of social relation. *Café Müller* thus indicates and reflects the fragmentation and declension of the social sphere, in a culture increasingly obsessed with the force of individualism, and its accordant economies of pleasure.

What I want to hold on to in Bausch's work, however fleetingly, is its capacity to transport its spectators, through this physical realm of broken gestures and relations, into alternate orders and experiences of time. The shape of occurrence here is organic, musical. Movement is not simply set to a score, but occurs, and is then found by music: Henry Purcell's *The Fairy Queen* and *Dido and Aeneas* emerging softly into audition, as it if it had always been there. The structural organisation of movement events resists narrative force; the fragments of relation are arranged within emotional and sensory logics of causality. The use of gestural repetition and difference, cyclical events and relations, creates suspensions and returns in our experience, problematises our tendency to rationalise time. The tempo of movement itself follows an errant order, an invisible dynamic, alternately volatile and slow, persistent and inconsistent. The flows of movement seemingly arise without the performer's volition: they are carried in a kind of transport from elsewhere. *Café Müller* seduces its spectator into a similar reverential temporality, where the predominant cultural orders of time – linear, progressive and accumulative – are suspended. These aesthetic manoeuvres plunge us into the suppressed orders of temporality in contem-

Figure 13.1   Jan Minarik, Malou Airaudo and Dominique Mercy in Pina Bausch's *Café Müller*. Courtesy Pina Bausch and Ulli Weiss. Photograph: Ulli Weiss.

Figure 13.2 Jan Minarik, Malou Airaudo and Dominique Mercy in Pina Bausch's *Café Müller*. Courtesy Pina Bausch and Ulli Weiss. Photograph: Ulli Weiss.

porary Western capitalist cultures: time as it is lived in felt experience, in the folds and flows of phenomenal relation.

Interlude on writing Bausch

> *The author of this essay writes the following words whilst watching an often-recited clip from Bausch's* Café Müller *in which the dancers, Jan Minarik, Dominique Mercy and Malou Airaudo, enact an increasingly frantic trio. Airaudo, drifting blind across the space, has come to rest, intimately facing Mercy. Minarik enters from behind and purposefully places the couple in a loving embrace that he evolves into a tableau of Airaudo carried in Mercy's arms. Minarik leaves to exit and Airaudo falls through Mercy's arms, collapsing to the floor. She then immediately resumes her initial pose of disconnected facing. Minarik returns and precisely repeats this failure-bound gestural sequence in loops of increasing speed and desperation until there is a transfer of impetus and it becomes apparent that Airaudo's compulsion towards Mercy is driven not by Minarik, but by her own volition. This volatile cycle eventually stills and Airaudo drifts away unheld. Mercy appears unmoved.*

Seeing them, he knows he writes in this relation too. The event slips through his hands just as he tries to hold it, to bear its weight, to feel its consequence. He is dumbfounded. He writes from necessity, to answer a call. He writes with 'good intention'; he wants to honour the event, to live beside its life, to touch it, to dance a little while arm in arm, and then leave towards some other moves. He is uncertain that his aim is true. He cannot stand outside of the event, for, as he sees, he is already part of it. He is its witness. But his dancing is terrible. His gesture in and toward the event is an empty and frozen form of holding. His leaden arms fail the caress. He feels the weight of the event slip away and wound him further. He would like to leave. Other agents return the event to him. Shadowy figures sit at his shoulder: they guide back the event. He is full of hope and thinks the event somewhat different, perhaps alluringly so. And so it begins again. Each failed meeting an echo of the last, an echo without origin. Eventually he finds names for the three figures in this little dance. He names his guide Time. His partner in the dance, well her name is Desire. Though he wishes he were both Desire and Time, because he longs for absolute fluidity, he knows that his name, his name is Memory.

What has happened now to the trajectories of these discourses of desire, time and movement in the contemporary scene of interdisciplinary dance practice? I want to explore this question, not in the residual scenes of physical theatre, as it is increasingly assimilated and dissipated into the theatrical mainstream, but in the highly energised terrain of contemporary dance-performance, or what some have termed new minimalist dance. I'll take the work of La Ribot as exemplary of many of the aesthetic and cultural concerns of this vibrant movement. La Ribot's dance takes place, like the dances of her contemporaries Jérôme Bel, Xavier Le Roy, Boris Charmatz, Tino Sehgal, Goat Island and Jonathan Burrows, at a new intersection of performance practice. The previous generation of experimental choreographers from the dance-theatre of Pina Bausch through to the physical theatre of Lloyd Newson and DV8 took the structures and forms of theatrical practice as a vital source of an interdisciplinary leap. In the hyper-connective context of contemporary culture, cross-art-form practice, including the work of movement artists, is now much more promiscuous, ambitious, intensive and eclectic in its affiliations and borrowings. La Ribot's oeuvre quietly exemplifies something of this openness, whilst focusing its extension towards traditions of performance art within a visual arts frame. The work draws on the aesthetics of conceptual and minimalist art, emphasises action in 'real' space and time, and is often located within galleries and complemented by aspects of installation. But despite its appearances, its un-dance-like qualities, I want to hold on to this link with older choreographic practices. This is not simply because La Ribot's identity is undeniably marked by her history as a dancer, but because the question of this lineage opens up some thoughts on the nature of her work and its aesthetic and cultural significance – perhaps even on the nature of the relation between movement and time.

La Ribot's work is intensely conscious of dance-theatre heritage and its conceptual arrangements, but articulates them somewhat differently. For here, the round of gallery spectatorship replaces the theatrical frame; the frontal cedes to panoramic exposure; and the binary division of the performer–spectator relation is dispersed. The spectator is liberated from a static place by the choice and fluidity of promenade. This aesthetic side-step of the theatrical plane deftly brings the spectator into a field of social and sensory engagement without need for the energised railing against the cleavage of the proscenium, which was so much a part of dance-theatre's and physical theatre's agitated aesthetics. La Ribot's persona and her drive to move are also highly present in relation to both the work's content and its form. However, the work eschews physical theatre's high-impact viscerality and the forceful assertion of the self in favour of a quieter, bare – though nonetheless edgy – being. Its terrain is the place where dance dissolves into action, the movement of stillness and the exposed materiality of the flesh. This too is work in which limits are tested, but the boundaries in question are those of the performing subject herself: her somatic, emotional and psychological constitution of her self. In common with the works of Bausch, La Ribot focuses on the relation between the female body, memory and time. But, as solo performances, La Ribot's works fix less on the wound in relation and more on the wound at the centre of the experience of embodied subjectivity itself. She traces the phenomenological inability of her body to ever constitute itself as a body with solid boundaries and integrity. Relation here is between the self and its own lived memory, between the self and the social body that it meets in its performances. Always restaging singular acts of self-dissolution, La Ribot enacts the wound of time in consciousness that renders its foundational experiences simultaneously constitutive and lost. In this meditation on the relation between time and a particular lived body, what makes and defines movement is insistently questioned.

Take, for instance, her short work *Another Bloody Mary*, which appears as part of the long-durational performance *Panoramix* (at the Tate Modern, London, in 2003). Here we should note that *Panoramix* is a work whose temporality is marked by paradox: a single durational work lasting around three and a half hours that brings together thirty-four much smaller works (*Piezas Distinguidas*), some as short as a few minutes, all made over a period of ten years. It is a kind of life work, a re-collection of a dispersed series of events. The constituent pieces seem too short to be performance proper – the overall work seems too long. This contradiction of conventions makes evident that it is time itself, its measurement and its flexibility, that is the subject of the work. In *Another Bloody Mary*, La Ribot carefully lays out pieces of red cloth and clothing on the floor. Each red is a different shade. Clearly, there is logic to their relation, as they are precisely placed, as if each object is personally implicated in some way in the scene it is coming to constitute. The whole thing starts to look like a big puddle of spilled blood. She is bare in bright-green heels, which suddenly appear even more incongruous in contrast with the plane of red in front of her. She puts on a scruffy blonde wig and attaches a pubic equivalent, then turns over on one heel so that she is off kilter, and takes a slow, slow fall over a number of minutes, until she is splayed across the floor. Her body is arched back, her face extinguished by the smudge of hair, the red river issuing, it seems, from between her legs. But in this event the body finds the blood.

Watching this work, which is founded on the effect of bareness, I am struck most of all by the presence of hair. Remember Bausch's tireless reiteration of long hair as the primary signifier of femininity. The hair in Bausch's work always flowed freely, released from the tight grips of ballet's scraped-back and pin-headed purity. The hair swung and fell, it followed the deathly gravitational pull on the performer's bodies, it came to rest veiling faces, entangled, dishevelled, a mark of embodied distress. But always the hair was authentic, it had been to ballet school with the dancers, and it seemed that Bausch had set it free. The hair was the perfect accessory of Bausch's imperfect feminine. The female figures in Bausch's work

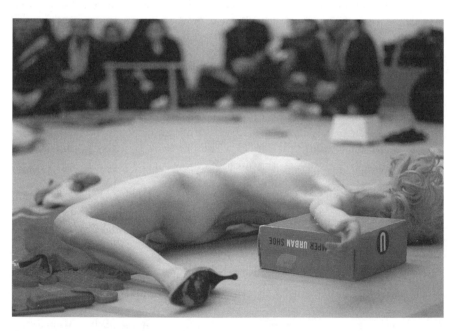

Figure 13.3   La Ribot, *Another Bloody Mary*. Photograph: Hugo Glendinning.

seem to reside in some perpetual condition of dishevelled night-time reverie, their silken slips barely lodged across exposed backs, their bodies just one step away from sleep, from a movement that would fully inhabit the life of the unconscious. Bausch's reconstitution of ballet's grace took the feminine form, but marked it as fallen: the female body was seen as torn, always already ruptured. What to make, then, of La Ribot's indisputably inauthentic mop, fixed on to an already dyed head of hair in front of our eyes, doubled, in case we were in any doubt, by a pubic wig, which lets us know that here is a question of veiling and exposure, of outsides and undersides, of the cloaking of sex? La Ribot is not so interested in the visual erotics of the fall, but in the idea that the visual order requires her to fall in order to constitute her as an image. Consequently she lets us see this falling – be with it, in all its detail, its muscular extension and somatic frailty – not as a resolved image, but as an extended moment, in which other instants arise.

In *Another Bloody Mary*, what is in question is the relation between movement and the image. Here it is a particular image of femininity that is subject to a thorough disarticulation. We stay for a long while in the grip of this image, watching the slow rise and fall of her breath inside this shattered feminine scene. It's a little like a kid's game of dress-up with its makeshift scenery and playing dead, but the game has gone seriously wrong. We are in a gallery, of course, and so it's a little like Marcel Duchamp's *Étant Donné*, but domestic and less anonymous, less furtive, less mythic. It's more like a forensic still from a crime scene, only very fake and very much alive. Perhaps I shouldn't think of it as an image at all: it's a feeling externalised, manifested in relation to objects and consequently relived. A life lived in the aftermath of the fall, bled out and empty, broken, dishevelled, but still interested in dissimulation, still breathing. What La Ribot does is first to inhabit and embody the image, then to subject that image to duration, where in the interplay between movement and stillness, life and death, the image is disarticulated, unfixed, brought to another articulation. I hear the lyrics of a song, overlaid, reiterating the confusion of tense – 'But my eyes still see', and later – 'I was dreaming of the past, and my heart was beating fast, I began to lose control, I began to lose control . . .'. Time slides in this duration, past and present intertwine and lose distinction, and I begin to lose control.

What seems to be at stake in the work of choreographers such as La Ribot is a reconsideration of the relation between the body, time and spectacle. Movement and stillness become key notions interrogated in these enactments, as a means to articulate and propose a resistant order of time. If Bausch's dance-theatre sought to initiate a phase-shift in the spectator's perception of time, to step aside from the culturally predominant perception of proper-time, and into another time more attuned to lived-time, it nonetheless installed a temporal model that was founded on conceptions of the economies and flows of desire. Whilst its aesthetic privileged sensual production and recognition on the part of the spectator, it constituted these exchanges, like those of its performers, as inevitably bound by psycho-sexual laws of relation. The spectator entered an experiential time–space configuration whose shape and rhythm was, if not cyclical, then at least spiral, composed of returns of attainment and loss within a descending trajectory. The fall was not just dance-theatre's predominant somatic trope, but its structural thought, its ur-gesture. Whilst the cultural value of this alternate time configuration can be seen as countering predominant models of temporality in Western late capitalist cultures – time as linear, progressive, accumulative – it nonetheless maintains a belief in time as continuous. La Ribot's experiments at the borders of dance and visual art continue this investigation of an alternate temporality, one closer to lived-time, but they do so uncertain of the very continuity of experiential time. Sensory-time is thoroughly instantiated as the time of spectatorship. This bringing back of time's repressed content necessitates an unfixing of the spectacle, which becomes a site where the mutual immanence of movement and stillness can be witnessed. La Ribot's body is the dispersed agent of this investigation, a displaced body, whose restlessness inside its long repose allows us access to that difference between the instant and what consciousness makes of it, to that vibration of being, where we touch once again time's discontinuity.

Chapter 14

What state am I in?

Or, How to be a spectator

Simon Bayly

> The word 'theory' derives from the Greek 'theorein', which means 'to look at'. According to some sources, it was used frequently in terms of 'looking at' a theatre stage, which may explain why sometimes the word 'theory' is used as something provisional or not quite real.[1]
>
> It is truth that is the new idea in Europe today.[2]

What can theatre be?

This oddly worded question has recently been posed by a five-year enquiry launched by the London International Festival of Theatre, an event which has played a prominent part in exposing London audiences to various flavours and forms of theatrical experience from Europe and beyond. On reflection, I hear what is being avoided in this question: it does not want to ask: 'What *is* theatre?' or even 'What *can be* theatre?' It is not interested in definitions or classifications or in annexing to the theatrical whatever vaguely resembles it. Instead, it appears to be hinting at an altogether different set of future possibilities. So, to rephrase, what *might* theatre be? To ask what theatre *might* be resonates as a plaintive request that it become different from what it is. To ask what theatre *might* be is to suggest that theatre as it actually appears does not yet answer to an imagined collective need for a certain experience *of* theatre. It is a plea for the re-imagination of the future of being together differently, of the stubborn communitarian impulse that is at the heart of the theatrical 'project'. To ask what theatre might be – a question that assumes a public address – is thus a question that demands the gathering together of impossibly disparate responses, a minimum form of assembly, as its guiding rationale.

The question of what theatre *might* be shies away from both the *can*, the *ought* and the *is*, replacing confidence or certitude with a fragile contingency that is unsure of tomorrow night. 'Might' here is very far from sure that it is right: theatre might turn out to be something vague, diffuse and overly diverse – or it might simply turn out to be nothing substantial other than the melancholic experience of its own desire to be something. There is a kind of all or nothing gambler's logic in this question, a sense that to ask it means to risk everything one has banked on, to give up whatever cultural capital has been accumulated in the hope of the big payoff.

What can theory be?

Arising as it does from looking at theatre stages, this essay must reckon itself as theory and so admit to the possibility that it is both provisional and not quite real. Similar to certain British views of Europe itself, in which things are never what they appear to be, cultural theory – a hetero-geneous body of largely 'continental', mostly French, writing that dates from somewhere in the mid-1960s – is variously characterised from British perspectives as either 'the largest body of self-serving, obscurantist, preten-tious emperor's tailoring bovine excrement to sully academic discourse since the gnostics or the alchemists'[3] or 'the way the greatest and most dramatic, rapid and universal social transformation in human history entered the consciousness of reflective minds who lived through it.'[4] Thankfully, I am not obliged to offer you a bracing summary of the theo-retical scene because, whatever view is taken, we are now (so theory goes, according to its finest exponents and explicators) so *post-theory*. Few of those of us who passed through the British university system between 1965 and 1995 will have escaped the far-reaching and possibly life-changing encounter with theory that became the educational orthodoxy in any self-respecting department of the arts and humanities (but conspicuously *not* of philosophy, where the reigning analytic tradition was largely content to deride 'continental' work as hopeless speculation or mysticism). And, if you have yet to undertake that passage, you can be sure that we will 'propose' a similar encounter to you when the time comes, though perhaps less sure of precisely why it might be necessary.

In this new life after theory, we are supposedly awakening into an alto-gether more moral, politically engaged and better existence, as if from a particularly thrilling but no less hallucinatory dream. One way in which academic discourses manage the transit to life after theory is to apply theory's basic tenets to itself and so read theory itself symptomatically: Derrida is deconstructed, the psychoanalytic theorists are psychoanalysed, post-modernism is hoist on its own petard. However, I want to suggest that the proper name of the pathology of which theory is a symptom is philosophy. Philosophy (continental flavour) itself passes via permutations of many other (masculine) names – Heidegger, Husserl, Bergson, Nietzsche, Kant, Spinoza, Leibniz, Hume, Descartes, Aristotle, Plato and so forth.[5] In turn, these names are the symptoms of another name – Socrates, the absent origin of philosophy, who, in writing nothing, appears as nothing other than a mutable figure of other people's speech and writing.

While philosophies might be fashionable, 'current' or of their time, philosophy itself is never contemporary. To make a wildly general assertion, philosophy is generated with a concern for what was 'originally' overlooked or forgotten, even as it constructs and deconstructs the very idea of an origin. Philosophy proceeds on the basis of a conviction that something important but very basic has been missed at some immemorial time, something that can only be recovered in an act of retracing steps not taken. Philosophers do not voyage out to make new discoveries – unlike theory, they never get near the 'cutting edge' of anything and rather prefer to stay indoors and rummage around in the attic for old, discarded problems. The question of what philosophy might actually be is itself a favourite pastime for philosophy, which would not benefit from the proffering of a further definition here, other than to say that it is not theory, though it may posit theories of many kinds (and some theory is excellent philosophy).

We are perhaps not familiar with the notion of philosophy as a practice, but a Socratic view of the history of philosophy would insist that in taking philosophy as consisting of ideas written in books and taught as such, we mistake philosophy for its shadow; philosophy exists not in its inscribed and collected history, but as something that *happens*, a dialogical practice that literally takes place between people and thus one that marks them out as a discrete unity of separate elements, allied in their commitment to find a common discourse that can integrate, rather than eliminate, or (as the current jargon has it) merely 'tolerate' or 'respect' their differences – which might simply be a method of ignoring them. To the extent that theatre and performance studies have wrested themselves away from their institutional origins in the study of literature, their success has been firmly based on the primacy of practice. Like the theatre in this understanding, philosophy as a practice is protective of its proprietary authenticity and ethical importance; it entertains a particular love–hate relationship with writing in particular and inscription in general; it attaches axiomatic value to the live, face-to-face encounter whilst seeking to absorb the distance lessons of representation and mediation; it wants to be both eternal and ephemeral, popular yet exclusive, open to all but truly appreciated by the dedicated few. Like the theatre, such an activity requires patience, perseverance and a great deal of rehearsal to yield results.

So, then, what *might* philosophy be? Or, rather, what might we want it to be, now? From my seat at the very front of the stalls, I can only venture this: philosophy is a shared attempt to pull the collective rug out from under our own feet in the hope that the experience of falling will bring us to a re-imagination of how life ought to be, but without anyone noticing until we hit the floor: the conversion of St Paul restaged as a pratfall. (By any account, this is a stupid definition of philosophy, but, as is suggested later, a confrontation with the stupid is a necessary consequence of the articulation of theatre and philosophy.) What, to this philosophical psychopathology, will then stand as exemplary of contemporary theatre in Europe will be theatre that permits a similar manoeuvre; as such, theatre and philosophy will be practices which will require a kind of built-in susceptibility to just such a sensibility in order to work its effects, a specific variety of participant-observer: the spectator open to his or her own undoing, someone for whom an encounter with the encounter is a necessity. Such a spectator might be one who seeks to evade a learned compulsion to read symptomatically and suspiciously in favour of some rather antiquated modes of engagement, among them commitment, fidelity, belonging. So, it might be that we need a theory of this hypothetical species of spectator, who does not quite fit the extant models: reader, critic, witness, observer, bystander, connoisseur, aficionado, follower of fashion.

What can Europe be?

If the descriptions given above of theatre and philosophy resonate obscurely with the project that is Europe, then it will be because Europe is no longer simply a question of geography. What is contemporary in Europe is that Europe is indeed not just a project, but also a theory (a model designed to explain, predict and master phenomena – nations and ethnicities among them), a philosophy (a staged re-imagination of how life ought to be) and an infinitely variable set of fine-grained, localised practices (like this essay, whatever you or I do that either chooses or is chosen to participate in the elaboration of this imagined life). Europe is at once a messy geopolitical reality and a pure abstraction, a club you can join if you know the bouncers and the dream of an ideal world republic purged of Platonic prejudice. On this account, the question of Europe represents a new order of political wager, whose stakes are often raised (as in Britain) to an artificially exaggerated level, on an act of fidelity to a highly variable conception of collectivity underwritten by equally variable notions of the philosophy, theory and practices of such a coming-together. What makes the question of Europe a painful, philosophical question is that it stages its own undoing, its very own pratfall, by begging all manner of other questions as it goes about the business of adapting itself to what happens. What will Europe be when, say, Morocco seeks formal admittance to the European Union, less than fifty years after its hard-won independence from French and Spanish colonialism? What are the limits of a union, or any kind of set of entities, when the qualifying rule for admission is that an element outside need only be physically adjacent to one element inside? What, literally on earth and beyond, could be excluded? If Europe is not simply the name of a new economic order for everybody everywhere who would rather not be American, how do we recognise and react to the advent of the new when the very act of recognition – the act of identifying a basic similarity between the new and the known – necessarily assimilates the new *to* the known and thus announces a desire for the disappearance of its fundamental otherness? How can a theory or philosophy of the new be raised to the level of conscious thought without pre-empting the very event it seeks to welcome?

There seems to be no escaping that, however one seeks to explain the phenomenon that is Europe, some symbolic surplus remains beyond all the economic, political and cultural specificities we might care to complicate it with. The French psychoanalyst and theoretician Julia Kristeva writes of Europe as a social ensemble possessed of both a *solidity* and a *fragility*, the latter arising from the former as a result of 'a particular mode of reproduction and its representations through which the biological species is connected to its humanity'. Europe thus becomes, against the better judgement of its post-colonial shame, the name of 'the good life' or, as Kristeva has it, 'a symbolic common denominator' created not in response to 'the *production* of material goods (i.e. the domain of the economy and of the human relationships it implies . . .), but, rather, to those of *reproduction*, survival of the species, life and death, the body, sex, symbol'. With typical far-sightedness (her essay dates from the late 1970s), she remarks:

> A new social ensemble superior to the nation has thus been constituted, within which the nation, far from losing its own traits, rediscovers and accentuates them in a strange temporality, in a kind of 'future perfect', where the most deeply repressed past gives a distinctive character to a logical and sociological distribution of the most modern type.[6]

As well as offering a more nuanced perspective on being 'in Europe', Kristeva's 'future perfect' – the grammatical way of talking about the past in the future ('you will have forgotten me by then') – strikes me as a good way to understand the meaning of the word 'contemporary' in the context of the occasion of this essay, beyond a simpler but redundant sense of 'whatever happens to be going on now'.

It seems the conflation of the questions of theatre, philosophy and the European contemporary staged above share a family resemblance of sorts at a structural level. Taken together, these questions invoke some future perfect possibility (for theatre, for philosophy, for Europe) as the cultivation of unaccommodating encounters with the alien, the new or the strange – as what will supply the necessary force to 'project', go forward, imagine a future – as *already inside and indiscernible from, but not identical with, what appears familiar*. The remainder of this essay sets out to give some substance to this proposal via a thinking that brings together theatre and philosophy.

Unaccommdating events

In his *Rhapsodie pour le théâtre*, the contemporary philosopher of the event and part-time dramatist, Alain Badiou, provides a humorous and polemical understanding of the theatre.[7] One of his more provocative assertions is the nature of the relationship between theatre and 'the State'. Here, the State is conceived both as a political entity and as the network of relations which structure what Badiou calls the 'situation', the latter being something akin to a set of discrete elements simply counted in a 'pure' numerical fashion as a multiplicity – in other words, what there literally *is*, say, students in the institution of a university – conceived as no more than that, prior to any effort at gathering together these elements into a higher-order system or theory.[8] It is 'stateliness' which performs that function, literally ordering the situation into a totality – the multiplicity of the set of students counted-as-one and so conceived as, say, the 'student body', regulated by a variety of opinions and knowledges.

Badiou opposes 'the theatre' to 'Theatre', echoing his philosophical distinction between the state and the situation. The former denotes the art of the state of things as a closed set of relations, a status quo governed by power grounded in a specific set of knowledges (what Badiou terms the 'encyclopaedia'). Representing representations, it states the State, so to speak, as the set of organised opinions that form the necessary basis of all sociality, but without saying anything about it. 'Theatre', on the other hand, *says* the State as a situation, not as a form of description or analysis at the level of content but rather as what delimits the 'stateliness' of theatre. The theatre (small 't') is the art of the State, isomorphic with politics. Thus, even today, all theatre is official in an obscure sense, with or without 'royal' or 'national' epithets: 'what is said in the theatre, even in a school hall with two lanterns, is said *en majesté*'.[9] This sense is particularly resonant in a British context, with its convoluted history of royal and aristocratic theatrical patronage and censorship. Theatre (small 't') demands a spectator whom it can address as a citizen-subject, someone who consents to being, as it were, put in his or her place.

For Badiou, Theatre (capital 'T') will thus be *an event* – something that happens, something particular, localised and situated – that upsets this address, emerging from within theatre itself, out of a certain 'void' within it. Each and every situation contains such a void, conceived not so much as pure emptiness but as an element that remains unnoticed or uncounted by the operation that produces the situation out of the counting-as-one of its other elements. As such, the event will neither have been planned nor anticipated. In such a saying, Theatre exposes 'the theatre' to the militancy of the event; Theatre will have been (future perfect) that which interrupted 'the theatre' and is thus a rare and anomalous phenomenon that can be encompassed by neither a political programme nor a theatrical style. As such, Theatre is a momentary but momentous event for the spectator equipped with a sensibility that is primed for such occurrences. The act of witnessing and subsequent public declaration for the event (*did you see that?*) inaugurates both the actualisation of the event itself and the *becoming-subject* of the one (or many) engaged in such an act of fidelity. Such a becoming is that of the spectator.[10]

Truth is an apparently implausible and redundant category within contemporary thought, but one which an ethics of the event desires to reanimate for philosophy, via one or other of its conditions: art, science, politics and love. Truths are not events that one can anticipate or preserve in a catalogue or album; rather, whatever manifests as a truth will do so as the perception of what has already taken place, of the eruption of the anomalous out of the status quo of a situation, which remains altered by this intrusion even as the event itself recedes.

What is meaningful – or, rather, truthful – is what Badiou calls the *generic* part of such an event, or what might be otherwise called the *anomalous*, a property akin to the relation between the situation-as-state and the event. From the point of view of the situation, the event is, as it were, invisible or indiscernible: it is literally *overlooked*. But one can declare publicly for the event, 'owning up' to being seized, pained or amazed by it and so making a relation between what is particular and what is universal. What was an event for me may have passed you by completely, but nevertheless, as capable of feeling such affections, we both know *what we are talking about*, not always to the extent that I might be willing to sign up for your declaration, but at least to the point where what was apparently indiscernible or 'void' has been raised up to a level of intelligibility and discursive possibility which fundamentally alters and reorganises the 'ongoing' situation.

One unavoidable conclusion of this line of thought is that a 'true' event is not an iterable phenomenon. This is perhaps the truly tragic condition that marks the struggle of much contemporary performance, sutured as it is to the processes of repetition. If an event can be said to be what punctuates experience and so becomes available to be produced itself *as* an event, the theatre evoked here is no more than a place where one attempts, against the odds, to solicit a density of events which are generically *rare* – infrequent, unanticipated, anomalous. In the end, such a theatre will simply be a circumscribed space where life as a generality is subject to an intensified discipline of controlled variables, in the hope of making something happen, constituted out of the following elements: actors, a director, decor, costumes, a text (or whatever stands in for one), a place, a public – which for Badiou is, or ought to be, an inconsistent, heterogeneous collection of *spectators*.

Unreasonable demands

There is, as many philosophies of performance declare, a void at the heart of appearing. But, rather than simply existing as something missing, a lack or gap, this void is possessed of a latent potentiality that is the point of purchase for a thinking of theatre in terms of the event. The discourses of performance offer the temptation to suture (in its curious double meaning of both to separate and to join) a denatured theatre to philosophy. Each appears to possess something the other desires: philosophy has the idea, the concept and the system; performance has desire, the phenomena and the event. The dedicated spectator, who finds reason to return the theatre night after night in the hope of an encounter with an event, is the main protagonist in this conception of theatre-philosophy.

On the other side of the auditorium, the Badioudian actor prepares to meet this demand, for what Herbert Blau describes as:

> [t]he inaugural moments and instances when the theater appears – unless all the world is a stage – from whatever it is that it's not. More theater, less theater: in the doing of theater we solicit, rebuff, try to entrap that thing (has it appeared again tonight?), though we're never quite sure we have it or that the audience can or should see it when, for a moment out of memory, we think we know what it is.[11]

The vagueness in Blau's use of 'thing' is entirely appropriate here. As Badiou suggests, this very vagueness or inability to find a name for that which appears as so essential attests to the fact 'that an event is supernumerary, not only with respect to its site but also to the language available to it ... the work of [its] naming ... is not yet complete, far from it'.[12] Such 'inaugural moments' are necessarily infrequent and one can never be sure that what one saw or heard was ever really there.

So what, then, is an event? What does it look like? The necessary scarcity of these inaugural moments and their all-too-apparent contingency prompts another demand: for evidence or proof in the form of an *example*. There is a demand here for something that is not constrained with the future perfect, which *will have* happened, but for something that *has* happened, something for which the work of naming has been completed and so can be entered into a list of genuine events. This would have to be an actual manifestation of the purely formal process outlined by Badiou – one example drawn from a limited class or kind whose members have something (almost everything?) in common. But such an example would also have to be *exemplary*, something singular and remarkable that sets a precedent worth a process of fidelity, but is also intrinsically inimitable. There is a subtle tension between the example and the requirement for it to be exemplary. It must be part of a collection or set (possessed of some shared formal properties by which it might be identified as an example), but it must also differentiate itself from other examples in the set and so take possession of its own idiosyncrasy.

Sensing the problematic nature of this demand, in *Rhapsodie pour le théâtre*, Badiou invents an imaginary interlocutor, 'the empiricist', who presses him for examples and lists, for the names of the events of Theatre that have, for him at least, cast a ray of light into the gloomy emptiness of theatre. And Badiou, under the pretence of duress, gives examples. There are writers: Claudel, Pirandello, Brecht, Beckett, Genet. There are directors and their particular productions: Vitez, Grüber, Chéreau, Stein, Strehler. There are even actors, but only in specific roles, and only female (for Badiou, according to an unexplicated logic of Lacanian psychoanalysis, only a woman can be an 'eventful' performer): Madeleine Renaud, Jany Gastaldi, Claire Wauthion, Madelene Marion . . .[13]

The list of actors goes on. But their names are entirely unfamiliar to me, and very likely, I hazard a guess, also to you. The names of the directors I do know, major players all, occupants past and present of some of the most heavily subsided state theatre institutions in Europe – yet I have never seen any of their work. And the writers? All too well-known, perhaps, central figures in the twentieth-century dramatic canon. These are indeed examples, both European and in Europe, that *have happened*. But, as Badiou's uneasiness with the list of exemplary examples testifies, that is precisely the problem. Within the context of the contemporary – the 'here and now' of your reading – the archetypal 'there and then' (France, Paris, late 1970s and early 1980s) of these examples ensures that they are rendered as names that cannot carry into the future (or elsewhere) the burden of eventful meaning they ought to bear. Under these conditions, fidelity to the act of naming an event as a central element of the inauguration of a truth process begins to seem misplaced.[14]

To elaborate such a fidelity is to attempt to make intelligible what would otherwise remain obscure or simply 'private': how to be a spectator, one who approves in advance and actualises an event into the possibility of a universal address? But this attempt confronts an impossible demand. Impossible, because how can one be faithful to an event that might very well be destroyed by the act of fidelity that makes it such? Because, in the end, after the house lights come up this was only theatre, the realm of make-believe, of pretending – wasn't it? What would my fidelity to a theatrical event mean *for its own sake*, other than becoming what the English call 'the luvvie', the one for whom a life in the theatre has taken on a little too much life of its own? What might you gain by my providing a list of theatrical greatest hits – in the literal sense of the event as a blow and the theatre as a place where the public goes, not to be educated, entertained or morally improved, but to be struck by 'theatre-ideas'?[15] Following Badiou, we would have to acknowledge that theatre is never enough; as an art, it is but one of the four conditions of philosophy – politics, art, science and love – which can only accede to its rightful function by thinking all of its conditions simultaneously. In this sense, Badiou's lists function as signs of their own philosophical failure, cataloguing events that cannot accede to a full-blown – and therefore public – process of a truth.

There is a sense, as with so many other overarching philosophical systems, that to fully admit the theatre into the realm of philosophical speculation is to flirt with the possibility of intellectual ridicule. Philosophy might be fond of the theatre, in that particularly patronising mode of feeble affection; it just doesn't go there any more.[16] Hence Badiou's rhetorical self-caricature in the dialogues with 'the empiricist' which he stages in *Rhapsodie pour le théâtre* and his self-consciously 'zany' suggestions for theatrical reform: compulsory attendance at four theatrical performances per annum for every citizen, tax refunds for those in compliance, fines for those who refuse; reinstatement of the interval; abandonment of the curtain call.

I want to suggest here that, from the perspective of philosophy, there is something intrinsically stupid and shameful about the entire theatrical apparatus and its mimetic procedures. This hints at a more widespread allergy to the paraphernalia of pretence, which goes beyond a simple anti-theatrical prejudice towards the supposedly subversive or radical qualities of mimesis. It is as if the theatre itself, with all its attendant rituals and procedures, serves as projective container for the latent stupidity of philosophy, or even of all forms of reflective or critical thought. Badiou insists that Theatre (as event that precipitates the process of a truth) is indeed a specific form of thought. Yet it seems that the closer thinking approaches the theatre, the more it flirts with the disaster of its own pretending. While, with Badiou, we might want to claim Theatre for a sophisticated philosophy of the event, to do so means we have to engage with theatre in all its showy tedium and irrepressible vanity, in its laboured striving for effect, and in its vulgar unsophistication, unassailable despite all manner of technological contrivance. To state it plainly: love of Theatre manifests itself via a hatred of theatre, but via an acknowledgement that it needs the theatre in all its hatefulness, just as the philosopher, the lover of wisdom, needs the sophist, the lover of specious reasoning and gratuitous dispute.

If one had to provide a compositional axiom for the likelihood of the creation of the event that is Theatre (the means by which, as Herbert Blau describes above, a performance might solicit or entrap that *thing*), then it is an explicit engagement with this paradox that, at least at this historical juncture, would seem to be required. At its simplest, this might manifest itself as a perpetual struggle between the hateful and constraining 'given' of theatre, the constituent elements that determine it *as* theatre (as opposed to, say, dance or live or performance art), and the contingency of the live encounter with that given. Furthermore, it would be up to each and every performance and performer to acknowledge or name what it considers as its given without the security of either the pseudo-*ethos* of a Brechtian critique or the pseudo-*pathos* of aesthetic suffering. Each and every performance and performer would have to delimit this given, take it very seriously, as a law laid down, a set of possibilities not to be disturbed by the distracting introduction of excessive novelty – something more akin to the accomplished pianist's relation to the musical score, for which the word 'interpretation' is entirely inadequate. At one level, this would then be an encounter that literally has a score to settle (the score, text or choreography being one of the theatre's constituent elements), requiring a return to some basic theatrical operations which might result in profound or even absurd simplification: a choreography reduced to variations on running around in circles; a performance that constitutes itself entirely out of obedience to the lyrics of a series of well-known pop songs; a performer who manages to construct a role out of simply appearing, generously and playfully, while simultaneously expressing a profound ethical unease with the very act of appearing itself.

What if the theatre is stupid?

But what, after all, will have been achieved by theatre-philosophy, if by itself it produces no truths, no events? Is it just a self-aggrandising abstraction, riding on the back of concrete examples of theatrical labour? Or, as Kristeva describes the name that is Europe, might it indeed be a 'symbolic common denominator', a discourse that gathers together a new ensemble or assemblage, not of nations, but of 'compossible' performance events that would make up the formation of a spectator? In such an assemblage, each event, to restate Kristeva's notion, 'far from losing its own traits, rediscovers and accentuates them in a strange temporality, in a kind of "future perfect", where the most deeply repressed past gives a distinctive character to a logical and sociological distribution of the most modern type'.[17] This is to say that a theatre-philosophy announces the return of the repressed past, of a primitive, even infantile, version of the theatre that we thought to have left behind many generations ago; not a historically identifiable theatre, but theatre as pure stereotype, a-historical and anti-cultural, theatre from which the theatre/Theatre opposition has yet to emerge. This would be theatre not as a form of thought but as a kind of mindlessness, a direct result of a degenerate mass psychology that theatre creates in its gathering together of an audience. This stereotype is still visible, most graphically in the iconic image used to promote all kinds of performance: a gurning face, with an open mouth, caught in the rictus of an utterly inauthentic laugh or scream, an all-too-living version of the cartoon cliché of the masks of comedy and tragedy. It is as if that only by confronting this 'given' face and what it represents, by owning up to it in some way, that what is contemporary in theatre – 'of the most modern type' – can manifest and intensify its own exemplary traits. In other words, the wager being placed here is that what is contemporary in theatre now is that which is able to recognise and integrate the theatre's own apparent idiocy, but without assimilating it into yet another theme or character.[18] Theatre's idiocy, resisting its projection into other containers, will then pervade the entire theatrical apparatus. In doing so, this generalised idiocy will replace the sophist as the proper counterpart to the theatre-philosopher, according to its ancient meaning of the generic, purely private person, the nameless 'layman' or nobody who seeks nothing of knowledge or learning and has no need of public reasons to pursue his interest. Thus the Theatre's ideal actor – and spectator, too – will be the idiot-philosopher, a Socratic identity that is not so much a role as a high level of *valency*, a capricious capacity for combination with other elements by which an essential identity is obscured in the formation of more complex compounds.

Sensing the hollowed-out names that populate Badiou's lists of exemplary examples, it feels difficult to go much further in generating any more in light of these difficulties. However, the task of going further falls elsewhere; to other encounters and to encounters with other events; in short, to you, dear spectator. What is required is the multiplication of Theatrical multiplicities beyond the confines of a single discourse that might seek to anticipate the form of their future occurrence. New lists will be required, and new thoughts will be necessary to elevate them into concepts that will permit 'the times' to be represented as:

> the time in which *this event of thought has taken place* . . . and which is henceforth the shared lot of everyone, whether they know it or not, since a philosophy has constituted for everyone the common shelter of this 'having-taken-place'.[19]

With respect to this proposition and the difficulties encountered above in testifying to it, the philosophical consolation provided by the theory of Michel Foucault, addressed to those who apparently cannot bear to hear it, now seems not just a consolation but an invitation: 'discourse is not life: its time is not your time'.[20] That is, one cannot possibly hope to 'say' and so grasp in one fell swoop the situation, state, event and its truth. Such a 'saying' must unfurl in the future perfect of what will have happened, a process of gradual coalescence and concentration in which the significant traits of the event and its subsequent intervention begin to emerge. And if this appears to privilege the retroactive processes of becoming a spectator in the process of epoch-making, will it suffice to remember that the great motivation for engaging in theatrical creation is simply to attempt to make what one would really rather enjoy watching, but is nowhere to be seen?

Notes

1 http://www.wordiq.com/definition/Theory, accessed 13 October 2004.
2 A. Badiou, *Manifesto for Philosophy*, New York: State University of New York Press, 1999, p. 101.
3 J. Atherton, 'Tools: Theory of Theory', 2002, available online http://www.doceo. co.uk/tools/theory.htm, accessed 12 October 2004.

4 E. Hobsbawn, *Age of Extremes – The Short Twentieth Century, 1914–1991*, London: Penguin, 1994.

5 In the Anglo-American analytic tradition of philosophy, the shared names are not of texts or thinkers, but of problems, such as the 'problem of other minds' – or of problems attached to names, such as 'Russell's Paradox' (a problem in set theory posed by Bertrand Russell in 1901).

6 J. Kristeva, 'Women's Time', in *The Kristeva Reader*, ed. T. Moi, London: Basil Blackwell, 1986, pp. 188–9 (emphasis in original).

7 Indeed, one could see this text as a miniature version of Badiou's complex mathematical ontology.

8 These terms derive from Badiou's complex ontology, set out systematically in *L'Être et l'événement* (Paris: Éditions du Seuil, 1988) and substantially revised in the forthcoming *Logiques des mondes*.

9 A. Badiou, *Rhapsodie pour le théâtre*, Paris: Imprimerie Nationale Editions, 1990 p. 47 (my translation, emphasis in original).

10 In a brief meditation on the problem of fidelity in Badiou's philosophy, Alexander Garcia Düttmann makes the following elliptical suggestion: 'What remains of fidelity in the wake of Badiou? Perhaps the thought that fidelity is *seeing* embodied.' And is not the *spectator* the very figure of such seeing? ('What Remains of Fidelity after Serious Thought', in *Think Again: Alain Badiou and the Future of Philosophy*, ed. P. Hallward, London: Continuum, 2004).

11 H. Blau, *The Audience*, Baltimore: Johns Hopkins University Press, 1990, p. 40 (emphasis in original).

12 Badiou, *Manifesto for Philosophy*, p. 85.

13 Badiou, *Rhapsodie pour le théâtre*, pp. 41, 77 9, 89 90.

14 Badiou has announced that he is in the process of modifying his conception of the 'situation' and also of the 'naming' of the event as its sole trace left after its actual occurrence. See the introduction to his *Ethics: An Essay on the Understanding of Evil*, London and New York: Verso, 2001, and in an interview that forms its appendix.

15 Badiou, *L'Être et l'événement*, p. 119.

16 To the best of my knowledge, none of the rapidly growing philosophical commentary on Badiou's work has paid even cursory attention to the significance of theatre in informing the philosophy of the event which is so central to his writing.

17 Kristeva, 'Women's Time', pp. 188–9 (emphasis in original).

18 It is not entirely surprising that it is particular works of contemporary cinema, which, to the extent to which they approach and encroach upon the theatrical, make a more convincing theme of the idiocy of theatre, most literally in Lars von Trier's controversial film *The Idiots* (1998). On the other hand, whatever von Trier's *Dogville* (2003) might be engaged in thematically, one thing it seems expressly engaged with is a much more generic, nameless theatrical idiocy, marked out not so much by its overtly theatrical sense of space, decor and casting as by its demand that it places on its collection of cinema celebrities of today and yesteryear to labour over endless excruciating mimes of opening nonexistent doors with nonexistent door handles: the stereotypical gesture par excellence of theatre's idiot.

19 Badiou, *Manifesto for Philosophy*, p. 88 (emphasis in original).

20 M. Foucault, *The Archaeology of Knowledge*, trans. A. M. Sheridan Smith, New York: Pantheon Books, 1972, p. 210.

Index

Acco Theatre Center 47–58
affect 106–7, 125–6, 133–4
Agamben, Giorgio 26, 67, 69
Alford, Violet 139
Arendt, Hannah 67
Artangel 107
Artaud, Antonin 141, 176
avant-garde 176

BAD.co 99–101
Badiou, Alain 203–10
Badovinac, Zdenka 73, 83, 85
Balibar, Etienne 65–8
Baktruppen 28–31
Banu, Georges 128
Barrett, John 143
Battistelli, Giorgio 43–4
Bausch, Pina 188–94
Bel, Jérôme 81, 194
Benjamin, Walter 63, 149–53, 181
Berio, Luciano 37
Berlin 42, 166
Bertolucci, Bernardo 34, 36–7
Bettelheim, Bruno 164–5, 168
Bey, Hakim 23
Blah Blah Blah 168–72
Blast Theory 81
Blau, Herbert 206
bodies 10, 89–102, 110, 114, 190
Borch-Jacobsen, Mikkel 112
borders 61–71
Borzik, Rolf 189
Boulez, Pierre 37–8
Bread and Puppet Theater 140
Brezovec, Branko 97–9
Brisley, Stuart 146
Brody, Alan 140
Bujas-Pristaš, Nikolina 99

Bunker 73
Burrows, Jonathan 194
Butler, Judith 65

Cage, John 34
Carnesky, Marisa 71
Cass, Eddie 141
Castellucci, Claudia 178
Céline, Louis-Ferdinand 43
Centre for Performance Research 107
Cesarani, David and Mary Fulbrook 66
Channel Tunnel 70
Charmatz, Boris 194
childhood 107, 153, 164
childrens' theatre and theatre for young people 16, 149–53, 163–73
Cohen, Robin 62
Clark, Kenneth 182
Conservas 74, 77–9
contemporary 3; and disavowal of realism 141; as 'future perfect' 203, 207; and historical legacy 22, 31, 58; and historicity 127–8; and temporality 188; and tragedy 179
Croatia 10, 87–102

dance-theatre, and dance-performance 117–18, 157, 188–98
Demuru, Monica 172
De Pauw, Josse 154
desperate optimists 81
Deyhim, Sussan 39
Diamond, Elin 90
Diderot, Denis 44, 179, 181
Dogme 154
Dood Paard 74, 79–82
Duchamp, Marcel 197

Eisler, Hanns 39
Einstürzende Neubauten 39
Elsaesser, Thomas 37, 40
encounter: and borders 61–71; and
    disorder 160; impossible 34; Israeli-
    German, and memory 47–58;
    theatrical 1–20, 106–7, 141, 177
England 136
Ensemble Modern 40–1
ephemerality of performance 121, 151
Europe 2, 61, 202–3; and children 107,
    164; Europeaness 73–4; European
    history 4–6, 18, 34–8, 58; European
    sensibilities 8–9; European Union 2,
    8, 24, 66, 69, 75, 202; see also
    migration
event 19–20, 152, 204–7

fascism 36, 43
Fassbinder, Rainer Werner 36, 38
festivals 8–9; see also Mladi Levi
fiction 15–16, 170–1
folklore 139–40; and fairy tales 164–5,
    172
Forced Entertainment 81
Foster, Hal 132
Foucault, Michel 210
Frank, Lars 167

German New Cinema 36
Germany 35–8, 41–2, 48, 53
gesture 24, 31, 151–3, 157, 191
Gibbons, Scott 183
Ginsborg, Paul 35
Goat Island 194
Goebbels, Heiner 38–41
Goodall, Jane 27
Gorky, Maxim 23–4
Green, André 106
Grotowski, Jerzy 58, 101, 140, 179
Gruppe 47 36
Guidi, Chiara 179

Handke, Peter 79–81, 84
Heathcote, Dorothy 171
Heidegger, Martin 25
Heinrich, Ines 167
Helm, Alex 140
Hermanis, Alvis 21–7
Herzog, Werner 36, 38
Holden, Jane 171
Holocaust 47–58
humans 21–2, 25–6, 176–7

iconoclasm 178
Indoš, Damir Bartol 101–2
Italy 35–8

Jameson, Fredric 114–15

Kaes, Anton 38
Kagel, Mauricio 37
Kaye, Nick and Giannachi, Gabriella
    178
Kieve, Paul 71
Kirshenblatt-Gimblett, Barabara 27
Knorr Cetina, Karin 125
Koprivšek, Nevenka 73, 85
Kristeva, Julia 160, 203, 209

Lacan, Jacques 111–12, 115–16
LaCapra, Dominick 49, 55
La Cubana 79
Laforgue, Jules 44
La Fura dels Baus 78–9, 146
Laplanche, Jean 114–16
La Ribot 194–8
Latour, Bruno 31–2
Latvia 21, 24
Lehmann, Hans-Thies 87, 89
Lemëtre, Jean-Jacques 124
Le Roy, Xavier 194
Levi, Primo 55, 63
Levi, Simona 79
Ligeti, György 37
Lindsay, Arto 39
Linnaeus, Carl 29
Living Theater 140
London International Festival of
    Theatre 199
Lyotard, Jean-François 159–61

magic 15–18, 71, 180–1
Marian, Radu 183
Marjanić, Suzana 102
Marshfield Mummers 136–47
Marthaler, Christoph 41–3
Massumi, Brian 121, 125, 133
Mazzini, Giuseppe 35
McKenzie, Jon 90
memory 47, 49, 51, 189–95
Michaelis, Ania 165–7, 169
Michaels, Anne 63
migration 6, 61–71
Migreurop 68–9
Midgley, Mary 25
Miller, Alice 164

mimesis 11, 14, 17; and innovation 144;
    and magic 180–1; and seduction
    116; and stupidity 208
Mladi Levi festival 73–85
Mnouchkine, Ariane 121–34
Montažstroj-Performingunit 95–7
Müller, Heiner 38, 40–1
mummers' play 136–47
Muselmann 54–7

nationalism 88–93
Nazism 36, 58
neanderthals 28–31
New Riga Theatre 21–7, 32
Nono, Luigi 37

Odin Teatret 140, 146
opera 34–7

performance studies xv-vi, 12, 63, 120,
    201; and academic writing 120–4,
    127; and performance practice 122
Perrault, Charles 173
philosophy xvii, 19; as practice 201–2;
    as theatre-philosophy 209
Platel, Alain 106, 109, 111, 117–18
play 13–14, 149–61, 169, 171
practitioner perspectives 12–13, 120–34
psychoanalysis 11, 111–16, 172
Puppen-Theater der Stadt Halle 166–7
Pusić, Vesna 87

Rampley, Matthew 180–1
realism 21, 89, 91–2, 168–72;
    naturalistic realism 24, 183–4
refugees 67–9, 169
Reinhardt, Bernard 84
Rokem, Freddie 48, 51–2, 55
Röszler, Gottfried 165

Schönberg, Arnold 37, 44
Sciarrino, Salvatore 44–5
Sebald, W.G. 63
Second World War 34–5, 42, 62
seduction 116–17
Sehgal, Tino 194
Šeparović, Borut 95
Sierens, Arne 107, 111

Slovenia 74–5, 83
Sociètas Raffaello Sanzio 43, 163,
    172–3, 175–85
Southern, Richard 141
Spectatorship: and agency 16; and
    belief 28; and complicity 55–6; and
    empowerment 168; and fidelity 202,
    207; and production of meaning 18;
    and remembering 6; self-reflexive 73,
    78, 106–18; and spectator studies 12,
    120–2; and temporality 192; see also
    witness
Stanislavsky, Konstantin 23–4, 175, 179
Stitt, André 146
Stockhausen, Karlheinz 37
Syberberg, Hans-Jürgen 38

Theater o.N. (Zinnober) 165–8
Théâtre du Soleil 121–34
theatre: basic operations 209; and event
    204–7; and theatricality 6, 63–5
theory 122, 129–30, 200–2
Tiezzi, Federico 179
time 18, 190–8
Tuđman, Franjo 92–3

Ulmer, Gregory 121–2, 126, 130, 132
Uninvited Guests 75–7

Victoria 107–18, 154–9
Virilio, Paul 25
Visconti, Luchino 36–7
von Trier, Lars 154

Warburg, Aby 179–82
Welfare State 146
Wenders, Wim 38
Williams, David 122
witness 51–7, 129, 204
Worthen, W.B. 65
wound 19; in embodied subjectivity
    195; and enigmatic signifier 115; in
    sexual and social relation 189
Yugoslavia 74–5, 84

Zimmerman, Berndt Aloys 37
Zipes, Jack 164, 168
Žižek, Slavoj 25, 128